First Workshop on Intelligent and Interactive Writing Assistants (In2Writing 2022)

Dublin, Ireland
26 May 2022

ISBN: 978-1-7138-6740-1

Printed from e-media with permission by:

Curran Associates, Inc.
57 Morehouse Lane
Red Hook, NY 12571

Some format issues inherent in the e-media version may also appear in this print version.

Printed with permission by Curran Associates, Inc. (2023)

For permission requests, please contact the Association for Computational Linguistics at the address below.

Association for Computational Linguistics
209 N. Eighth Street
Stroudsburg, Pennsylvania 18360

Phone: 1-570-476-8006
Fax: 1-570-476-0860

acl@aclweb.org

Additional copies of this publication are available from:

Curran Associates, Inc.
57 Morehouse Lane
Red Hook, NY 12571 USA
Phone: 845-758-0400
Fax: 845-758-2633
Email: curran@proceedings.com
Web: www.proceedings.com

In2Writing 2022

The First Workshop on Intelligent and Interactive Writing Assistants

Proceedings of the Workshop

May 26, 2022

The In2Writing organizers gratefully acknowledge the support from the following sponsors.

grammarly wordtune

Introduction

We are excited to welcome you to the First Workshop on Intelligent and Interactive Writing Assistants (In2Writing 2022). The workshop is being held in a remote/in-person hybrid format, on May 26, 2022, in conjunction with ACL 2022, which will take place from May 22-27, 2022.

This interdisciplinary workshop aims to bring together researchers from the NLP and human-computer interaction (HCI) communities and industry practitioners and professional writers to discuss innovations in building, improving, and evaluating intelligent and interactive writing assistants. For the first edition of this workshop, the program includes 6 invited talks, 1 presentation session (best paper), 1 poster and demo session, and 2 panel discussions entitled "Understanding the impact of writing assistants on ownership, authenticity, originality, and confidence" and "Bridging NLP and HCI community to design and build writing assistants."

We received 19 submissions this year, which comprised 17 long papers and 2 short papers. Every submission received a meta-review and at least three reviews. When making our selections for the program, we carefully considered the reviews, meta-reviews, and fit for the theme of the workshop. The 20 members of the Program Committee did an excellent job reviewing the submitted papers. We sincerely thank them for their essential role in selecting the accepted papers and helping produce a high-quality program for the conference. Our goal was to create a balanced program that encompasses topics across NLP and HCI while accommodating as many favorably rated papers as possible. Among 19 submissions, we accepted 8 papers (leading to an overall acceptance rate of 42.11%) and conditionally accepted 6 papers. For conditionally accepted papers, authors were allowed to revise their submissions based on reviews, and the final acceptance was given after ACs reviewed the revised version. Among the accepted papers, 4 papers were cross-submissions, which were already presented in other venues, but went through the same review process as other submissions. They have been included in these proceedings as extended abstracts.

A conference of any scale requires advice, help, and enthusiastic participation of many parties, and we have a big 'thank you' to say to all of them. We thank our six invited speakers, Lillian-Yvonne Bertram (Northeastern University), Elizabeth Clark (Google NY), Claire L. Evans, Daniel Gissin (AI21 Labs), Timo Mertens (Grammarly), and Melissa Roemmele (RWS Group) for enriching the workshop with their talks. We would also like to thank all our invited panelists Jill Burstein (Duolingo), Courtney Napoles (Grammarly), Melissa Roemmele (RWS Group), Qian Yang (Cornell University), Simon Bouisson, Sherry Wu (University of Washington), and Ekaterina Kochmar (University of Bath) and making our workshop a vibrant and diverse place for stimulating discussions on a variety of relevant topics.

We would also like to gratefully acknowledge the support of our sponsors: Grammarly and AI21 Labs.

We thank our program committee members for committing their time to help us select an excellent technical program. We also thank all the authors who submitted to the workshop and all conference participants for making the first edition of In2Writing a success and for their contributions to growing the research areas of intelligent and interactive writing assistants with their fine work.

Finally, it is our great pleasure to welcome you in-person and virtually to the conference. We hope that you will have an enjoyable and productive time and leave with fond memories of In2Writing 2022!

John Joon Young Chung, Katy Ilonka Gero, Daniel Gissin, Ting-Hao 'Kenneth' Huang, Dongyeop Kang, Mina Lee, and Vipul Raheja
The In2Writing Workshop Organizing Committee

Organizing Committee

Organizing Committee

Ting-Hao 'Kenneth' Huang, Pennsylvania State University
Vipul Raheja, Grammarly
Dongyeop Kang, University of Minnesota
John Joon Young Chung, University of Michigan
Daniel Gissin, AI21Labs
Mina Lee, Stanford University
Katy Ilonka Gero, Columbia University

Program Committee

Program Committee

Jordan Huffaker, University of Michigan
Minsuk Chang, Naver AI Lab
Hwaran Lee, Naver AI Lab
Risako Owan, University of Minnesota
Shirley Anugrah Hayati, GaTech
Chieh-Yang Huang, Penn State University
Alex Tamkin, Stanford University
Gabriel Poesia, Stanford University
Dae Hyun Kim, Stanford University
Joon Sung Park, Stanford University
Alex Calderwood, UCSC
Kenneth Arnold, Calvin University
Melanie Subbiah, Columbia University
Chris Kedzie, Rasa
Wanyu Du, University of Virginia
Dhruv Kumar, Grammarly
Arjun Akula, UCLA
Xinyu Hua, Bloomberg AI
Melissa Roemmele, RWS Language Weaver
Vivian Liu, Columbia University

Invited Speakers and Panelists

Lillian-Yvonne Bertram, Northeastern University
Claire L. Evans
Elizabeth Clark, University of Washington
Timo Mertens, Grammarly
Melissa Roemmele, RWS Group
Daniel Gissin, AI21Labs
Ekaterina Kochmar, University of Bath
Jill Burstein, Duolingo
Sherry Wu, University of Washington
Qian Yang, Cornell University
Simon Bouisson

Table of Contents

Data-to-text systems as writing environment

Adela Schneider and **Andreas Madsack**
Johanna Heininger and **Ching-Yi Chen** and **Robert Weißgraeber**
AX Semantics, Stuttgart, Germany
{firstname.lastname}@ax-semantics.com

Abstract

Today, data-to-text systems are used as commercial solutions for automated text production of large quantities of text. Therefore, they already represent a new technology of writing. This new technology requires the author, as an act of writing, both to configure a system that then takes over the transformation into a real text, but also to maintain strategies of traditional writing. What should an environment look like, where a human guides a machine to write texts? Based on a comparison of the NLG pipeline architecture with the results of the research on the human writing process, this paper attempts to take an overview of which tasks need to be solved and which strategies are necessary to produce good texts in this environment. From this synopsis, principles for the design of data-to-text systems as a functioning writing environment are then derived.

1 Introduction

Natural Language Generation (NLG) systems are computer systems that automatically generate texts in human languages, using advanced techniques from artificial intelligence and/or computational linguistics (Carlson, 2015). Non-academic NLG systems are used in different areas of text production and result in fundamental changes for content creation and publication processes: They form a new type of writing technology and create a new environment for humans in which texts are generated automatically, but humans still (co-)design the rules and specifications for this generation.

While NLG systems based on pre-trained large language models function more as writing assistants for authors on an individual level, the NLG systems that are the subject of this study have a different aim: They are configured to be able to produce large amounts of text automatically.

In this context, writing is regarded in a broader sense and means creating a blueprint for producing specific texts. So this new type of writing can be described as meta-writing: However, since the requirements of text structure, expression, and realisation of a communication goal cannot be solved on an abstract level only, many traditional writing tasks remain to be done by the author. Mahlow and Dale (2014) have described this new condition as follows: "Automated text production – when the author is not the writer". This observation raises the question, what a writing environment should be like in which a machine is guided by an author to write a text?

In this research, we use the framework of creating a writing environment to set out the requirements for an NLG system. So, the human writer is considered here as the agent, while the software functions as the environment. This setting is due to the fact that writing, in general, is primarily perceived as an individual action, even though some instances of writing are performed in collaboration. But of course, it is not the only possible framework. The interaction between humans and machines has recently been discussed, especially in the communicative field of AI, where both humans and the instances of AI are seen as agents and the aspect of collaboration is much more prominent (for the field of journalism: Lewis et al. (2019); for fiction writing: Manjavacas et al. (2017); Clark et al. (2018)).

And indeed, it may be that statistical approaches and deep-learning methods, in particular, bring the software's autonomy more to the fore. Autonomy is, after all, the distinctive property of the agent (Henrickson, 2018). This then would call for a reassessment of the situation, looking more closely at the requirements of collaboration within this described environment. However, data-to-text systems in real-world applications still require such a share of human configuration and control and the creative contribution share of the software, at least in the NLG systems focused on in this paper, is still so limited that it would not be adequate to claim

Proceedings of the First Workshop on Intelligent and Interactive Writing Assistants (In2Writing 2022), pages 1 - 10
May 26, 2022 ©2022 Association for Computational Linguistics

creative autonomy of the software in the process.

The environmental framework with its orientation towards the writing processes also offers the advantage of shifting the focus in the evaluation of NLG systems (Howcroft et al., 2020) from the evaluation of the output to an evaluation of the processes, that Gehrmann et al. (2022) recently postulated: "Evaluating NLG tasks only through the lens of outputs is thus insufficient and we should strife (sic) to deliver a more fine-grained breakdown (...)". For traditional writing it is set that the principle of having control over the writing and editorial processes is the most effective method of influencing text quality (Wyss, 2013; Perrin, 2001). And we assume it remains valid also for working with NLG systems. Thus, our approach could open up new perspectives for the evaluation of NLG systems.

What Perrin stated in 2002 for writing per se also applies to automated text production nowadays: "Writing is thus changing from a field of largely intuitive language design to a language technology that becomes aware of its compositional principles and purposefully uses its means, tools, and strategies" (translated from German (Perrin, 2002, page 7)).

As a starting point to achieve such an awareness and methodology for this new kind of writing, including a system of rules, strategies, and cues that guide action, we want to make the action steps, tools and decisions within the processes explicit:

1. In order to approach this, we take a look at the structure and design of NLG systems, because from these the special requirements and conditions are derived to which the user is subject with their text generation task. (*The different categories of NLG systems* and *Overview of the NLG pipeline*)

2. To identify the factors that are conducive to the production of (good) texts, we will outline how the human writing process is organized (*A model of the human writing process*). In doing so, we will refer to the results of writing process research as well as to the approaches to the development of modern writing software. (*Requirements for writing software*)

3. With these findings in mind, we try to take a closer look at automated text production with NLG systems. How can the phases of NLG systems be coordinated with the human writing process? And how should the parameters of the various phases be designed so that texts can be produced with good quality? (*NLG systems in real life: writing on a meta level*)

4. As a result, we will formulate the requirements for the design of NLG systems that take into account the human writing process (*Principles for designing NLG systems*). These requirements ensure creating an environment in which the production of complex written texts is possible. The texts generated in this way should use the full potential of language and not just provide simple data descriptions

2 The different categories of NLG systems

In the basic reference work on NLG it is characterized as 'the subfield of artificial intelligence and computational linguistics that is concerned with the construction of computer systems that can produce understandable texts in English or other human languages from some underlying non-linguistic representation of information' (Reiter et al., 2000).

There are already a number of implemented applications for the data-to-text approach in different areas. They range from the media sector, where they have been a much-discussed topic as "robot journalism", to medical reports, business and finance reports or product descriptions in e-commerce. NLG systems are useful when large amounts of text are needed or information is only available in formats that are not easily understood (such as measurement data from medical examinations), and verbalisation facilitates or enables understanding.

In this study, a further classification concerning the organization of NLG systems is to be discussed. On the one hand there are the so-called *pipeline solutions* that modularize the procedures and then execute the tasks (one after the other). The *end-to-end solutions* on the other hand leave the modular approach behind and aim for *end-to-end* generation based on the successes of deep learning. They can be trained with (data, text) tuples that can be efficiently collected at scale (Castro Ferreira et al., 2019; Harkous et al., 2020). Large pre-trained language models such as GPT-3 or BERT can be integrated into all of these solutions.

At present, end-to-end solutions are not yet suitable for commercial production of great amount of texts because they have two fundamental limitations: First, they are very domain-bound, so they can only generate texts for very limited segments. In addition, they lack semantic fidelity, this means how accurately the generated text conveys the meaning (Harkous et al., 2020). As described, end-to-end systems based on deep learning combine all NLG steps in one function. This means that the only possible intervention is to select or edit the results (Gehrmann, 2020). Due to this too tight restriction of interaction these approaches fall out of consideration for this research. Modular data-to-text systems, on the other hand, offer more points of connection and reflect parallels between humans and systems in the text generation process.

Since this study analyses the application under real-life conditions, the focus is on implementable solutions, not on academic NLG projects. In the commercial sector, rule-based pipeline solutions are established first and foremost, which differ in handling, architectures and purposes. Some of the solutions are offered as self-service, requiring limited or no programming skills. The leading companies in this fields are ARRIA NLG, Narrative Science, AX Semantics, Yseop and Automated Insights (Dale, 2020).

3 Overview of the NLG pipeline

There are different ways to structure the tasks and decisions of text generation. The most cited model for this is the NLG architecture constructed by Ehud Reiter and Robert Dale that performs tasks in sequence related to document planning, sentence planning and linguistic realization (Reiter et al., 2000).

Module	*Content task*	*Structure Task*
Document planning	Content determination	Document structuring
Microplanning	Lexicalisation Referring expression Generation	Aggregation
Realisation	Linguistic realisation	Structure realisation

Table 1: Overview over the most important modules and tasks in the NLG pipeline (Reiter et al., 2000)

The function of the *Document Planner* is to specify the text's content and structure based on domain and application knowledge about what information fits the specified communication goal and other generating objectives. In this module decisions are made about which information will be included (*Content determination*) and in what order this information will appear (*Document structuring*).

The task of the *Microplanning* component is to take the results of the Document Planning module and refine it to produce a more detailed text specification. At this point, sentences and paragraphs are planned (*Aggregation*) and the linguistic elements to be used to express the information are determined (*Lexicalisation*), i.e. which specific words or certain phrases are to be used. Within the *Referring expression generation*, it is decided which properties are used to describe an object unit, for example, a person's proper name and profession. It is therefore necessary to determine which properties are important so that the reader can identify the object.

In the process of *Surface Realisation*, the system converts abstract representations of sentences into grammatically well-formed text (*Linguistic realisation*) and ensures that the abstract structures of sections and paragraphs are assembled as a document in the appropriate format.

4 A model of the human writing process

From the best-known model that illustrates how human writing functions at the cognitive level – the so called Flower-Hayes-Model (Flower and Hayes, 1981) – three important features can be derived that are characteristic of the human individual writing process:

1. There are distinguishable cognitive processes.
2. These processes are organized recursively.
3. Text passages that have already been written have an influence on further text production.

The three distinguishable cognitive processes are controlled by a monitor. This central executive directs attention and switches from one sub-process to another.

The first process is *planning* of a text, where information is collected and thoughts are made about the form and structure of the text. What should the text achieve? Whom does it address? What aspects, data, information should appear in it? It comprises three types of sub-operations: First there is *generating*, in which the writer retrieves information relevant to the writing task from long-term memory. Then there is *organising*, during which the most useful of the retrieved elements are arranged in a plan; finally the writer sets further goals to guide the writing (*goal setting*).

After the *planning* follows the phase of linguistic implementation (*translating*). While many ideas in the planning phase are not really linguistically available, a kind of translation process now takes place during which the thoughts are translated into language: One now decides on the concrete vocabulary.

The third main process is *reviewing* with its two sub-operations *editing* and *revising*. Now, the writer re-reads the text and aims to improve the quality of the written text by changing the text at the time it was written to correct errors, or fit the plans (*editing*). Or they intentionally revise the text to look for problems and errors at all levels of the text (*revising*).

4.1 Recursiveness in writing

One of the most important findings of Flower and Hayes, which is also confirmed by later analyses of the writing processes, is the observation that writing is recursive: The writer jumps back and forth between the processes, again and again. There is no sequential proceeding in which one process is completed and then the next begins.

In principle, it is possible to activate any process at any time, but it can be seen that the frequency and duration of the processes change throughout a writing session. The activation of translating remains constant while that of planning decreases and that of revision increases (Olive, 2004). In the concrete act of writing, the *recursive procedure* shows itself in different facets:

- There is no fixed sequence of the individual operations. It seems that the individual writer develops certain patterns of sequences that remain relatively stable (Olive, 2004).
- Individual activities always refer to each other and overlap.
- All processes can be repeated as often as required.
- Each formulation can be the trigger for a subsequent revision, which results in a new formulation, which in turn can be a trigger for another new formulation.

Text passages written previously have influence on the further text and the arrangement of the processes. Reading and rereading the actual text is an important mental process in which the idea of the text is compared with the actual implementation. The deviations either lead to immediate changes in the written text or to a modification of the idea of the text - which, of course, in the further course of time influences both the text that is still being written and corrections of the pre-existing text passages.

5 Requirements for writing software

In general, technology and writing have always been interdependent: the writing tool and the writing medium influence writing in terms of how the problems at hand can be solved. In most writing settings today, the pen, pencil or typewriter has ceased to be the tool, and paper is no longer the medium. Rather, computers, tablets and smartphones with input functions and screens are the extended writing environment today (Mahlow and Dale, 2014).

The writing environment in the narrower sense is the associated software. There have been and still are approaches to investigate which conditions serve the authors to write without interference and receive the appropriate support during the writing process.

The investigation of the results of writing process research played an important role in this context (Sharples, 1999). It was criticised that the writing tool and the medium were not included in former research. The most important results of the critique are, first, Sharples' (Sharples, 1999) re-evaluation of recursiveness and writing phases and second, the description of certain objects (external mental representations) as a bridge between the writer's ideas and the emerging text. He emphasises the biphasic nature of two activities within the writing process: *engagement* - this means the actual writing, where new material is created and *reflection*, the thinking (about the writing) where the generated material is revised. The two processes are separate and cannot occur simultaneously, forming cycles of engagement and reflection in writing (Sharples, 1999).

From these results, guidelines for the development of writing environment software were derived (Sharpies and Pemberton, 1990) with elaborating the following aspects:

- Because one cannot think about the structure of the text while writing, it is necessary to have a macrostructure (a kind of plan of the text), but this cannot be kept in our working memory. One needs an external representation of these macrostructures (Sharples, 1999).
- It must be possible to store mental representations of information (which can be in linear

language or in other forms such as networks, mind maps, drawings or structures).

- Writers need to be able to switch quickly between tasks (i.e. between notes, outline and linear text or spell check) this facilitates the interleaving of tasks.
- Writers need to switch freely between different parts of the document as well, and should simultaneously be able to choose an appropriate level of focus. So, they should have an overview display and then be able to zoom in. At the same time, it has to be possible at all levels to delete or merge parts of the text or to change the order.

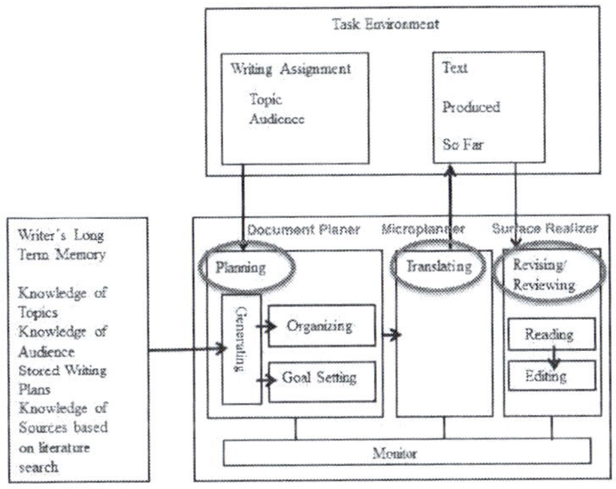

Figure 1: The Flower-Hayes-Model, Flower and Hayes (1981)

Today there are a handful of software tools that take this non-linear writer-centred approach as their starting point (such as PageFour, Liquid Story Binder, RoughDraft (discontinued), Ulysses, Scrivener), but they tend to be used for specific professionalised, often narrative, writing (Bray, 2013).

However, functions are built into conventional text processors as well that support individual phases of the writing process, such as the outline view, comment functions, text and grammar checks (Piotrowski and Mahlow, 2009).

6 NLG systems in real life: writing on a meta level

At this point, the phases of the human text production process and the modules of the NLG pipeline architecture are juxtaposed in order to find out which principles can be derived for an NLG system that is not designed for experts, but as a writing environment for the (automated) production of large numbers of texts.

6.1 NLG: document planner – human writing: conceptual planning

The characteristic of this phase lies in the significance of alignment with the overall goals of the text: What are the interests of the target audience? What are the communication goals? This provides orientation for the selection of content and the structuring of the resulting text.

The result depends on what goal is to be achieved with the texts and in which environment the text should be published. The editorial strategies as well as the narrative angles for the stories are developed.

In individual writing, the writer derives such text assignments and keeps them either in long-term memory or in the form of a text brief or sample text. How detailed such specifications are worked out depends on the text assignment and the experience of the writer.

In NLG systems the output of the document planner is a document plan which is a structured and ordered representation of messages. Often it is realized in form of a tree, whose leaf nodes are messages and whose internal nodes specify document elements such as paragraphs and sections and discourse relations between the elements. The representations of this plan are partly structural in nature, partly they are already connected with verbal elements (Reiter et al., 2000; Gatt and Krahmer, 2018).

Up to now humans were in most cases also responsible for designing handcrafted rules during the planning phase of automated text production, but there are some examples for developments of modelling genres with Machine Learning and statistics as long as there is a corpus of manual written text available for this specific case (Reiter and Williams, 2010).

At this point, it is worth considering how to transfer the author's implicit knowledge about the communication goal, text genre and document structure into explicit knowledge, such as rules, which can be applied to text generation. Many approaches are possible for the production of such a machine-processable document plan by the writer: The necessary elements can be requested via a kind of questionnaire or forms can be filled out, based on briefing forms (Reiter and Williams, 2010). Since in both areas a form of (internal) representation is created, that is still not translated into words, and for the reasons outlined above, namely that human

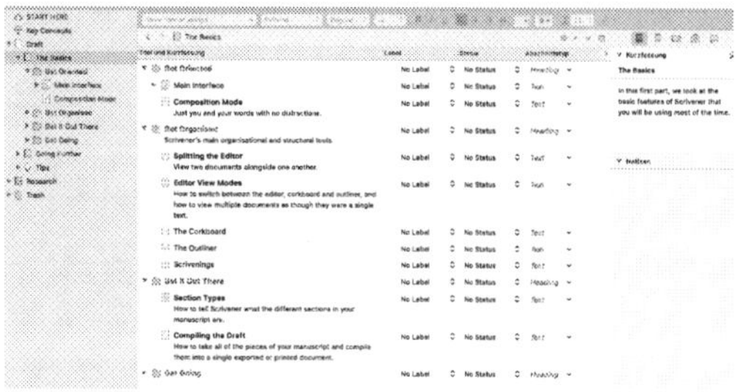

Figure 2: This is the main view in the writing software *Scrivener*. This is an example how a graphic representation with verbal elements can look. On the right there is the option to label and annotate the text parts. (Source: `https://www.literatureandlatte.com/scrivener/overview`)

mental representations of the document structure are often visual, graphic solutions are a suitable choice. A good example for this is the main page of the writing software *Scrivener (Literature and Latte)* (see Figure 2).

Also in this phase, knowledge and information is inserted either by collecting data and doing research by the human author or by working with the database in NLG systems. In NLG systems data has to be filtered, mapped and combined to achieve the information needed. The results are semantic representations of information which are often expressed in logical or database languages (Gatt and Krahmer, 2018). Commonly, in these systems the authors link particular data situations into abstract meaning which then can be used to trigger specific statements, phrases or document planning decisions. During production, data situations of the various data sets are then evaluated by the system and possible choices determined and executed upon. Especially compared to end-to-end neural systems, this makes sure that all aspects in the output are grounded in the underlying data.

6.2 NLG: microplanning (aggregation) – human writing: text structuring

In this step, it is decided in which order information should appear in a text. As with planning what content is to be included, the orientation towards the reader group and the communication goal also applies here.

In addition, there are some basic rhetorical rules and conventions for the individual text genres. For example, there is a rhetoric rule to place more general information at the top, while the details appear further back. In journalistic text forms on the other

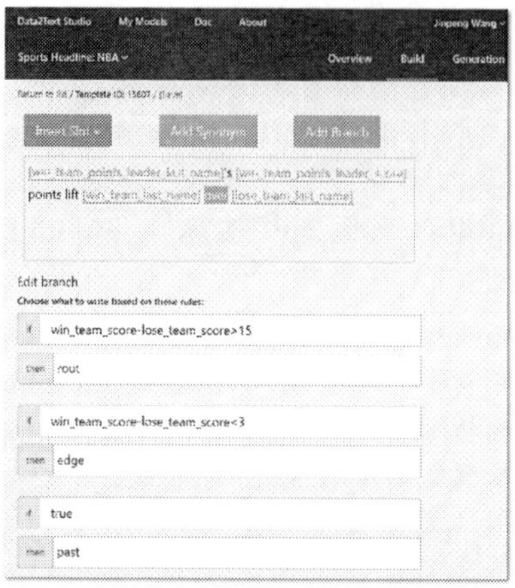

Figure 3: This is a view of the logical structures of the statements and the first step to translating into language. (Data2Text Studio Interface, source: (Dou et al., 2018))

hand, the news, i.e. the special points, are mentioned first, while more general information comes later. There are some recent approaches to use machine learning techniques for content structuring, but since the text structure is very domain-oriented, its design is still produced on the basis of handwritten rules.

This is where requirements for different levels of focus (Sharpies, 1992) come into play: It is advisable to be able to name or label the sentences and to represent them graphically so that they can be arranged by drag and drop, for example. Via the graphical representation, one can then access the assigned sentence and the appropriate data in order to be able to make changes at this level.

6.3 NLG: micro planner – human writing: translating

In this phase, the resulting nonverbal knowledge is translated into actual language. Now decisions have to be made about the words used and the syntax of the text.

In NLG systems, one would basically have to transfer the non-linguistic concepts developed in the document planning phase directly into lexical elements. However, this is not easy for various reasons.

First, the aspect of vagueness, which is tolerated in natural language, plays a major role here. Statements that are transferred as closely as possible directly from the data into words lead to a precision that is quickly perceived as unnatural in natural language. A certain degree of vagueness is necessary for expression in human languages.

The second basic difficulty with this transferring task is that there are always several different ways to verbally describe a piece of information or an event. So there is not one solution for this task, but always multiple ones (Gatt and Krahmer, 2018). For example, Reiter et al. (2005) discussed time expressions in the context of weather-forecast generation. A direct transfer of these time stamps into a record leads to the described overprecision (*At 3:14 it was raining*). Reiter et al. (2005) are also pointing out that e.g. a timestamp 00:00 could be expressed as *late evening*, *midnight*, or simply *evening*. Not surprisingly, humans show considerable variation in their lexical choices.

Another consequence of this direct transmission would be the uniformity of expression, which is usually poorly tolerated in a text. If, for example, in weather texts a rise in temperature occurs several time and is expressed as follows:

```
[time]+ [temp. rise in degrees]
+ {the temperature rose by}
```

The weather report for a day would look like this: *In the morning the temperature rose by 4 degrees. In the afternoon the temperature rose by 5 degrees. In the the evening the temperature rose by -2 degrees.*

First the verbal expression *rise* for a negative rise would be *fall*. And in addition, such a formal structure would be identified very quickly and classified as unreadable. For this reason, several linguistic expressions must be available for a single pre-linguistic event, which are then selected by the system either randomly or based on a formulated condition derived, for example, from the communication goal or the rhetorical strategy. These linguistic variations also serve to ensure sufficient variance in the production of serial texts (see Figure 4).

The formulation of a larger set of different expressions for the data events is a task that in NLG systems still has to be performed by writers and is basically subject to the same principles as in the human language process.

Unlike planning, the phase of *translate* is not related to spatial-visual functions of memory, but rather to phonological working memory: In principle, it is as if the writer now hears the words they write (Olive, 2004; Kellogg et al., 2007). An abstract representation such as a plan or a formula does not provide support during this phase. For this reason, the user is always shown a real-time preview of what a possible instance of the statement would actually look like. Only in this form a statement can be *heard*.

Figure 4: This is a preview of multiple generated text for one data set to guarantee variance. (Data2Text Studio Interface, source: (Dou et al., 2018))

In this manner the user first develops an abstract formulaic representation of the text, then takes the intermediate step via preview and subsequently inserts the corrections into the formula (as an example of a separated preview table see Figures 3 and 4).

The sequence of this procedure, however, narrows the linguistic range of expression in comparison to the conventional formulation of an event. At this point, it is more suitable to give the writer the opportunity to phrase the sentence on the basis of a specific data set as if they were only producing an individual text. And only in a second step express the formula for this expression by providing the software with the labels and logics that it needs for further processing and that it cannot itself recognise on the basis of the text produced.

At this stage, the application of an AI-based component is feasible. They can deliver suggestions based on e.g. keywords or paraphrases of the sentences created by the writer. Just as described earlier, the self-written text and the suggestions of the software take over the function of the *already written text passages*, which in turn can lead to new ideas for the next sentence or to revisions of previous text parts.

6.4 NLG: surface realizer – human writing: reviewing

Linguistic Realisation is concerned with mapping the phrase specifications to the specific words and syntactic constructs which the target language provides such as making subject and verb agree, capitalizing the first letter of a sentence or building the correct plural of a noun. Most decisions in this stage are related to grammar (Reiter et al., 2000).

There are three approaches for implementing this task into NLG systems (Gatt and Krahmer, 2018): Human-written templates that are easy to control, but require a lot of time and effort and offer only limited variability for texts; rule-based systems that make their choices on the basis of the grammar of the language; and statistic related solutions that rely on corpus data.

In the human writing process, an important part of these tasks is already accomplished in the verbalisation phase, but the validation of linguistic and grammatical accuracy takes place in the review phase. For checking syntax and grammar in the native language, the author usually relies on their linguistic intuition and looks up rules in case of doubt. In principle, however, they immediately recognise whether a concrete sentence is syntactically correct or not.

It is less simple for them to assess correctness on the basis of abstract representations. For this reason, a separate review process for linguistic expression and correctness always has to be carried out on the basis of a sample of generated texts. In order to strategically adjust this review, it should be possible to compile this sample group on the basis of different criteria, such as the selection of specific evaluation data sets.

It is noteworthy that NLG systems offer significant advantages in the review process over conventional word processors. Since they retain much more detailed linguistic information about the text, they can perform more targeted correcting operations than word processors. Thus, they fulfil the requirements that Piotrowski and Mahlow (2009) have formulated as to how a software must look like that supports the writer in their editing: (1) Specific views for highlighting linguistic phenomena, and (2) functions to perform operations on linguistic units.

With NLG systems every change made in the text is automatically grammatically adjusted to ensure congruency: For example, changing the number of the subject initiates changing the number of the finite verb and vice versa.

7 Principles for designing NLG systems

The following principles for the design of an NLG system can be derived from the observations presented above:

1. **Build modular systems in alignment with the writing processes:** The modular design of conventional NLG systems suits the writer in that it can be used to provide them with the material and environment to support the specific stage of the writing process. Set up separate views for each main process, which are restricted to the processes in terms of their functionality.

2. **Keep tasks flexible**: To comply with the recursiveness of human writing, it must be possible to edit each task at any time. On the one hand, this means that it must be possible to switch between tasks without any obstacles. And secondly, all changes within a task must be immediately passed on to all instances of the system.

3. **Provide external (non-verbal) representations**: In each phase, the writer must be able to draw on material that are not yet available as linear text. This includes not only overviews of the planning or outlines, but also the option of notes on the existing data material, formulated conditions, templates or text sections.

4. **In the planning view give preference to visual information**: This ranges from representations of the structure to illustrations of logics and data material.

5. **Facilitate the possibilities for linguistic expression**: The writer should always be able to write concrete sentences (without having to include formulas or other abstractions). Provide vocabulary or synonyms and ensure that the writer has the option of formulating multiple variations for the same statement.

6. **Display instances of real text**: The instance of a real text remains an important variable in the process. Only when real text is visible and editable linguistic creativity and grammatical correction can be adequately implemented. Even though this type of automated

text production has different requirements as the production of an individually written text.

7. **Enable linguistics-based editing**: In rule-based data-to-text NLG systems, there is enough meta-information about the grammatical structure of the text that can be used for this task.

8 Conclusion

We showed that there are considerable similarities between the NLG modules and the writing phases of humans in terms of the tasks and decisions involved, which is a significant prerequisite for establishing these systems as a new extended writing technology.

The analysis of these processes is of particular relevance in that quality assurance for data-to-text systems – whose goal is the mass generation of texts – is only attainable by optimizing the processes, since an evaluation of the entire output is not feasible.

However, it also became clear that the human writing process has special features that need to be taken into account when designing NLG systems, especially the consistent and fast change between the processes and the distinctive cognitive activities that require access to different components of the human working memory (e.g. visio-spatial or phonological loop). To neglect these characteristics would mean confining the human involved in a linear process and to strict rules of formal language (i.e. code) to produce natural language texts. This kind of environment would impede the capacity of human writing and, with it, the quality of the text generated. In other words, it would stand in the way of a further successful development of the *technology of writing* which is to be expected in the course of adapting NLG systems in text production.

References

Nancy Bray. 2013. Writing with scrivener: A hopeful tale of disappearing tools, flatulence, and word processing redemption. *Computers and Composition*, 30(3):197–210.

Matt Carlson. 2015. The robotic reporter. *Digital Journalism*, 3(3):416–431.

Thiago Castro Ferreira, Chris van der Lee, Emiel van Miltenburg, and Emiel Krahmer. 2019. Neural data-to-text generation: A comparison between pipeline and end-to-end architectures.

Elizabeth Clark, Anne Spencer Ross, Chenhao Tan, Yangfeng Ji, and Noah A. Smith. 2018. Creative writing with a machine in the loop: Case studies on slogans and stories. In *23rd International Conference on Intelligent User Interfaces*, IUI '18, page 329–340, New York, NY, USA. Association for Computing Machinery.

Robert Dale. 2020. Natural language generation: The commercial state of the art in 2020. *Natural Language Engineering*, 26(4):481–487.

Longxu Dou, Guanghui Qin, Jinpeng Wang, Jin-Ge Yao, and Chin-Yew Lin. 2018. Data2Text studio: Automated text generation from structured data. In *Proceedings of the 2018 Conference on Empirical Methods in Natural Language Processing: System Demonstrations*, pages 13–18, Brussels, Belgium. Association for Computational Linguistics.

Linda Flower and John R. Hayes. 1981. A Cognitive Process Theory of Writing. *College Composition and Communication*, 32(4):365–387.

Albert Gatt and Emiel Krahmer. 2018. Survey of the state of the art in natural language generation: Core tasks, applications and evaluation.

Sebastian Gehrmann. 2020. *Human-AI collaboration for natural language generation with interpretable neural networks*. Ph.D. thesis, Harvard University.

Sebastian Gehrmann, Elizabeth Clark, and Thibault Sellam. 2022. Repairing the cracked foundation: A survey of obstacles in evaluation practices for generated text. *ArXiv*, abs/2202.06935.

Hamza Harkous, Isabel Groves, and Amir Saffari. 2020. Have your text and use it too! end-to-end neural data-to-text generation with semantic fidelity. In *Proceedings of the 28th International Conference on Computational Linguistics*, pages 2410–2424, Barcelona, Spain (Online). International Committee on Computational Linguistics.

Leah Henrickson. 2018. Tool vs. agent: attributing agency to natural language generation systems. *Digital Creativity*, 29(2-3):182–190.

David M. Howcroft, Anya Belz, Miruna Clinciu, Dimitra Gkatzia, Sadid A. Hasan, Saad Mahamood, Simon Mille, Emiel van Miltenburg, Sashank Santhanam, and Verena Rieser. 2020. Twenty years of confusion in human evaluation: Nlg needs evaluation sheets and standardised definitions. In *INLG*.

Ronald T. Kellogg, Thierry Olive, and Annie Piolat. 2007. Verbal, visual, and spatial working memory in written language production. *Acta Psychologica*, 124(3):382–397.

Seth Lewis, Andrea Guzman, and Thomas Schmidt. 2019. Automation, journalism, and human–machine communication: Rethinking roles and relationships of humans and machines in news. *Digital Journalism*, 7:1–19.

Cerstin Mahlow and Robert Dale. 2014. Production Media: Writing as Using Tools in Media Convergent Environments. In Eva-Maria Jakobs and Daniel Perrin, editors, *Handbook of Writing and Text Production*, volume 10 of *Handbooks of Applied Linguistics*, pages 209–230. De Gruyter Mouton, Berlin, Germany.

Enrique Manjavacas, Folgert Karsdorp, Ben Burtenshaw, and Mike Kestemont. 2017. Synthetic literature: Writing science fiction in a co-creative process. In *Proceedings of the Workshop on Computational Creativity in Natural Language Generation (CC-NLG 2017)*, pages 29–37, Santiago de Compostela, Spain. Association for Computational Linguistics.

Thierry Olive. 2004. Working memory in writing: Empirical evidence from the dual-task technique. *European Psychologist*.

D. Perrin. 2002. *Schreiben: von intuitiven zu professionellen Schreibstrategien*. Westdt. Verlag.

Daniel Perrin. 2001. *Wie Journalisten schreiben. Ergebnisse angewandter Schreibprozessforschung*. UVK Verlag.

Michael Piotrowski and Cerstin Mahlow. 2009. Linguistic editing support. In *Proceedings of the 9th ACM Symposium on Document Engineering*, pages 214–217.

Ehud Reiter, Robert Dale, and Zhiwei Feng. 2000. *Building natural language generation systems*, volume 33. MIT Press.

Ehud Reiter, Somayajulu Sripada, Jim Hunter, Jin Yu, and Ian Davy. 2005. Choosing words in computer-generated weather forecasts. *Artificial Intelligence*, 167:137–169.

Ehud Reiter and Sandra Williams. 2010. Generating texts in different styles. In *The Structure of Style*, pages 59–75. Springer.

Mike Sharpies. 1992. Representing writing: External representations. *Computers and Writing: State of the Art*.

Mike Sharpies and Lyn Pemberton. 1990. Starting from the writer: Guidelines for the design of user-centred document processors. *Computer Assisted Language Learning*, 2(1):37–57.

Mike Sharples. 1999. *How we write. Writing as creative design*. Routledge.

Vinzenz Wyss. 2013. *Qualitätsmanagement in Redaktionen*, number 1 in Aktuell : Studien zum Journalismus, pages 89–105. Neuberger, Christoph and Meier, Klaus, Baden-Baden.

A Design Space for Writing Support Tools Using a Cognitive Process Model of Writing

Katy Ilonka Gero
Columbia University
katy@cs.columbia.edu

Alex Calderwood
University Of California, Santa Cruz
alexcwd@ucsc.edu

Charlotte Li
Columbia University
li.zihao@columbia.edu

Lydia B. Chilton
Columbia University
chilton@cs.columbia.edu

Abstract

Improvements in language technology have led to an increasing interest in writing support tools. In this paper we propose a design space for such tools based on a cognitive process model of writing. We conduct a systematic review of recent computer science papers that present and/or study such tools, analyzing 30 papers from the last five years using the design space. Tools are plotted according to three distinct cognitive processes—planning, translating, and reviewing—and the level of constraint each process entails. Analyzing recent work with the design space shows that highly constrained planning and reviewing are under-studied areas that recent technology improvements may now be able to serve. Finally, we propose shared evaluation methodologies and tasks that may help the field mature.

1 Introduction

The development of large-scale language models (sometimes called foundation models) is dramatically changing what technology can achieve and support (Bommasani et al., 2021). Language models like GPT3 (Brown et al., 2020) and Meena (Adiwardana et al., 2020) have led to an increasing interest in how these new technologies may support writers, for instance by providing a journalist with text in the style of The New Yorker (Seabrook, 2019) or giving a novelist a new story ending (Marche, 2021). In this paper we seek to understand where research on writing support tools currently stands, and what areas of research may be important but currently under-served.

Computational approaches to writing support have a long and rich history, certainly dating back to before the introduction of modern computation, at least to the early 1900s with the cut-up method (Burroughs, 1961) and 'plot genie' books (Hill, 1931), and likely even further back when considering the long history of generative traditions such as tarot cards (Sullivan et al., 2018). In more contemporary understandings of computation, technology developed by the natural language processing (NLP) community is often taken up as a writing tool.[1] We believe the advent of foundation models poses an exciting inflection point at which these technologies can be used to support the evergreen activity of writing in new ways.

In this paper, we draw on a cognitive process model of writing that considers writing to be a goal-directed thinking process with three distinct and non-linear cognitive processes: planning, translating, and reviewing (Flower and Hayes, 1981). We use this model to propose a design space for writing support tools. This allows us to understand what a writing support tool is attempting to support, and identify gaps or opportunities in the field. It provides a shared vocabulary for researchers, and we hope it will help the field mature and provide common goals and methodologies.

To demonstrate the use of the design space, we perform a systematic literature review of research on writing support tools from the last five years (2017-2021). This shows areas of active research and under-served areas, as well as limitations of current technology to support different aspects of writing. We also use these papers to investigate how to evaluate writing support tools.

The contributions of this paper are:

- A design space for writing support tools, based on a cognitive process model of writing.
- A systematic literature review of writing support tools ($n_{papers} = 30$) from 2017-2021.
- A gap analysis highlighting opportunities for designing future writing support tools.
- A series of common evaluation methodologies for future work to draw on.

[1] For example, spell-checking was an early use of point-wise mutual information (Peterson, 1980), the exciting NLP technology of its time.

Proceedings of the First Workshop on Intelligent and Interactive Writing Assistants (In2Writing 2022), pages 11 - 24
May 26, 2022 ©2022 Association for Computational Linguistics

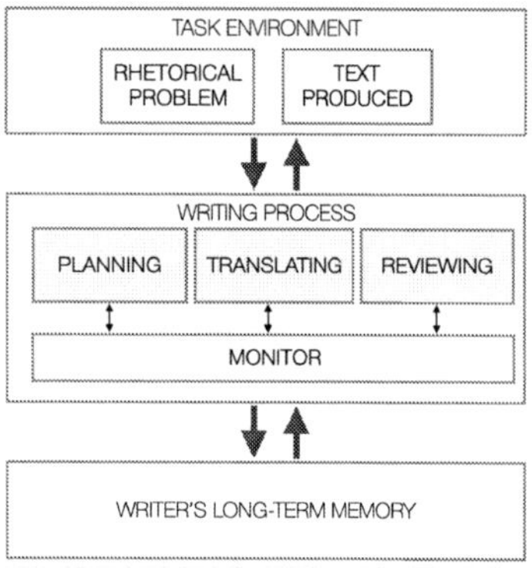

Figure 1: The cognitive process model for writing, as proposed by Flower and Hayes (1981).

2 Related Work

2.1 A Cognitive Process Model of Writing

Flower and Hayes (1981) theory of the cognitive processes involved in writing laid the groundwork for a plethora of research on the psychology of writing over the past four decades. This process model, backed by empirical studies, proposed that writing is best understood as a set of distinct hierarchical thinking processes. Figure 1 shows a schematic of the model, with the three main writing processes—planning, translating[2], and reviewing—highlighted in yellow. When Flower and Hayes state that these processes are hierarchical, they mean they can be called upon iteratively, being embedded within each other. For example, when a writer is constructing a sentence (translating), they may call in a compressed version of the entire writing process. Flower and Hayes' are also quick to note that these processes are not linear. While a common mantra is to 'plan, then write, then review', in reality writers are making plans and reviewing what they have written all throughout the writing process.

Flower and Hayes also proposed that the act of writing is propelled by goals, which are created by the writer and grow in number as the writing progresses. These goals, which span in complexity and abstraction from 'appeal to a broad audience' to 'don't use that cliche', are what direct the writer to different processes. We can model the writing process by considering the writer's goals and what processes they enlist to achieve them.

While this model has since been updated with an increase in complexity[3], considering how goals propel the writing process remains a useful model. Writing has long been considered a mode of learning, as it is both a process and a product, which allows near-constant reflection on the ideas the writer is trying to express (Emig, 1977). By considering a writer's shifting goals, writing researchers have understood why mature writers are able to learn from their writing (Scardamalia and Bereiter, 1987).

We make use of this theory to structure a design space for writing support tools: to understand what these tool actually help with, and how we might design new ones. While there are many ways to think about writing and how computers may support it, we focus on the cognitive process model as it emphasizes writers' intentions, rather than their actions. We believe that this abstraction away from the mechanics of writing will help researchers articulate their intentions with writing support tools, and share results across disparate writing tasks.

2.2 Design Spaces

One way to synthesize a multitude of designs is to envision it in a 'design space', or a metaphorical laying out of designs according to some metrics or measures. MacLean et al. (1996) describe design space *analysis* as an approach to representing design rationale. In this view, a design space places a design in a "space of possibilities" and uses this placement to explain why a design was chosen among all the various possibilities. This frames design spaces as a useful way of communicating with stakeholders. By explaining why a design was chosen, stakeholders can better sell, maintain, and otherwise interact with a product.

Woodbury and Burrow (2006), addressing the growing popularity of design spaces in computational research, describe design space *exploration* as the idea that we can use exploring alternatives as a compelling model of design. This involves representing designs in a meaningful way, and using the representation to explore the space.[4]

A popular and highly-cited example of a design space comes from wireless sensor networks (Romer and Mattern, 2004). As the use of such networks

[2]They use the word 'translating' to refer to the act of putting words on the page, as 'writing' is used to describe the whole process and 'composing' can also be ambiguous. While 'translating' is typically used in NLP communities to denote converting text between languages, we use it here as a technical term to aligns with relevant psychology research.

[3]Hayes adds much more detail to the long-term memory component, and adds components for working memory and the motivation and affect of the writer (Hayes, 1996)

[4]It can also be used to build computer systems to aid in the exploration.

increased globally, "it was very difficult to discuss specific application requirements, research directions, and challenges." The proposed solution was a sensor network design space: its various dimensions would be categorized in order to both understand the existing research as well as discover new designs and applications. One conclusion was that a small set of platforms could cover the majority of the design space, rather than requiring numerous, application-specific platforms.

In this paper we introduce a design space both to think about what writing support tools currently do, and what we might want them to do in the future. In this sense we take both MacLean's and Woodbury's view: the design space is both a way to talk about why existing tools are the way they are, as well as a way to design new ones.

2.3 Related Literature Reviews

Related work has looked at a design space for non-visual word completion (Nicolau et al., 2019) and hybrid paper-digital interfaces (Han et al., 2021). We look to these for methodologies and areas of overlapping interest. Perhaps more related is work from Strobl et al. (2019) in which they perform a review on digital support for academic writing. They review 44 papers addressing essay writing needs in US secondary school instruction. Many of these papers come from educational research communities, and few use NLP technologies. Our review focuses more on human-computer interaction communities and leans more towards system that incorporate NLP technologies. When performing our literature review, we follow the checklist outlined in PRISMA[5] for performing a systematic literature review, including specifying inclusion / exclusion criteria and all sources searched.

3 Writing Goals Design Space

Flower and Hayes (1981) describe writing in the following way:

> The act of composing itself is a *goal-directed thinking process*, guided by the writer's own growing network of goals.

These writing goals may be large, like to write up an experiment for an academic paper, or small, like to make a sentence sound more formal. They may be open-ended, like to come up with the name for a character, or quite limited, like to spell a word correctly. The goals may require imagining the reader, like to determine if a sentence is too confusing, or they may require diving deeper into what's already written, like to ensure a technical topic is discussed consistently throughout an article. Writing goals may start as external motivators—someone may ask one to write something—but as one writes, writing goals are created by the writer and propel the writing process forward.

We propose using this to structure a design space for writing support tools. Whether we call them support tools, assistants, co-creators or machines-in-the-loop, we believe what unites these systems is that they take on goals inherent in the writing process. We propose two axes for the design space:

1. Which part of the writing process the system aims to support. Flower and Hayes, in their original model of writing, propose three components: planning, translating, and reviewing. These three components align with models of creativity, which often cite ideation, implementation, and evaluation (Amabile, 1983). In both cases the components are accessed iteratively, and often hierarchically. A writer may start with a high-level plan, and then in the act of 'translating' the plan may create a smaller plan within it. Splitting up writing support tools into these processes helps us understand how, when, and why a writer may use a tool.

We acknowledge that there can be some ambiguity in distinguishing between these processes. For instance, consider a tool that, upon request, completes a writer's sentence. This tool may be supporting translating, if the completion is intended to articulate what the writer already had in mind. Or it could be supporting planning, if the completion is intended to provide the writer with new ideas or directions for their writing. When annotating papers, we rely on how the researchers describe the tool, though we acknowledge the ambiguities involved in this and that writers may use a tool in unexpected or unintended ways.[6]

2. The amount of constraint the goal has. A highly constrained goal has very few possible solutions, like when writing a technical definition. A lightly constrained goal has many possible solutions, like when describing a newly introduced fictional character. The amount of constraint gives

[5] http://prisma-statement.org/documents/PRISMA_2020_checklist.pdf

[6] An alternate approach is to rely on how writers describe their usage, but given that many papers did not include this in their evaluation, we would not have been able to annotate all papers using this method.

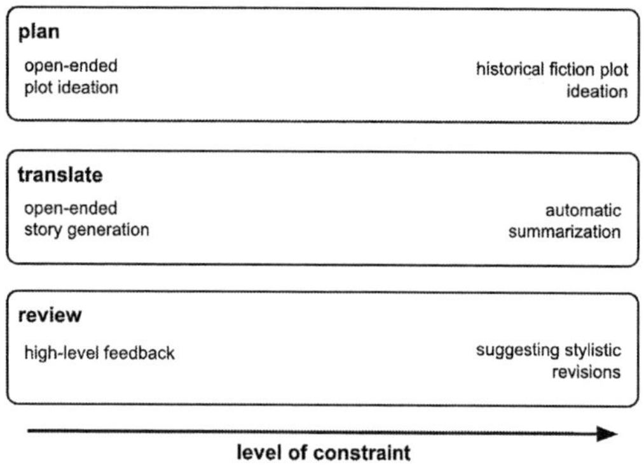

Figure 2: The writing goals design space is defined by the part of the writing process a tool wants to support and the level of constraint of the goal. This shows some example writing goals a tool may want to support.

us a measure of how particular the support must be to achieve the goal. This may be considered a measure of difficulty—writing a technical definition is very constrained, and supporting this writing task requires a high level of world understanding from a system—but constraint doesn't always imply difficulty. A writing goal may be very constrained, for instance make a particular sentence more positive, but the support may be fairly straightforward, like providing a list of positive words.

Figure 2 shows some hypothetical writing support tools in this design space, to better understand the space. Further details and descriptions of the design space can be found in the Appendix.

4 Methodology

We perform a preliminary, systematic literature review such that we can plot tools in the design space. This validates the utility of the design space and provides insights into the landscape of writing support tools.

4.1 Designing a Search Query

We design a query for searching the ACM Digital Library for relevant papers. Our goal for this query is to find as many relevant papers as possible, while minimizing the number of irrelevant papers needed to sort through. This proved more difficult than expected because search terms like 'writing' and 'support' are quite common in other subfields, like those studying memory architecture. We iterated on a query that returned many of the papers we expected to be included (such as (Roemmele and Gordon, 2018a) and (Wambsganss et al., 2020)), while also returning less than 300 results, such that we could visually inspect them all in a timely manner. We chose to only look at papers from the last five years as we wanted to focus on where the field is currently going. We didn't require an average yearly download or number of citations, as done in other systematic reviews like Frich et al. (2019), because we wanted to include very recent work that may not be well-distributed yet.

Our final query can be found in the Appendix. It resulted in 216 items.

4.2 Selecting Papers to Include in Review

First we had one researcher read the titles of all papers and perform a quick 'desk reject' on any papers that were clearly off topic.[7] After this, 77 papers remained. Of these papers, two researchers read all the abstracts and noted if they thought a paper should be included based on the inclusion criteria below. They did this separately, and then came together to discuss and resolve disagreements.

Our inclusion criteria was:

1. a conference or journal publication[8]
2. a contribution that presents or studies a tool that aids in the translation of ideas into text

We include additional examples of what would and would not be included (which the researchers used as guidelines) in the Appendix.

This resulted in 30 papers. A list of these papers can be found in the Appendix. Each paper was assigned a nickname which allowed for easier reference than the paper title or author list.

4.3 Annotating the Selected Papers

Three members of the research team participated in the annotations. The selected papers were split up, and each paper was annotated by a single researchers. Some of these annotations were to allow us to plot tools in the design space, others were to align with Frich et al. (2019), a systematic review of creativity support tools, and still others were to quantify the type of contribution. The full list of annotations, as well as details on how ambiguities in the annotations were resolved, can be found in the Appendix. The results of our annotations can be found at `https://github.com/kgero/writing-support-tools-2022`.

[7]For example, a paper with the title 'A Tool for Visualizing Classic Concurrency Problems' was rejected for clearly being about a different topic.

[8]i.e. not a course description, workshop proceedings, etc.

5 Results and Analysis

5.1 The Writing Goals Design Space

In this section we consider how tools are distributed in the design space, which looks at the type of goal the tool supported, and how constrained that goal is. The 30 papers represented 33 systems, with some papers presenting multiple systems.[9] Three papers studied tools that supported all parts of the writing process: Writing Together (Olson et al., 2017) studied Google Docs, Writing on Github (Pe-Than et al., 2018) studied GitHub, and Literary Style (Sterman et al., 2020) presented an early stage exploratory tool. We exclude these because it is difficult to locate them in a single part of the design space; future work may consider how tools can be distributed across multiple parts of the design space. Excluding these, we are left with 27 systems to analyze in this section.

Figure 3 shows all tools in the writing goals design space. We color them by the size of the goal being supported. We see most parts of the design space covered, with tools in all three parts of the writing process and spanning many different levels of constraint. The papers also operate on all different sizes of writing goals.[10]

The design space shows that planning and reviewing lack work on highly constrained support, suggesting an area for future work. As the constraint for the goal increases, tools tend to support narrower and more structured writing tasks. In planning, MiL (stories) (Clark et al., 2018) and BunCho (Osone et al., 2021) (both constraint=1) support any kind of story writing, while MiL (slogans) (Clark et al., 2018) and Metaphoria (Gero and Chilton, 2019b) (both constraint=4) support slogan and metaphor writing, which have rules and syntactic structures to guide the generation process. Reviewing similarly sees this move towards the niche as constraint increases. Textlets (Han et al., 2020) (constraint=1) is a general purpose reviewing tool based on a sophisticated usage of the 'find' command. In contrast, MepsBot (Peng et al., 2020) (constraint=4) focuses on comments in online mental health forums and Dajke (Schmidt, 2020) (constraint=5) is about adjusting the reading level of Tibetan learning material. Lightly constrained support for planning often relies on newer text generation technologies: MiL (stories) (constraint=1) and MiL (slogans) (constraint=4) come from the same paper (Clark et al., 2018), but the lightly constrained work on stories relies on a neural network while the more constrained work on slogans relies on templates.

Does a highly constrained writing goal need to be niche or highly structured? It may be that language technologies have not yet been capable of supporting more general purpose but still highly constrained writing goals. For instance, brainstorming often happens at multiple points throughout a creative process, with later brainstorming being more constrained by previous choices. Early stage brainstorming may be easier to support because there are less constraints needed to get right. An area new technologies could explore is later-stage brainstorming, which could be quite general purpose—input any piece of writing and a brainstorming prompt—but still lie in the highly constrained planning part of the design space.

The design space shows that highly constrained support for translation is well studied; these systems tend to support highly structured writing tasks. AmbientLetter (Toyozaki and Watanabe, 2018) supports spell-checking while writing on paper; LyriSys (Watanabe et al., 2017) generates topically relevant song lyrics based on a syllabic pattern; Play Write (Iqbal et al., 2018) supports writing microtasks; StoryAssembler (Garbe et al., 2019) supports writing dynamic / non-linear stories. Because the writing goals are quite diverse, these systems use a variety of technologies. Some are about providing text to the writer but most provide support in some other way, like structuring tasks or ensuring constraints are met.

As in planning and reviewing, the translating tools for highly constrained goals are more highly structured. Likely this structure is what allows the tool to be supportive, or is developed by designers to provide traction for the problem. We also saw these tools being quite niche. More general writing tasks like storytelling (e.g. MiL (stories) (Clark et al., 2018), BunCho (Osone et al., 2021), and Writing with RNN (Roemmele and Gordon, 2018b)) were lightly constrained, but this isn't inherent to storytelling. Subtasks within storytelling can be quite constrained, but we didn't see them turn up in our literature review. An interesting

[9] UI Design (Gonçalves and Campos, 2017) studied four systems, but since they were all very similar, for this section we consider them to be a single system (as they would be in the same part of the design space anyway).

[10] 5 at the level of words, 6 at sentences, 8 at paragraphs, 3 at more than the paragraph, and 5 on the writing experience.

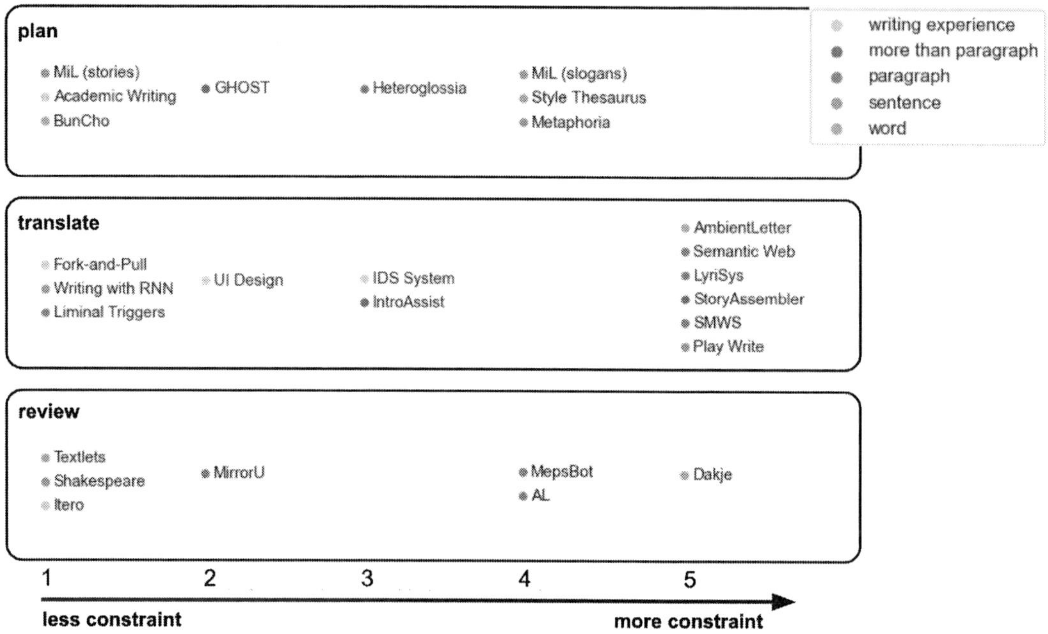

Figure 3: Twenty-seven writing support tools plotted in the writing goals design space. We can see that highly constrained planning and reviewing are under-explored areas.

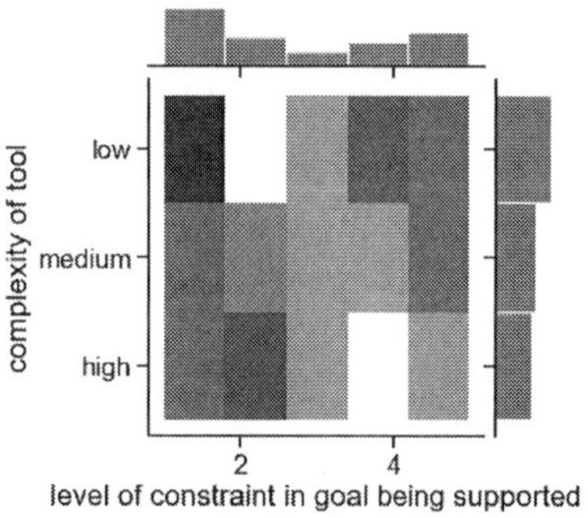

Figure 4: There were more tools with 1-2 features (low complexity). The distribution of constraints being supported was U-shaped.

example of highly constrained translation that we didn't see is taking bullet points and turning them into prose. This is another example of a highly constrained but more general purpose task we believe is an interesting area for future work.

5.2 Complexity of Tool and Technology Used

The tools studied had various levels of technical complexity, drawing on a wide spectrum of user interactions and language technologies. They ranged from full document editors such as Microsoft Word and OmniFocus, which provide rich interface's on top of feedback such as spell checking, to collaboration software such as GitHub, to text generation technologies such as context-free grammars and neural algorithms. Figure 4 shows the distribution of tools according to complexity and level of constraint. For annotating the complexity of a tool we followed Frich et al. (2019), where high complexity refers to an entire system or suite of tools, and low complexity refers to tools with only one or two features. (That is, complexity here is not a measure of technical difficulty.) The tools reviewed were slightly skewed towards low complexity (14 of the 33 tools). Most of the tools (78%) were contributions of the authors.

A third (11 of 33) of the tools used a neural algorithm for text generation or translation and five used some other form of grammar, template, or external knowledge source for text generation. BunCho (Osone et al., 2021) was one of the handful of non-English tools (5 of 33), using GPT-2 to generate Japanese story titles and summaries. Predictive text completion was used by a number of tools, like Storytelling Assistance (Roemmele and Gordon, 2018a), to insert text in a way that might provoke the writer to explore new directions and see their work in a new light.

A number of the tools were more highly constrained, providing some form of scaffold or guidance. Tools like IntroAssist (Hui et al., 2018) use cognitive writing theories to produce static scaffolds that assist writers in their goals, in this case to write an intro email. Style Thesaurus (Gero and Chilton, 2019a) and Metaphoria (Gero and Chilton, 2019b) were among the more highly constrained tools that served as ideation support; the latter generating metaphors from input terms rather than producing sentence-level text.

A number of the tools were interested in analyzing and improving written text at various intermediate points in the writing process. Itero (Türkay et al., 2018) visualized document revision statistics to let writers get a better sense of their own interaction with their written words. AL (Wambsganss et al., 2020) used natural language processing to provide feedback on the quality of essays in terms of their argument structure, readableness, and coherence. Of these, some went the further step of correcting or altering the writer's text. SMWS (Wu et al., 2019) used the paradigm of neural text translation to 'translate' a Dyslexic writer's Facebook comments into non-Dyslexia style writing.

The front-end user experience was primary to many of the tools. UI Design (Gonçalves and Campos, 2017) investigated how various interfaces promoted focus and other such writing considerations, and which led to increased writing quality. Liminal Triggers (Gonçalves et al., 2017) built an editor to investigate the effectiveness of subliminal priming to reduce writer's block. Textlets (Han et al., 2020) turned selected text into manipulable objects for intradocument organization. A few of the studies were interested in situating writing interfaces into alternative environments, such as a smartphone app for mixed-attention environments (Iqbal et al., 2018) and game-text writing tool embedded right into the game engine (Guarneri et al., 2017).

Many of the tools employed networking. Writing Together (Olson et al., 2017) examined the collaborative effects of Google Docs, a full web-based writing interface with inline comments and tracked revision histories. IDS (Tian et al., 2021) provided a mechanism to collaboratively turn summary writing into the form of a final document. A few of the studies explored how GitHub's pull/push workflow, which differs subtitantively from the live-editing affordances of Google Docs, can be used to improve writing quality. Heteroglossia (Huang et al., 2020) expands the typical idea of collaboration with a system that had Mechanical Turkers roleplay for individual characters within a creative story.

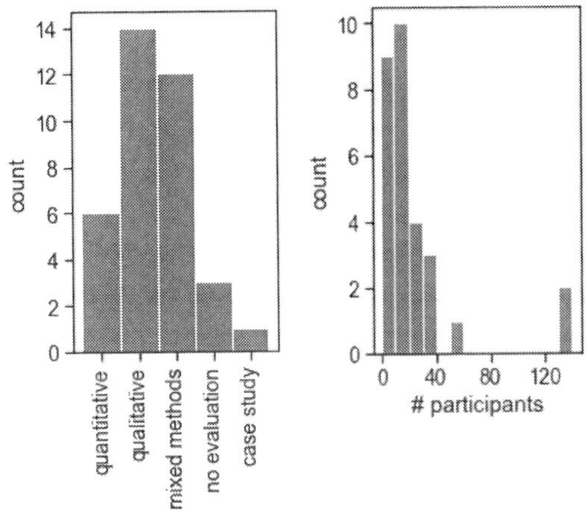

(a) Evaluation Type (b) Number of Participants

Figure 5: Histograms representing the distribution of evaluation methodologies.

5.3 Analysis of Evaluation Methodologies

A total of 33 evaluations were conducted among the 30 papers we studied. Several papers conducted more than one evaluation for their research, while three papers had no evaluation: Shakespeare (Liu et al., 2019), Dakje (Schmidt, 2020), and Ambient Letter (Toyozaki and Watanabe, 2018).

Figure 5 shows the distributions of evaluation type and number of participants. On average, 25 participants were recruited for evaluation of writing tasks. 75% of the evaluations were conducted with fewer than 40 participants and these evaluations were either qualitative or mixed methods, likely because qualitative evaluations produce large and unorganized data that does not allow easy manipulation and analysis for too many participants. Writing Together (Olson et al., 2017) and Storytelling Assistance (Roemmele and Gordon, 2018a) conducted studies with about 130 participants, and both were quantitative only evaluations.

Looking at the papers that had some component of qualitative evaluation, there was a wide range of criteria studied, including quality of writing, usability, usefulness, coherence to context, enjoyment, satisfaction, impact on flow, impact on confidence, and many more. Qualitative studies tended to assess their tools through semi-structured interviews with a small group of target users, such as creative writers or students. Around 50% of qualitative evaluations were done alongside a quantitative evaluation. Studies with only quantitative evaluations, such as Storytelling Assistance (Roemmele and

Gordon, 2018a), assessed quality of the tool with questionnaires reported on a Likert scale and used measures specific to the tools they are studying, like Levenshtein edit distance or simultaneous time spent on writing, to evaluate user's attitudes and collaborative usage of the tool.

Around half of the evaluations reported did not include the time participants spent writing with the system, which makes it difficult to assess this in relation to other aspects of the studies. Among the evaluations that reported time spent writing, quantitative evaluations done without the addition of a qualitative evaluation have a much shorter average time spent with the user (5-10 mins) than the others (25 mins). However, there's nothing inherent about quantitative or larger-scale evaluations that precludes writing for a longer period of time.

Quality of writing corresponds to a variety of different task-specific measures. MiL (stories) (Clark et al., 2018) has Amazon Mechanical Turk workers rate outputs for creativity, coherence, grammaticality, and entertainment. AL has annotators rate an argument according to a formal schema. Writing Together (Olson et al., 2017) studied writing done during a project writing course; writing quality was determined by course graders.

Given so much variety in the evaluation methodologies, we make several recommendations on how evaluations could become more comparable:

- Report more details of the actual writing done in the study, for instance amount of time spent writing, amount of words written, and the type of participants recruited (novice, expert, etc.).
- Use shared surveys rather than develop new ones each time. The Creativity Support Index (Cherry and Latulipe, 2014), NASA Task Load Index (Hart and Staveland, 1988), and Technology Acceptance Model (Venkatesh and Davis, 2000) may all be useful. We also encourage researchers to propose writing-specific surveys that can be used by others.
- Report user interaction measures, like edit distance, and number and frequency of interactions, that can be shared across different writing tasks.

Perhaps the biggest barrier for comparing research is the lack of shared tasks. These papers represent a broad range of writing tasks, from slogan writing to dynamic storytelling to argumentative writing. While we do not believe that writing is a monolith, and nor should be writing support tools, a set of shared tasks may help consolidate the work.

We suggest three shared writing tasks: story writing (fiction), argumentative essay writing (nonfiction), and personal essay writing (creative nonfiction). Personal essay writing has many elements of fiction, like relying on character and narrative, while being constrained to the reality of the writer's lived experience. These tasks span from being completely open-ended (story writing) to partially constrained (personal essay) to quite constrained (argumentative essays). Within each task are many subtasks which span from being very open-ended (how to start the argumentative essay) to very constrained (how to describe an existing character).

We choose these tasks because they each contain goals which could span the entire design space and a variety of genres. There are many tasks we did not include, like emails, explainers, and poetry. These were not chosen because we felt they were too niche (like poetry) or too broad-reaching (like emails) to help unify research.

Below we discuss some variation within each task, and some potential subtasks to focus on:

- Story writing. This already-common task contains within it diverse goals from plot development to scene description. The length can vary its complexity and they can be constrained to varying degrees by a prompt. We recommend two specific tasks. The first is writing stories in response to a prompt. (Again, this is already common and can be continued to be worked on.) The second is adding detail to an existing or partially written story, for instance adding character or scene descriptions. This will allow work to look at some of the more constrained parts of story writing.
- Argumentative essay writing. This task is common in U.S. secondary education and can be extended to include journalistic forms like opinion pieces. It contains subtasks like defending propositions, writing an engaging introduction, and appealing to the audience. We recommend two specific avenues of research: Supporting argumentative structure, and supporting introductory remarks. While supporting structure gets to complicated technical elements of the ideas of a piece of writing, supporting introductory remarks requires more modeling of the reader and understanding what makes text interesting and engaging.

- Personal essay writing. This task can include private journaling as well as more public forms like memoir or even personal statements. It can contain subtasks like finding relevant historical information or identifying potential narratives. The utility of this task is how writers are self-motivated. For this task we recommend focusing less on the quality of writing, and more on the experience of the writer. While stories and argumentative essays have many formal elements that can be used in evaluation, we recommend this task be about immersion and self-expression.

6 Limitations

Our systematic review was limited in scope, as we focused only on the last five years, and our query for selecting papers may not have caught all relevant papers. For instance, one clear problem with using the ACM Digital Library is that many NLP conferences are not included. Future work should investigate more sources for papers, and look further into the archive. Additionally, we did not include commercial or open source writing tools that exist outside of the academy, which likely would improve the findings of any large-scale, systematic review of writing support tools.

There are also many more questions that could be asked about writing support tools. For instance, we found that user type was not widely reported, but user type may be implied by the writing task, or inferred by the evaluation methodology. Relatedly, further analysis could be done on how much work is dedicated to fiction v. nonfiction or short v. longer writing. We hope that by making our selected papers easily accessible, others may use this to do their own investigations with other focuses.

7 Conclusion

We present a design space for writing support tools based on a cognitive process model of writing. We perform a systematic literature review, reviewing 30 papers from the last five years (2017-2021). We find that highly constrained planning and reviewing are under-studied areas. We see that evaluation methodologies vary widely, and propose validated surveys and interaction measures as ways to make evaluations more comparable across systems. We also propose three shared tasks—storytelling, argumentative writing, and personal essays—to aid in propelling work on writing support tools forward.

References

Daniel Adiwardana, Minh-Thang Luong, David R. So, Jamie Hall, Noah Fiedel, Romal Thoppilan, Zi Yang, Apoorv Kulshreshtha, Gaurav Nemade, Yifeng Lu, and Quoc V. Le. 2020. Towards a Human-like Open-Domain Chatbot. *arXiv:2001.09977 [cs, stat]*. ArXiv: 2001.09977.

Teresa M Amabile. 1983. The social psychology of creativity: A componential conceptualization. *Journal of personality and social psychology*, 45(2):357.

Rishi Bommasani, Drew A Hudson, Ehsan Adeli, Russ Altman, Simran Arora, Sydney von Arx, Michael S Bernstein, Jeannette Bohg, Antoine Bosselut, Emma Brunskill, et al. 2021. On the opportunities and risks of foundation models. *arXiv preprint arXiv:2108.07258*.

Tom B. Brown, Benjamin Mann, Nick Ryder, Melanie Subbiah, Jared Kaplan, Prafulla Dhariwal, Arvind Neelakantan, Pranav Shyam, Girish Sastry, Amanda Askell, Sandhini Agarwal, Ariel Herbert-Voss, Gretchen Krueger, Tom Henighan, Rewon Child, Aditya Ramesh, Daniel M. Ziegler, Jeffrey Wu, Clemens Winter, Christopher Hesse, Mark Chen, Eric Sigler, Mateusz Litwin, Scott Gray, Benjamin Chess, Jack Clark, Christopher Berner, Sam McCandlish, Alec Radford, Ilya Sutskever, and Dario Amodei. 2020. Language Models are Few-Shot Learners. *arXiv:2005.14165 [cs]*. ArXiv: 2005.14165.

William S Burroughs. 1961. The cut-up method of brion gysin. *The third mind*, pages 29–33.

Erin Cherry and Celine Latulipe. 2014. Quantifying the Creativity Support of Digital Tools through the Creativity Support Index. *ACM Transactions on Computer-Human Interaction*, 21(4):1–25.

Elizabeth Clark, Anne Spencer Ross, Chenhao Tan, Yangfeng Ji, and Noah A. Smith. 2018. Creative writing with a machine in the loop: Case studies on slogans and stories. In *23rd International Conference on Intelligent User Interfaces*, IUI '18, page 329–340, New York, NY, USA. Association for Computing Machinery.

Janet Emig. 1977. Writing as a Mode of Learning. *College Composition and Communication*, 28(2):122–128. Publisher: National Council of Teachers of English.

Linda Flower and John R. Hayes. 1981. A Cognitive Process Theory of Writing. *College Composition and Communication*, 32(4):365.

Jonas Frich, Lindsay MacDonald Vermeulen, Christian Remy, Michael Mose Biskjaer, and Peter Dalsgaard. 2019. Mapping the Landscape of Creativity Support Tools in HCI. In *Proceedings of the 2019 CHI Conference on Human Factors in Computing Systems*, pages 1–18, Glasgow Scotland Uk. ACM.

Jacob Garbe, Max Kreminski, Ben Samuel, Noah Wardrip-Fruin, and Michael Mateas. 2019. Storyassembler: An engine for generating dynamic choice-driven narratives. In *Proceedings of the 14th International Conference on the Foundations of Digital Games*, FDG '19, New York, NY, USA. Association for Computing Machinery.

Katy Ilonka Gero and Lydia B. Chilton. 2019a. How a stylistic, machine-generated thesaurus impacts a writer's process. In *Proceedings of the 2019 on Creativity and Cognition*, C&C '19, page 597–603, New York, NY, USA. Association for Computing Machinery.

Katy Ilonka Gero and Lydia B. Chilton. 2019b. Metaphoria: An algorithmic companion for metaphor creation. In *Proceedings of the 2019 CHI Conference on Human Factors in Computing Systems*, CHI '19, page 1–12, New York, NY, USA. Association for Computing Machinery.

Frederica Gonçalves and Pedro Campos. 2017. Understanding and evaluating the user interface design for creative writing. In *Proceedings of the European Conference on Cognitive Ergonomics 2017*, ECCE 2017, page 85–92, New York, NY, USA. Association for Computing Machinery.

Frederica Gonçalves, Ana Caraban, Evangelos Karapanos, and Pedro Campos. 2017. What shall i write next? subliminal and supraliminal priming as triggers for creative writing. In *Proceedings of the European Conference on Cognitive Ergonomics 2017*, ECCE 2017, page 77–84, New York, NY, USA. Association for Computing Machinery.

Andrea Guarneri, Laura A. Ripamonti, Francesco Tissoni, Marco Trubian, Dario Maggiorini, and Davide Gadia. 2017. Ghost: A ghost story-writer. In *Proceedings of the 12th Biannual Conference on Italian SIGCHI Chapter*, CHItaly '17, New York, NY, USA. Association for Computing Machinery.

Feng Han, Yifei Cheng, Megan Strachan, and Xiaojuan Ma. 2021. Hybrid Paper-Digital Interfaces: A Systematic Literature Review. In *Designing Interactive Systems Conference 2021*, pages 1087–1100, Virtual Event USA. ACM.

Han L. Han, Miguel A. Renom, Wendy E. Mackay, and Michel Beaudouin-Lafon. 2020. *Textlets: Supporting Constraints and Consistency in Text Documents*, page 1–13. Association for Computing Machinery, New York, NY, USA.

Sandra G Hart and Lowell E Staveland. 1988. Development of nasa-tlx (task load index): Results of empirical and theoretical research. In *Advances in psychology*, volume 52, pages 139–183. Elsevier.

John R. Hayes. 1996. A new framework for understanding cognition and affect in writing. In *The Science of Writing: Theories, Methods, Individual Differences, and Applications*. Lawrence Erbaum Associates.

Wycliffe Aber Hill. 1931. *The Plot Genie*. EE Gagnon Company.

Chieh-Yang Huang, Shih-Hong Huang, and Ting-Hao Kenneth Huang. 2020. *Heteroglossia: In-Situ Story Ideation with the Crowd*, page 1–12. Association for Computing Machinery, New York, NY, USA.

Julie S. Hui, Darren Gergle, and Elizabeth M. Gerber. 2018. *IntroAssist: A Tool to Support Writing Introductory Help Requests*, page 1–13. Association for Computing Machinery, New York, NY, USA.

Shamsi T. Iqbal, Jaime Teevan, Dan Liebling, and Anne Loomis Thompson. 2018. Multitasking with play write, a mobile microproductivity writing tool. In *Proceedings of the 31st Annual ACM Symposium on User Interface Software and Technology*, UIST '18, page 411–422, New York, NY, USA. Association for Computing Machinery.

Eric LaBouve, Erik Miller, and Foaad Khosmood. 2019. Enhancing story generation with the semantic web. In *Proceedings of the 14th International Conference on the Foundations of Digital Games*, FDG '19, New York, NY, USA. Association for Computing Machinery.

Xiaotong Liu, Anbang Xu, Zhe Liu, Yufan Guo, and Rama Akkiraju. 2019. Cognitive learning: How to become william shakespeare. In *Extended Abstracts of the 2019 CHI Conference on Human Factors in Computing Systems*, CHI EA '19, page 1–6, New York, NY, USA. Association for Computing Machinery.

Allan MacLean, Richard M Young, Victoria M E Bellotti, and Thomas P Moran. 1996. Questions, Options, and Criteria: Elements of Design Space Analysis. page 51.

Stephen Marche. 2021. The computers are getting better at writing. *The New Yorker*.

Hugo Nicolau, André Rodrigues, André Santos, Tiago Guerreiro, Kyle Montague, and João Guerreiro. 2019. The Design Space of Nonvisual Word Completion. In *The 21st International ACM SIGACCESS Conference on Computers and Accessibility*, pages 249–261, Pittsburgh PA USA. ACM.

Judith S. Olson, Dakuo Wang, Gary M. Olson, and Jingwen Zhang. 2017. How people write together now: Beginning the investigation with advanced undergraduates in a project course. *ACM Trans. Comput.-Hum. Interact.*, 24(1).

Hiroyuki Osone, Jun-Li Lu, and Yoichi Ochiai. 2021. *BunCho: AI Supported Story Co-Creation via Unsupervised Multitask Learning to Increase Writers' Creativity in Japanese*. Association for Computing Machinery, New York, NY, USA.

Ei Pa Pa Pe-Than, Laura Dabbish, and James Herbsleb. 2021. Open collaborative writing: Investigation of the fork-and-pull model. *Proc. ACM Hum.-Comput. Interact.*, 5(CSCW1).

Ei Pa Pa Pe-Than, Laura Dabbish, and James D. Herbsleb. 2018. Collaborative writing on github: A case study of a book project. In *Companion of the 2018 ACM Conference on Computer Supported Cooperative Work and Social Computing*, CSCW '18, page 305–308, New York, NY, USA. Association for Computing Machinery.

Zhenhui Peng, Qingyu Guo, Ka Wing Tsang, and Xiaojuan Ma. 2020. *Exploring the Effects of Technological Writing Assistance for Support Providers in Online Mental Health Community*, page 1–15. Association for Computing Machinery, New York, NY, USA.

James L. Peterson. 1980. Computer programs for detecting and correcting spelling errors. *Commun. ACM*, 23(12):676–687.

Olaf Resch and Aglika Yankova. 2019. Open knowledge interface: A digital assistant to support students in writing academic assignments. In *Proceedings of the 1st ACM SIGSOFT International Workshop on Education through Advanced Software Engineering and Artificial Intelligence*, EASEAI 2019, page 13–16, New York, NY, USA. Association for Computing Machinery.

Melissa Roemmele and Andrew S. Gordon. 2018a. Automated assistance for creative writing with an rnn language model. In *Proceedings of the 23rd International Conference on Intelligent User Interfaces Companion*, IUI '18 Companion, New York, NY, USA. Association for Computing Machinery.

Melissa Roemmele and Andrew S. Gordon. 2018b. Automated assistance for creative writing with an rnn language model. In *Proceedings of the 23rd International Conference on Intelligent User Interfaces Companion*, IUI '18 Companion, New York, NY, USA. Association for Computing Machinery.

K. Romer and F. Mattern. 2004. The design space of wireless sensor networks. *IEEE Wireless Communications*, 11(6):54–61.

Marlene Scardamalia and Carl Bereiter. 1987. Knowledge telling and knowledge transforming in written composition. In *Advances in applied psycholinguistics*. Cambridge University Press.

Dirk Schmidt. 2020. Grading tibetan children's literature: A test case using the nlp readability tool "dakje". *ACM Trans. Asian Low-Resour. Lang. Inf. Process.*, 19(6).

John Seabrook. 2019. The next word: Where will predictive text take us? *The New Yorker*.

Sarah Sterman, Evey Huang, Vivian Liu, and Eric Paulos. 2020. *Interacting with Literary Style through Computational Tools*, page 1–12. Association for Computing Machinery, New York, NY, USA.

Carola Strobl, Emilie Ailhaud, Kalliopi Benetos, Ann Devitt, Otto Kruse, Antje Proske, and Christian Rapp. 2019. Digital support for academic writing: A review of technologies and pedagogies. *Computers & Education*, 131:33–48.

Anne Sullivan, Mirjam Palosaari Eladhari, and Michael Cook. 2018. Tarot-based narrative generation. In *Proceedings of the 13th International Conference on the Foundations of Digital Games*, pages 1–7.

Sunny Tian, Amy X. Zhang, and David Karger. 2021. A system for interleaving discussion and summarization in online collaboration. *Proc. ACM Hum.-Comput. Interact.*, 4(CSCW3).

Xaver Tomihiro Toyozaki and Keita Watanabe. 2018. Ambientletter: Letter presentation method for discreet notification of unknown spelling when handwriting. In *The 31st Annual ACM Symposium on User Interface Software and Technology Adjunct Proceedings*, UIST '18 Adjunct, page 36–38, New York, NY, USA. Association for Computing Machinery.

Selen Türkay, Daniel Seaton, and Andrew M. Ang. 2018. Itero: A revision history analytics tool for exploring writing behavior and reflection. In *Extended Abstracts of the 2018 CHI Conference on Human Factors in Computing Systems*, CHI EA '18, page 1–6, New York, NY, USA. Association for Computing Machinery.

Viswanath Venkatesh and Fred D. Davis. 2000. A Theoretical Extension of the Technology Acceptance Model: Four Longitudinal Field Studies. *Management Science*, 46(2):186–204.

Thiemo Wambsganss, Christina Niklaus, Matthias Cetto, Matthias Söllner, Siegfried Handschuh, and Jan Marco Leimeister. 2020. *AL: An Adaptive Learning Support System for Argumentation Skills*, page 1–14. Association for Computing Machinery, New York, NY, USA.

Liuping Wang, Xiangmin Fan, Feng Tian, Lingjia Deng, Shuai Ma, Jin Huang, and Hongan Wang. 2018. Mirroru: Scaffolding emotional reflection via in-situ assessment and interactive feedback. In *Extended Abstracts of the 2018 CHI Conference on Human Factors in Computing Systems*, CHI EA '18, page 1–6, New York, NY, USA. Association for Computing Machinery.

Kento Watanabe, Yuichiroh Matsubayashi, Kentaro Inui, Tomoyasu Nakano, Satoru Fukayama, and Masataka Goto. 2017. Lyrisys: An interactive support system for writing lyrics based on topic transition. In *Proceedings of the 22nd International Conference on Intelligent User Interfaces*, IUI '17, page 559–563, New York, NY, USA. Association for Computing Machinery.

Robert F. Woodbury and Andrew L. Burrow. 2006. Whither design space? *Artificial Intelligence for Engineering Design, Analysis and Manufacturing*, 20(2):63–82.

Shaomei Wu, Lindsay Reynolds, Xian Li, and Francisco Guzmán. 2019. Design and evaluation of a social media writing support tool for people with dyslexia. In *Proceedings of the 2019 CHI Conference on Human Factors in Computing Systems*, CHI '19, page 1–14, New York, NY, USA. Association for Computing Machinery.

A Appendix

A.1 Methodology

The query we searched for searching the ACM Digital Library was:

> [[Abstract: writing] OR [Abstract: writer]] AND
>
> [[Abstract: interface] OR [Abstract: system] OR [Abstract: prototype] OR [Abstract: tool]] AND
>
> [[Abstract: assistant] OR [Abstract: support] OR [Abstract: tool]] AND
>
> [Publication Date: (01/01/2017 TO 12/31/2021)] AND
>
> [CCS 2012: Human-centered computing]

The results of the query can be found at the following url:

`https://dl.acm.org/action/doSearch?fillQuickSearch=false&target=advanced&expand=dl&CCSAnd=60&AfterMonth=1&AfterYear=2017&BeforeMonth=12&BeforeYear=2021&AllField=Abstract%3A%28writing+OR+writer+OR+writers%29+AND+Abstract%3A%28interface+OR+system+OR+prototype+OR+tool%29+AND+Abstract%3A%28assistant+OR+support+OR+tool%29`

Below are examples of types of papers that would or would not be included. We used these examples when determining which papers would be included.

- Some examples that would not be included: a general purpose productivity tool, where writing is an example use case; a study/analysis where the data analyzed is writing data; a study about writing-adjacent tools, like handwriting recognition; a tool that generates writing with little human interaction; a non-writing tool with a language interface; language learning tools.

- Some examples that would be included: a design fiction about a writing tool; a writing tool that has no evaluation; a writing tool that writes the first draft and then a human revises it; a study of a commercial writing tool; a tool that supports a very specific writing task; a tool that supports writing and something else (but is not a general purpose tool).

We chose this inclusion criteria subjectively, to focus on our particular interest in writing support tools and their relation to improvements in language technology. We do not intend to present this inclusion criteria as an objective definition of writing support tools. For instance, handwriting recognition may be considered a writing support tool in some contexts, but would not fit our purposes. Another small group of papers we rejected were papers that supported the collection or organization of data that would later be written about, such as a tool for quickly extracting sports-game highlights for sportswriters, and another that solicited reflections throughout the day to support memoir writing. Journalists and others may consider these writing tools, but we excluded them on the rationale that they were somewhat disconnected from the final text produced.

Table 1 shows all annotations done for the papers selected. Table 2 shows all 30 papers selected for this review, with brief descriptions and ordered by the year they were published.

There was some ambiguity in the annotations. Some tools straddled multiple parts of the writing process, or the paper didn't frame the tool in a way that clearly defined the intention of the support. Systems that provided generated text were sometimes framed as providing ideas for the writer, and these labeled as supporting 'planning', whereas others that provided generated text were framed as actually writing, and these were labeled as supporting 'translating'. However, the distinction can be subtle, and sometimes, in a user study, participants used the tool in a different way than the designers intended. Some tools had a single main feature and many small 'satellite' features, making the level of complexity unclear. Our intention with these annotations is not to provide a perfectly objective representation but rather to understand the breadth and similarities within a field of study. When an annotator was unsure about an annotation, they consulted with the rest of the team.

Some papers presented or studied more than one tool; others presented more than one evaluation for a single tool. In the case of multiple tools, we give each tool its own nickname and consider them separate entities. In the case of multiple evaluations, we consider them separate entities only when analyzing evaluation methodologies. (Multiple tools evaluated together are considered a single entity when analyzing evaluation methodologies.)

How support aligns with the cognitive process model	
part of writing process	plan / translate / review
level of constraint	1: low constraint (almost anything could be helpful) 3: medium constraint (constrained but with variety in "right" answers) 5: high constraint (support must be very specific, few "right" answers)
size of goal being support	word / sentence / paragraph / more than paragraph / writing experience
Matching creativity support tool review (Frich et al., 2019)	
complexity of tool	low: one or two features medium: multiple features, semi-complex system high: entire system or suite of tools
evaluation type	no evaluation / case study / qualitative / quantitative / mixed methods
number of participants	(numeric response)
evaluation criterion	(open response)
time spent writing with tool	(numeric response in minutes)
Quantifying type of research	
tool is exclusively about text	yes/no
tool is about collaborative writing	yes/no
tool is contribution	yes/no
technology tool uses	(open response)

Table 1: List of all annotations done for the papers. Most annotations have options, while some are open response.

Some papers studied existing commercial writing tools, and others presented novel tools developed by the researchers. The commercial writing tools studied tended to be word processors, like Microsoft Word or Google Docs. We include all of these in our analysis.

A.2 Design Space

Below are further details articulating the design space.

- Plan: Support for ideation would be included in the planning portion of the design space, as would tools that aid in structuring writing. Some brainstorming support would be lightly constrained planning, for instance during early-stage story telling, whereas other brainstorming might be highly constrained, as in when writing about historical events or in an already-constructed story world.
- Translate: We can place existing NLP tasks like automatic story generation and automatic summarization as supporting translation, where story generation tends to be only lightly constrained by a prompt and summarization is highly constrained by the document it is summarizing.
- Review: A tool that provides the writer with feedback would support reviewing, as would one that involves revising what has already been written. A lightly constrained reviewing tool might provide generic or high-level feedback like "what narrative structure are you using?" whereas a highly constrained tool might provide feedback on specific word choice, stylistic patterning, or argument coherence.

UI Design (Gonçalves and Campos, 2017): Presents a user study of four writing environments – Microsoft Word, Scrivener, OmniWriter and Ulysses. They found OmniWriter to be the most satisfying tool, and propose design guidelines for such tools, including full-screen mode for distraction-free writing.

LyriSys (Watanabe et al., 2017): Reports on a lyric generation system, which generates full song lyrics according to strain and accent constraints, and provides plenty of user control including semantic topic transitions.

Writing Together (Olson et al., 2017): Studies data traces of collaborative writing in student teams' use of Google Docs.

Liminal Triggers (Gonçalves et al., 2017): Investigates how subliminal triggering may help to relieve writer's block.

GHOST (Guarneri et al., 2017): Presents a tool to support non-writers creating stories for video games. The resulting tool, GHOST, is built into Unity and aids in the creation of plot roadmaps.

Writing with RNN (Roemmele and Gordon, 2018b): Presents Creative Help, an interface that suggests new sentences in a story using an RNN language model. Study varies the degree of randomness.

MiL (Clark et al., 2018): Presents and studies creative writing support tools: a next-sentence generator for story telling, and a slogan generator for writing slogans.

AmbientLetter (Toyozaki and Watanabe, 2018): Proposes a technique to support writing activity (via autocorrection and predictive conversion) in a confidential manner with a pen-based device.

Play Write (Iqbal et al., 2018): Introduces a microproductivity tool that allows users to review and edit Word documents in small moments of spare time from their smartphone.

IntroAssist (Hui et al., 2018): Presents a tool for supporting writing introductory help requests via email by providing checklists and examples.

Itero (Türkay et al., 2018): Presents a study on how integrating writing revision analytics and visualization into writing practices can impact writing self-efficacy.

Writing on Github (Pe-Than et al., 2018): Presents the preliminary findings of a mixed-methods, case study of collaboration practices in a GitHub book project.

MirrorU (Wang et al., 2018): Presents a mobile system to support reflecting and writing about daily emotional experiences; provides assessment and feedback across level of detail, overall valence, and cognitive engagement.

Semantic Web (LaBouve et al., 2019): Presents a mixed initiative tool for story generation, designed to take as input a story generating grammar in addition to generic keywords and uses the semantic web to contribute real-world details.

Shakespeare (Liu et al., 2019): Presents a web application that helps with educating different writing styles through automatic style transfer (with deep learning), visual stylemotry analytics, and machine teaching (by picking out examples of a particular writing style). The authors propose a use case of this system with Shakspeare's writings.

Metaphoria (Gero and Chilton, 2019b): Presents a tool that shows how words might be metaphorically related.

StoryAssembler (Garbe et al., 2019): Presents StoryAssembler, an open source generative narrative system that creates dynamic choice-driven narratives, and a case study.

SMWS (Wu et al., 2019): This paper describes a tool built by the Facebook researchers to automatically 'translate' text written by people with dyslexia to non-dyslexic style writing. Having built the tool into the Facebook comment interfcae, they conduct a week long study to measure its efficacy.

Academic Writing (Resch and Yankova, 2019): Presents OKI, a chatbot tool that helps with project management, assistance in applying scientifc methods, and search in open access literature.

Style Thesaurus (Gero and Chilton, 2019a): Presents a series of automatically generated thesauruses, using word embeddings trained on custom corpuses, which reflect the stylistic preferences of the corpus text.

AL (Wambsganss et al., 2020): This paper presents an NLP tool to aid student argumentative writing by providing automatic feedback on their argumentation structure.

Dakje (Schmidt, 2020): Introduces a new readability tool alongside a specific use case, and demonstrates how it can help benefit literacy in the Tibetan languages. Users have instant access to statistics on the readability of their word choices so they can make edits for easy-to-read text.

Heteroglossia (Huang et al., 2020): Presents a crowd-sourcing tool that allows writer to elicit story ideas based on a role-play strategy. The tool is developed as Google Doc add-on.

Textlets (Han et al., 2020): Introduces Textlets, interactive objects that reify text selections into persistent items, and show how Textlets can be used for selective search and replace, word count, and alternative wording.

MepsBot (Peng et al., 2020): Presents in-situ writing assistance for people commenting in online mental health communities; compares support that assesses text versus recommends text.

Literary Style (Sterman et al., 2020): Develops a model of style by training a neural net, and present novel applications including an interactive text editor with real-time style feedback.

Fork-and-Pull (Pe-Than et al., 2021): Investigates the utility of the GitHub "fork and pull" workflow for writers through a mixed-methods case study of collaborative writing. They looked at two collaborative writing cases, the first to write a mathematics textbook on homotopy type theory, and the second a set of open source public policies.

IDS System (Tian et al., 2021): Presents Wikum+, a website that allows you to create instances of interleaved discussion and summarization.

BunCho (Osone et al., 2021): Presents a tool for generating titles and synopses from keywords. Additionally, an interactive story co-creation AI system is proposed. (Japanese language)

Table 2: List of all 30 papers, ordered by the year their were published, with short description of contribution.

A Selective Summary of *Where to Hide a Stolen Elephant: Leaps in Creative Writing with Multimodal Machine Intelligence*

Nikhil Singh[§*] **Guillermo Bernal**[§*] **Daria Savchenko**[†*] **Elena L. Glassman**[†]
[§]MIT Media Lab
{nsingh1,gbernal}@mit.edu
[†]Harvard University
{daria_savchenko@g,glassman@seas}.harvard.edu

Abstract

While developing a story, novices and published writers alike have had to look outside themselves for inspiration. Language models have recently been able to generate text fluently, producing new stochastic narratives upon request. However, effectively integrating such capabilities with human cognitive faculties and creative processes remains challenging. We propose to investigate this integration with a multimodal writing support interface that offers writing suggestions textually, visually, and aurally. We conduct an extensive study that combines elicitation of prior expectations before writing, observation and semi-structured interviews during writing, and outcome evaluations after writing. Our results illustrate individual and situational variation in machine-in-the-loop writing approaches, suggestion acceptance, and ways the system is helpful. Centrally, we report how participants perform *integrative leaps*, by which they do cognitive work to integrate suggestions of varying semantic relevance into their developing stories. We interpret these findings, offering modeling and design recommendations for future creative writing support technologies.[1]

1 Introduction

Much remains unexplored about how emerging methods in AI, machine learning, and natural language processing might influence creative writing, in part due to the ambiguity and variability of human writing processes. These processes go beyond the linear projection from idea to a full text; research shows how planning narratives, translating ideas into visible textual material, and reviewing are all happening and interacting throughout the process rather than simple sequential stages (Nold, 1981; Flower and Hayes, 1981). However, this is a very familiar process for humans when communicating through writing; as every writer knows, having good ideas does not automatically produce a good text progression. The need for that "good idea" to be anchored and developed so that the reader can be invested takes a great deal of effort. In today's world, language generation models like GPT-2 (Radford et al., 2019), GPT-3 (Brown et al., 2020), and new ones coming down the line are typically silent on the inner processes of negotiation and decision that a human writer is working through. Additionally, contributions from these systems might take forms to influence writing other than text; writers are able to engage multiple perceptual channels through their work: they may activate multisensory imagination through evocative imagery, invoking auditory and olfactory phenomena, and other forms of sensory description.

We investigate how participants engage with a multimodal writing support system that bridges generated writing suggestions with multimedia retrieval to produce concept representations simultaneously in sight, sound, and language. We pair this interface with an extensive study that combines surveys, interaction, and semi-structured interviews during observed, think-aloud writing sessions. We examine and report in detail how participants receive, consider, and integrate suggestions from an intelligent tool into their writing. We explore prominent axes of individual and situational variation in these integrative behaviors, noting the different kinds of "leaps" participants make to understand suggestions and make the necessary compositional decisions to incorporate new information contained in them, ranging from copying and pasting to re-writing core aspects of their entire story.

In summary, our findings suggest that participants perform different kinds of *integrative leaps*, involving cognitive work to make suggestions useful to their writing. We interpret these and make commensurate design recommendations for future creative writing support tools.

[1]This work is a cross-submission and is published as Singh, Bernal, Savchenko, and Glassman, 2022.

Proceedings of the First Workshop on Intelligent and Interactive Writing Assistants (In2Writing 2022), pages 25 - 26
May 26, 2022 ©2022 Association for Computational Linguistics

Acknowledgements

This material is based upon work supported by the NSF under Grant No. 2107391.

References

Tom Brown, Benjamin Mann, Nick Ryder, Melanie Subbiah, Jared D Kaplan, Prafulla Dhariwal, Arvind Neelakantan, Pranav Shyam, Girish Sastry, Amanda Askell, Sandhini Agarwal, Ariel Herbert-Voss, Gretchen Krueger, Tom Henighan, Rewon Child, Aditya Ramesh, Daniel Ziegler, Jeffrey Wu, Clemens Winter, Chris Hesse, Mark Chen, Eric Sigler, Mateusz Litwin, Scott Gray, Benjamin Chess, Jack Clark, Christopher Berner, Sam McCandlish, Alec Radford, Ilya Sutskever, and Dario Amodei. 2020. Language models are few-shot learners. In *Advances in Neural Information Processing Systems*, volume 33, pages 1877–1901. Curran Associates, Inc.

Linda Flower and John R Hayes. 1981. A cognitive process theory of writing. *College composition and communication*, 32(4):365–387.

Ellen W Nold. 1981. Revising. *Writing: the nature, development, and teaching of written communication*, 2:67–79.

Alec Radford, Jeffrey Wu, Rewon Child, David Luan, Dario Amodei, and Ilya Sutskever. 2019. Language models are unsupervised multitask learners. *OpenAI blog*, 1(8):9.

Nikhil Singh, Guillermo Bernal, Daria Savchenko, and Elena L. Glassman. 2022. Where to hide a stolen elephant: Leaps in creative writing with multimodal machine intelligence. *ACM Trans. Comput.-Hum. Interact.* Just Accepted.

A text-writing system for Easy-to-Read German evaluated with low-literate users with cognitive impairment

Ina Steinmetz and **Karin Harbusch**
Universität Koblenz-Landau
Computer Science Faculty
Universitätsstraße 1, 56070 Koblenz, Germany
inaschroeder@uni-koblenz.de | harbusch@uni-koblenz.de

Abstract

Low-literate users with intellectual or developmental disabilities (IDD) and/or complex communication needs (CCN) require specific writing support. We present a system that interactively supports fast and correct writing of a variant of *Leichte Sprache* (LS; German term for *easy-to-read German*), slightly extended within and beyond the inner-sentential syntactic level. The system provides simple and intuitive dialogues for selecting options from a natural-language paraphrase generator. Moreover, it reminds the user to add text elements enhancing understandability, audience design, and text coherence. In earlier development phases, the system was evaluated with different groups of substitute users. Here, we report a case study with seven low-literate users with IDD.

1 Introduction

Recent studies report that more than 10 percent of German-speaking adults have low literacy skills (cf. Anke Grotlüschen et al., 2020). People with intellectual and developmental disabilities (IDD) and/or complex communication needs (CCN) often belong to this group (Light et al., 2019; Grotlüschen and Buddeberg, 2020; hereafter referred to as *the target group,* or simply *the users*).

Leichte Sprache (*LS;* easy-to-read German), a simplified variety of German, was developed for the target group as part of the plain language movement of the 2000s (cf. Inclusion Europe, 2009; BITV2.0, 2011, Netzwerk Leichte Sprache, 2013, or Bredel and Maaß, 2016).

Inclusion necessitates technical assistance to barrier-free participation in all social spheres (Hirschberg and Lindmeier, 2013). In the following, we investigate the extent to which *natural language processing* (NLP) can support the users while writing. An increasing variety of writing-support systems based on *natural language generation* (NLG) attract attention (for their prospects, see, e.g., Dale and Viethen, 2021; for approaches based on deep learning, see Otter et al., 2021). Adaptive behavior like automatically modifying the written text incurs the risk that users—due to low-literacy—do not carefully check whether or not the changes express the intended meaning. Missing is a text base produced by the target group. In general, text in LS is produced by authors proficient in standard German[1]. Thus, suggestions by the system that are automatically extracted from given LS text might not be perceived as helpful but irritating, let alone unintentionally patronizing. In addition, interactions with the user pose additional challenges, such as designing an accessible interface (cf. Nganji and Nggada, 2011). In essence, supportive interaction patterns should not overtax the user.

In the present paper, we describe *EasyTalk* for fast, correct and reader-centered writing in *Extended Leichte Sprache* (*ELS*; Harbusch and Steinmetz, 2022; ELS extends LS in several respects, for instance, with high frequent constructions from spoken German that incorporate the target group's ways of articulating their thoughts; for previous prototypes of *EasyTalk*, see Steinmetz and Harbusch, 2020; 2021a/b). On the sentential level, a natural-language paraphrase generator suggests correctly inflected word forms. It pursues the overall correctness and completeness of the sentence and provides the correct German word ordering. In order to improve text-understandability and text-coherence over the entire text, *EasyTalk* reminds the user to add *audi-*

[1] They may be supported by rule-based validation tools (for LS, see, e.g., languagetool.org/de/leichte-sprache/) or automatic text-simplification (cf. Ebling et al., 2022; for English, see, e.g., paperswith-code.com/task/text-simplification)

Proceedings of the First Workshop on Intelligent and Interactive Writing Assistants (In2Writing 2022), pages 27 - 38
May 26, 2022 ©2022 Association for Computational Linguistics

ence-design features within a clause (Bell, 1984). The user is invited to clarify the discourse structure by adding connectors (inspired by *Rhetorical-Structure Theory* (RST); see Hovy, 1988 and Mann and Thompson, 1988), thus explicitly marking the relationship between the simple clauses. (SVO order is mandatory in declarative main clauses of (E)LS).

In the following, we first summarize the state of the art in writing-support systems. Then, we outline *EasyTalk*'s mechanisms for supporting text-production both within and between sentences. In Section 4, we report the results of a case study we recently conducted with seven users from the target group. The results are compared with observations from earlier evaluations with other user groups, in particular with L2 learners of German. The paper ends with a discussion of open issues and desirable future work.

2 Writing support systems for users with IDD and/or CCN

This section summarizes the state of the art in writing systems focusing on German where particular problems arise from rich morphology and free word ordering. In Section 2.1, we present symbol-based systems that go beyond needs-based, functional communication supporting the expression of personal thoughts in the context of social closeness and sharing information (cf. Light, 1988). In Section 2.2, we outline text-based systems designed for the target group. Finally, we address systems for teaching text-writing.

2.1 Symbol-based writing systems

Augmentative and Alternative Communication (AAC) offers a wide range of support to people with CCN, for example, the use of symbols as visual representation of a word or idea (cf. Figure 1, Figure 2, and Figure 3[2]). Technical solutions for symbol-based AAC are increasingly available on mainstream devices like smartphones and tablets (Ascari, 2018), ranging from simple concatenation of symbols for needs-based, functional communication (see, e.g., the popular free apps *SymboTalk*[3]

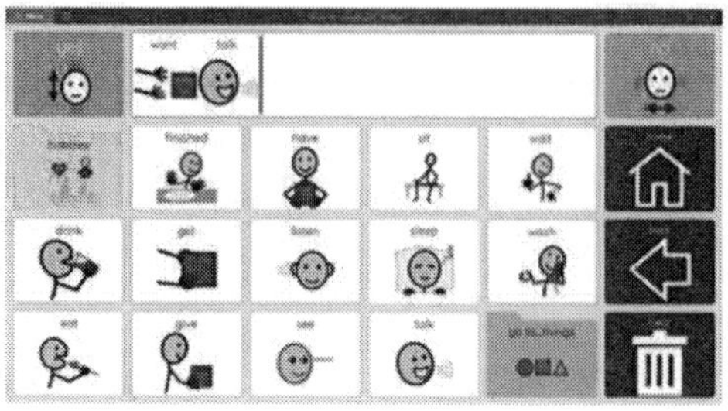

Figure 1: A simple *Mind Express* symbol-grid.

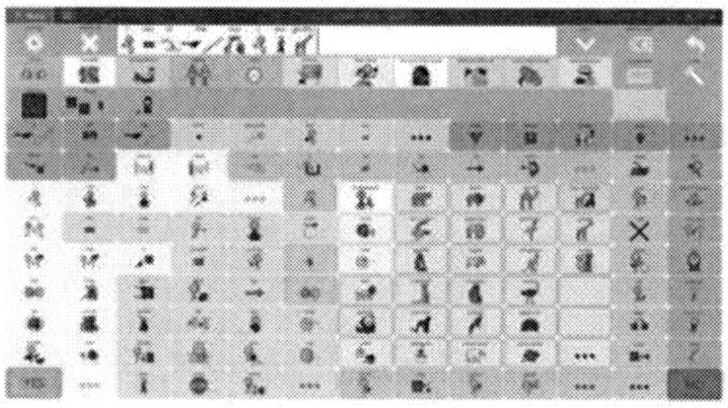

Figure 2: A complex *Mind Express* symbol-grid where symbols are grouped and colored by category (e.g., verbs in green, nouns in orange).

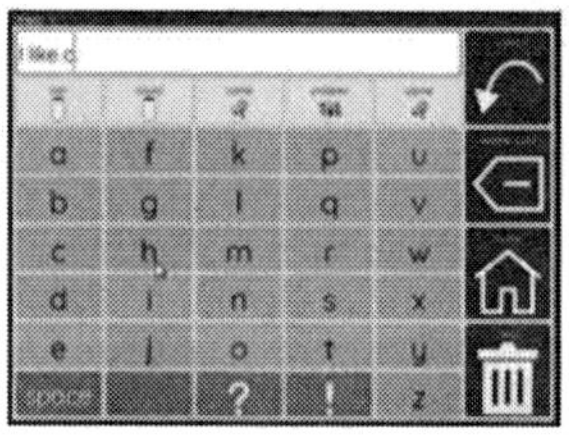

Figure 3: A *Mind Express* alphabet page, offering symbols and letters to access words.

and *LetMeTalk*[4] for German) to complex (commercial) systems (cf. Lancioni et al., 2019, for a thorough survey). Although language support through linguistic processing by computer is increasingly in demand, the full potential of support through NLP for AAC is not yet exploited (Waller, 2019).

Gateway[5], *Mind Express*[6] and *TD Snap Core First*[7] offer a representative sample of widely provided features in complex, commercial symbol-based AAC systems. Primarily, these systems enable users to participate actively in real-time spoken dialog. In addition, they aim to help users to increase the grammatical and lexical diversity

[2] The three snapshots (accessed 17.02.2022) are taken from: `www.jabbla.com/en/mind-express/` and `www.jabbla.com/en/tutorials/steps-to-language-the-alphabet-page-in-level-1/`.

[3] `www.symbotalk.com/`

[4] `apps.apple.com/de/app/letmetalk-gratis-aac-talker/id919990138`

[5] `www.gatewaytolanguageandlearning.com/`

[6] `www.jabbla.com/en/mind-express/`

[7] `de.tobiidynavox.com/pages/td-snap-core-first#`

of their written output. For writing, they provide basic linguistic support, such as adaptive word prediction and automatic inflection of simple sentence constituents. The more complex the linguistic variety, the stronger the need for grammatical knowledge on the part of the users. For instance, they may have to specify the correct word endings manually due to the lack of correct predictions by the systems.

As shown in Figure 1 and Figure 2, the systems typically offer customizable *grid layouts* of varying complexity, suitable for different access methods like eye-control, touch, or scanning[8]. Grid cells may contain symbols, words, letters, and function buttons like 'undo' or 'enter menu'. Accordingly, activating a grid cell can select a word, lead to another grid page containing more words of a certain category, or access grammatical functions, respectively. Users with basic spelling skills can use a mixture of letters and symbols to choose the words (cf. Figure 3).

Generally, these systems presuppose individualized teaching and year-long practice (see, e.g., McNaughton et al., 2008, and Waller, 2019, addressing various challenges). Progression from easier to more advanced keyboards is supported by the constant positioning of the typed sentence. The layout examples in Figure 1 and Figure 3 place the current sentence prominently at the top. Preceding sentences are only visible to advanced users (e.g., Figure 2, two consecutive sentences are displayed in the white box). By design, the writing support focuses on the sentence level.

2.2 Text-based writing support systems

Writing instruction with appropriate technology positively impacts people with IDD (Smith et al., 2020). Modern text editors implement barrier-free access by features like read-aloud functionality. The database by the German foundation *barrierefrei kommunizieren!*[9] lists systems for users with disabilities: standalone systems like *Kurzweil3000*, *Penfriend*, and *MULTiTEXT;* and next-word predictors like *WoDy, EMU,* and *FTB-TippFixx* that can be integrated with MS Word and other text editors to support the user.

Text-based writing support suits users with a modest level of computer skills, who can write short sentences in a (simplified or customized) text editor. A variety of visual highlightings and color encodings (e.g., color keys for different word types, parts of a sentence, punctuation symbols) facilitates navigation through the text. Flexible read-aloud functions reproduce the written text letter by letter, word by word or sentence by sentence (with or without punctuation marks), thus providing memory support and spelling assistance. On demand, all systems employ grammar checkers. Adaptive word predictions (partially for customizable vocabulary) are usually offered in the form of word lists searchable via hotkeys for quick selection. However, all systems present the users with an empty page. The process of building up the text structure is not supported.

2.3 Teaching text-production

In German-language primary and secondary schools, the method of the *Schreibwerkstatt/Schreibkonferenz* 'writing workshop' is widely applied (see, e.g., Reichardt et al, 2014, for a broad survey). The students learn how to introduce every protagonist of a story in a way that allows the reader to identify them while the story progresses. Also taught is the appropriate use of elements of text coherence, discourse structure, and audience design. At the sentence-formulation level, students are instructed to integrate sets of short, choppy sentences into longer, more effective ones (cf. *sentence-combining techniques;* see Nordquist, 2018, for an online introduction; Ney, 1980, for the history, and Saddler and Preschern, 2007, for the school context). Beside computer systems for the above-mentioned topics[10], there is a wide range of NLG systems for automatic text production, such as parameterized interactive storytelling by Lukin and Walker (2019), or interactive story modeling using recurrent neural networks by Fortuin et al. (2018). However, none of these systems are available in German. Moreover, there is no straight-forward way to equip any of these systems with an interface appropriate for the target group.

3 Text-writing assistance by *EasyTalk*

EasyTalk targets the creation of text beyond the genre of simple chat messages with an interface that does not overtax the user. In particular, it aims

[8] A scanning system iterates sequentially through all options until the user instructs the system to stop and select.

[9] www.barrierefrei-kommunizieren.de/datenbank/

[10] See, e.g., the *WritingPal* (www.igi-global.com/chapter/the-writing-pal/88184)

to alleviate the need for a lengthy learning and practicing period. All barrier-free concepts cited previously should be available. To interlace with the user's word-by-word formulation process, we suggest a bottom-up approach employing a natural-language paraphrase generator on the sentential level (cf. Section 3.1). To meet the concepts the target group is likely to use to express their thoughts, the generator is based on an extension of LS. As the extension does not deviate from the mandatory SVO word order in declarative main clauses, we propose to add discourse-structure clues between sentences (see Section 3.2) to improve text coherence. We demonstrate that all dialogues with the user can be restricted to easy wording and simple choices—irrespective of the complexity of the linguistic task.

3.1 Text functions

EasyTalk's user interface comprises three layers embedded in the Menu Panel: Top: Text Panel; Middle: Sentence and Connector Panel in alternation; Bottom: Next-Word Panel (see the two snapshots in Figure 4 depicting that either the Sentence Panel or the Connector Panel is active).

Eventually, the users can export their texts from *EasyTalk* with or without symbols via the option '*save text*' from the meta-level Menu Panel (cf. A in a gray hexagon in the lower snapshot). In addition, this panel offers various settings (B) providing further customization features, which we will not discuss here due to space limitations. For instance, extending the vocabulary or changing the symbols enable personalization of the system.

Framed by the Menu Panel, the top layer displays all previously typed text (e.g., finishing the sentence currently in the upper snapshot updates the Text Panel in the lower one). The user can activate the read-aloud functionality by clicking on a sentence (cf. C in a green pentagon in the lower snapshot). For backing up the train of thoughts, the user can scroll through the text (D). If desired, lines from the text can be erased (E).

Next, we explain our approach to the design of the individual writing panels.

3.2 Within-sentence support

At the sentential level, *EasyTalk* aims at fast and correct writing. The user is supported by: symbols for finding words in their correct spelling, the correct inflectional endings in any sentential context, mentioning all obligatory arguments accord-

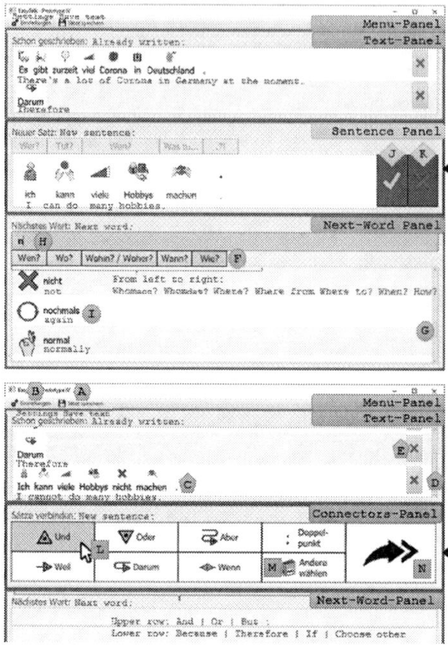

Figure 4: Two consecutive snapshots of *EasyTalk's* overall interface. Top: typing the sentence *Ich kann viele Hobbys nicht machen*; Bottom: adding the connector *Und* after the sentence is finished. The interface elements are explained in the text.

ing to the verb-valency frame, and maintaining the correct word ordering. On the premise of supporting the user according to the document planning, constituents can be freely entered in any desired order. However, guidance by a default execution-strategy is always active. To fulfill audience design[11] aspects, *EasyTalk* reminds the user to add attributes such as time and place. All interactions with the user are presented in an intuitive manner.

To this end, *EasyTalk* employs a natural-language paraphrase generator originally designed for L2 learners of German (cf. the *COMPASS* system for explorative language learning; Harbusch and Kempen, 2011) based on a *lexicalized, unification-based Performance Grammar* (Harbusch and Kempen, 2002; Kempen and Harbusch, 2002). The user assembles all constituents of a correct sentence interactively with the system, including revisions (cf. *scaffolded writing*). *EasyTalk* appropriately simplifies the decision dialogues with the generator. Moreover, the Per-

[11] We use the original term by Bell (1984) to refer to the wide area of how to enrich a text for making it understandable for the reader, i.e., taking a third-person perspective for understanding the text (reader-centered writing).

formance Grammar version we use is restricted to syntactic constructions of *Extended Leichte Sprache (ELS)*. ELS is a slight extension of LS. In LS, only easy words should be used. Abbreviations, genitive case, subjunctive mood, passive voice, and subordinate clauses are forbidden. Declarative main clauses should use the canonical SVO word order only. ELS covers constructions beyond the scope of pure LS that have been attested to be easy in experiments with LS readers (Bock, 2019). For instance, negation with *nicht* 'not' or passives with *werden* 'be' are licensed. The scope of constructions tested by Bock (2019) is extended with frequent constructions in LS text that are also frequent in spoken German (e.g., negation with $kein_{inflected}$ 'no', or simple past tense for auxiliaries and modals; cf. Harbusch and Steinmetz, 2022, for a corpus study into treebanks of LS text, spoken and written German to determine the range of constructions that the target group likely uses to articulate their thoughts).

The overall lexicon of *COMPASS* covers CELEX[12] (Gulikers et al., 1995). In *EasyTalk*, it is restricted to CEFR[13] L2-learner level A2. However, personalized entries or entries from specific contexts—like writing essays in school for a specific genre or topic—can easily be added.

To support low-literate users, all lemmas can be associated with symbols from the user's preferred set[14]. Moreover, the system provides a read-aloud function for all text elements.

Now, we cursorily highlight the supportive features during a typing session. A new sentence—thus, the overall session with *EasyTalk*—starts with a prefilled punctuation element (header = '.?!' and filler = '.') in the Sentence Panel (for details, see Steinmetz and Harbusch, 2021b). Elements in this panel and in the Next-Word Panel are always divided into a header and a filler.

Initially, the punctuation element is interactive. Clicking it changes the sentence type. By clicking repeatedly, it cycles through the different modes. Each choice sets up the ordered sentence constituents (e.g., verb-first for yes/no questions and imperatives) according to the ELS word order. The period as the default sentence type refers to a declarative main clause. If this option is selected, the header 'who' is displayed in the sentence-initial position. This header asks in easy words for the subject of the declarative main clause. Once the user has selected the first word form, the sentence type for the current sentence cannot be changed without backtracking, i.e., erasing all yet typed words—a precaution to avoid confusing word-order changes all over the yet typed sentence.

The upper snapshot of Figure 4, illustrates a later stage throughout typing. Now, cues referring to the grammatical functions for the overall sentence are displayed in the preferred ELS word order. If desired (e.g., a specific argument/attribute figures prominently in the user's mind), the user can select any header directly. Otherwise, the user follows the consecutive order provided by the system.

In addition to the advantage of offering the filling of the constituents in the order the user prefers, communicating the grammatical function of a word gives rise to presenting the suggestions for the word in its correct inflectional form—thus, speeding up typing. For instance, the finite verb is inflected according to the subject-verb agreement. Moreover, the system supports the correctly inflected typing of complex phrases filling any grammatical function position (like die_{ACC} $Katze_{ACC}$ *auf* dem_{DAT} $Dach_{DAT}$ *von* der_{DAT} $Nachbarin_{DAT}$ 'the cat on the roof of the neighbor'). In particular, all arguments are displayed as soon as the verb is known. *EasyTalk* checks whether obligatory arguments according to the verb valency are filled. The system refuses any instruction to finish the sentence before it is complete. The correct German word order for the entire sentence is yielded by the generator (cf. the sentence-final nonfinite verb in Figure 4)—another feature that reduces the user's mental load.

The word-by-word entering of sentences of the text takes place in the Next-Word Panel. It is subdivided into three components: (1) a text-input window at the top, (2) the pre-ordered header line in the middle controlling the content of (3) the suggestion list at the bottom. The user can type according to a personal strategy. The default prompting always highlights an active header in green (cf. F in an orange circle in the upper snapshot) and offers matching word forms in the suggestion list (with the correct inflectional ending in the current context). If desired, the user changes the currently active header. In Figure 4, we illus-

[12] CELEX is also available for Dutch and English. Thus, *EasyTalk* can be ported to these target languages with minor efforts.

[13] `www.coe.int/en/web/common-european-framework-reference-languages`

[14] By default, *EasyTalk* uses the ARASAAC symbol set: `www.arasaac.org`

trate the active choice of the header *Wie?* 'How'. In turn, the system updates the suggestions for appropriate fillers. Words not visible in the suggestion list can be accessed by scrolling through the list (G), or by starting to type a word's prefix (H)—given that the user knows the spelling. To select a word form, the user navigates to the desired list item and confirms the selection (I). Directly pressing 'Enter' quickly selects the topmost list item.

By the perpetual list of attribute headers, *EasyTalk* reminds the user to add cues that cannot be clarified as with face-to-face communication. In the upper snapshot of Figure 4, assumingly, the user has first typed all obligatory elements of the sentence. Due to the available headers in the Next-Word Panel, the user has activated the header *Wie?* 'How'. (N.B. the header *Wen?* is still present for a potential extension of the most recently entered direct object *viele Hobbys*, for instance, by a prepositional object.) Accordingly, the suggestion list offers appropriate fillers. Typing the letter "n" in the text-input window shows the negation *nicht* 'not' as topmost item. Previous usability studies with different groups of L2 learners of German show that presenting attribute headers is stimulating to advanced users without disturbing tendencies for beginners (Harbusch and Steinmetz, 2022).

In addition, the Sentence Panel provides the meta-level commands to finish the sentence, or to erase the last word, respectively (cf. J and K in yellow spades in the upper snapshot). In order to avoid unintended operating errors, these elements are put far away from the typing keys. We expect the user to notice them when reading the finished sentence.

3.3 Sentence-combining support

On finishing a sentence, the middle area switches from the Sentence Panel to the Connector Panel.

Studies into an LS corpus with more than 29,000 sentences from a variety of LS text from the internet (Harbusch and Steinmetz, 2022) describe a problem. In order to provide text coherence, declarative main clauses deviate in 50 percent of the cases from the SVO order—although any deviation from SVO word order is very hard to understand by the target group (Bock, 2019). Moreover, the standard German writers of the LS text often resort to subordinate clauses—also forbidden in LS.

Es gibt zurzeit viel Corona in Deutschland.	'There's a lot of Corona in Germany at the moment.'
Darum	**'Therefore'**
Ich kann viele Hobbys nicht machen.	'I cannot do many hobbies.'
Und	**'And'**
Es ist sehr langweilig.	'It is very boring.'
Aber	**'But'**
Ich habe eine Idee:	'I have an idea:'
Ich schreibe jetzt eine Geschichte für meine Freunde.	'I will write a story for my friends now.'

Figure 5: A short example text illustrating the impact to text coherence stimulating the use of connectors (in bold, red) in *EasyTalk*. The colon is a very frequent, yet ambiguous connector in LS. When selected, *EasyTalk* replaces the full stop with a colon instead of adding a separate line.

We suggest a very easy (E)LS-conform method to provide coherence cues. The idea is inspired by the German *weil*-V2 phenomenon in spoken German (the subordinating conjunction *because* is followed by a clause with main-clause V2-word order; cf. Reis, 2013 for a thorough survey). Based on audio and transliteration data from spoken German, Kempen and Harbusch (2016) argue that speakers start a new sentence after having uttered the conjunction. We reason that the concept of going on with a main clause after any conjunction or a sentential adverb in the Frontfield is a feasible generalization that circumvents subordinating clauses and focused elements in the Frontfield position in German without losing the information carried by these items. Looking at this claim from a sentence-planning perspective, any abstract relation known from the Rhetorical-Structure Theory becomes available as sentence connector between two main clauses. The resulting text reflects the writer's conceptual message. Thus, the overall discourse structure, is conveyed much better than by choppy sequences of main clauses (cf. the text in Figure 5 with highlighted connectors preserving the constraints of (E)LS).

Via the Connector Panel (cf. Figure 4, lower snapshot), all abstract RST-relations are made accessible by using an intuitive wording from the target users' vocabulary (e.g., REASON = *because*). The menu provides seven connectors—recommended by Netzwerk Leichte Sprache (2013)—for direct access (cf. the coordinating *and* (cf. L in a blue square) highlighted as active choice). Operating *Andere wählen* 'Choose other' (M) offers additional options in the Next-Word

Participant	P1	P2	P3	P4	P5	P6	P7	P8
Age	20-25	20-25	18-20	20-25	20-25	20-25	20-25	18-20
Gender	M	M	F	F	M	M	F	F
Condition(s)	ASD	ASD, VI	HoH, CCN	IDD	IDD, VI	IDD	IDD, MI	IDD, VI
Uses spelling checker	N	Y	N	Y	Y	Y	N	N
Uses a mouse	N	Y	N	N	N	N	Y	N
Regular computer use	N	N	N	N	N	Y	N	Y
Eye tracking recorded	Y	Y	Y	Y	Y	N	N	Y

Table 1: Data on the participants (Genders: M = Male, F= Female; Conditions: ASD = Autism Spectrum Disorder, VI = Visual impairments, HoH = Hard of Hearing, CCN = Complex Communication Needs, MI = Motor impairments, IDD = intellectual or developmental disorders). P8 opted out of the test on her own wish.

Panel. *EasyTalk* appends the selected connector at the end of the Text Panel. Initially, we leave the Next-Word Panel empty to avoid additional reading during the decision making for a connector. Choosing the arrow button (N) skips the selection of a connector. For details on the selection process, see Steinmetz and Harbusch, 2021b).

Now, we report the recent evaluation study.

4 Evaluation

In general, it is best practice to identify and correct usability flaws in software before it is made available to the user (see, e.g., Holzinger, 2005). For the target group, the first impression is particularly crucial for the acceptance of a system. AAC software is often abandoned after a short period of use (see, e.g., Dawe, 2006; Fager et al., 2006; Waller, 2019).

Maturing versions of *EasyTalk* were previously evaluated in several tests with substitute user groups (see, e.g., Steinmetz and Harbusch, 2020, 2021a) such as experts in the field of accessible communication and L2 learners (CEFR-level A1-B1 and differing computer skills). Nevertheless, it is essential to test the system with the actual target group (cf. Newell and Gregor, 2000; Henry, 2007; Nganji and Nggada, 2011, for user sensitive, inclusive design of accessible, disability-aware software). Here, we compare the previous findings with observations from the recent study.

4.1 Test setup and participants

Testing with people with disabilities presents unique challenges and increased organizational effort (cf. Lazar, 2017: Chapter 16, for an overview)—for example, special precautions currently need to be taken in direct contact with the target group which is particularly vulnerable to COVID-19 (cf. Rödler, 2020; Portal et al., 2021). Therefore, we conducted a qualitative case study aiming to uncover the biggest usability flaws in our software with only a handful of participants (cf. *discount testing*; Nielson, 1989).

For this purpose, we asked eight German-speaking participants, aged 18-25, with different conditions, writing and computer skills (cf. Table 1), to exploratively test the system in sessions from 25 to 40 minutes. The tests were performed under normal room lighting on a laptop with 15" display screen resolution of 1920x1080. *EasyTalk* had to be operated in the same setup (e.g., displaying the ARASAAC symbols) by all participants using the provided laptop keyboard and an external mouse.

4.2 Test procedure

Since predefined tasks—like in a usability study—might exert unnecessary pressure and frustration on the target group which could distract from evaluating the specific communication features in question we aimed to create casual situations in our experimental set-up that avoids unintentionally scrutinizing our participant's personal skills. To provide a feeling of security, the individual caregiver (or the writing workshop leader) and only one person from the evaluation team (the *interviewer*) were present during the sessions. Each session started with a brief warm-up to break the ice.

Standard evaluation techniques like thinking aloud or UX questionnaires[15] would overtax the target group. Complex, open-end questions are particularly difficult for participants with CCN or severe ASD. Thus, we abstained from systematically switching between typing and judging this process in a structured interview with post-task question as another potential source of irritation

[15] www.ueq-online.org/

due to test subjects feeling pressured to make a statement. Nevertheless, we encouraged the participants to give comments. As far as the participants complied, we elaborated on raised topics. Besides observing the participants as they typed their conceptual message and logging the users' actions, we decided to employ eye tracking as far as the participants gave their permission and conditions allowed for recording eye movements with a *Tobii Pro Nano*[16] to obtain objective information (cf. Bojko, 2005).

To explain how the system works, the interviewer wrote one sample sentence in *EasyTalk*: *Die Sonne scheint heute.* 'The sun shines today.'. The participants could opt for rehearsing the example interactively with the interviewer. Afterwards, all participants were invited to explore the system freely. (Before the experiment, the leader of the *Schreibwerkstatt* had advised participants with spontaneous decision-making problems to think up in advance the sentences they wanted to write during the experiment.) If needed, the participant received help with spelling or interacting with the computer either from the interviewer or the caretaker. At the end of the typing session, the interviewer exported the text from *EasyTalk* with or without symbols according to the participants preference to hand it to them as receipt for participating in the experiment. One final yes/no-question was asked to all participants: Would you like to use *EasyTalk* in the writing workshop in the future?

4.3 Results

In general, the evaluation corroborates the easy and intuitive interface design of *EasyTalk*. All participants successfully typed at least three sentences, with each sentence being an average of four words long with *EasyTalk* (see Figure 6 for the text typed in two sessions). Four participants spontaneously skipped the interactive example rehearsal and typed their own sentences without problems. Participant P8, who can write texts beyond the scope of LS in *MS Word*, stated that *EasyTalk* did not benefit her and opted out of the test after writing a four-word sentence. We exclude P8 in the following. Spontaneously, P5 judged: "*The headers help with concentration*" and *"The connectors between sentences are important. Sometimes there are longer sentences.*

Figure 6: Two sample sessions. Top: Participant P1 chose to type the interviewer's example himself as first sentence. P1 skipped the choice of connectors all of the text; Bottom: P5 typed four sentences without rehearsing the interviewer's example and used an explicit connector once (*und* 'and').

You can do them piece by piece in this manner.". P2 stated: *"It works great but I have to concentrate a bit here."*. We attribute the overall positive result to improvements of the overall interface that were based on several evaluation rounds with substitute users. The current test confirms that the communication with the system is easy to learn due to intuitive dialogues all over the system.

The eye-tracking data supports this claim. We defined areas of interest (AOIs) in the interface to be able to track task-accomplishment paths. All users focused on the dialogue elements in the intended manner. With respect to effectiveness, we did not find traces of searching around for items. The eye-tracking data documents the inspection of the Text Panel after a sentence was finished.

One person spontaneously wrote a question. Participants P1–P7 supplemented their sentences with modifiers (e.g., *when?* or *how?* cues were spontaneously selected in the Next-Word Panel). Six participants completed the decision dialogue for complex verb constructions (Steinmetz and Harbusch, 2020). Although we had not demonstrated this decision dialog in the introduction, four participants typed verbs in present perfect tense, and two users selected a modal as finite

[16] www.tobiipro.com/product-listing/nano/

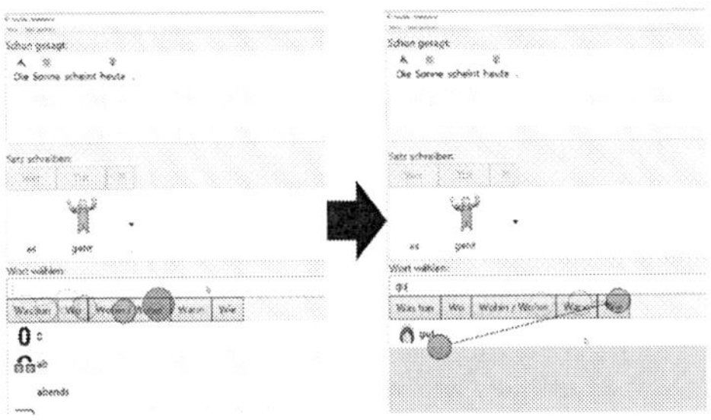

Figure 8: Two consecutive snapshots of P1 typing the third word of the second sentence. First, P1 focuses the headers in the Next-Word panel. In turn, P1 starts typing the word. Finally, P1 focuses the element *gut* 'good' in the suggestion list.

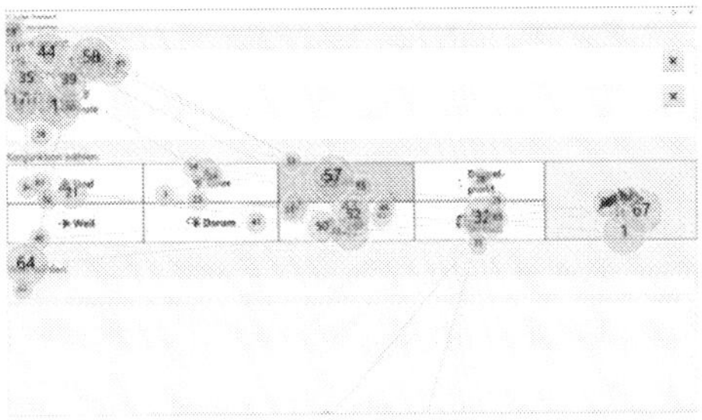

Figure 7: Gaze plot of P1while connecting sentences 2 and 3 using the Connector Panel. P1 looked at the previous text in the Text Panel and read through all connector options before operating the arrow button to skip the connector.

verb followed by an infinitive (cf. the example sentence in Figure 4). Two participants spontaneously erased words in the Sentence Panel using the red X-button—also not shown in the introduction. Clicking the green √-button in the Sentence Panel was shown, and completing a sentence was successfully performed by all participants. These observations also reflect that *EasyTalk* is easy and intuitive to use for the target group beyond explicitly demonstrated features.

With respect to efficiency, P4 systematically selected the words as soon as they appeared in the completion list in favor of writing the words to the end. In contrast, P6 initially typed every word from start to finish. Later on, P6 selected the words from the completion list as soon as possible. P2 commented: *"Writing to the end is better."* and judged the completion list as helpful to prevent spelling mistakes.

According to the eye-tracking data, the participants' focus while writing the current sentence was mainly on the Next-Word Panel. The Text Panel and the Sentence Panel were used to back up the flow of thoughts. In detail, the participants exhibited different interaction strategies (Figure 8, e.g., illustrates P1's word selection strategy of focusing the wh-cues). To connect a sentence, all participants looked at the previous text in the Text Panel and read through the Connector Panel (see Figure 7 for an example gaze plot). However, the eye-tracking data unveiled shortcomings of the Connector Panel's layout. Often, the second row of connector options was considerably less likely inspected. Unfortunately, nobody felt inclined to add a connector systematically after reading through all/some options. Accordingly, we plan to shorten the list of mentioned options. Moreover, we intend to set up an active training mode in *EasyTalk* that teaches when and how to use text connectors (Reid et al., 2013).

Because of the participants' overall positive response to the question of whether they wanted to use the system, the leader of the writing workshop asked for a copy of EasyTalk for using it in future.

5 Conclusions

We presented *EasyTalk*, an intuitive-to-use writing assistant for fast and correct text writing in ELS for low-literate users with IDD and/or CCN. The evaluation verified the claim that users can instantaneously type complete and correct sentences with *EasyTalk*. However, the offer of connectors should be improved. As mentioned above, we plan a make-over of the Connector Panel combined with an active teaching unit. It is an open question to which extent automatic storytelling concepts (cf. Section 2.3) can be incorporated into the active training mode of our system (cf. Steinmetz and Harbusch, 2021a). We intend to evaluate this new feature in longitudinal studies with the target user group.

Besides further above-mentioned future work, personalized features for specific user groups will be realized. Moreover, a native smartphone version is under development.

Acknowledgments

We owe a huge dept of gratitude to the *Schreibwerkstatt* of the *Habila Tannenhof Ulm* for the comprehensive support for the case study.

In addition, we are extremely grateful to the anonymous reviewers for their constructive and insightful suggestions and comments. All remaining errors are our own responsibility.

References

Rúbia Ascari, Roberto Pereira, and Luciano Silva. 2018. Mobile Interaction for Augmentative and Alternative Communication: a Systematic Mapping. *Journal on Interactive Systems,* 9: 105-118. http://dx.doi.org/10.5753/jis.2018.704

Allan Bell. 1984. Language Style as Audience Design. *Language in Society,* 13(2): 145–204. https://doi.org/10.1017/S004740450001037X

BITV2.0. 2011. Verordnung zur Schaffung barrierefreier Informationstechnik nach dem Behindertengleichstellungsgesetz (Barrierefreie Informationstechnik-Verordnung – BITV 2.0). Barrierefreie-Informationstechnik-Verordnung vom 12. September 2011 (BGBl. I S. 1843), die zuletzt durch Artikel 1 der Verordnung vom 21. Mai 2019 (BGBl. I S. 738) geändert worden ist http://www. gesetze-im-internet.de/bitv_2_0/BJNR184300011.html

Ursula Bredel and Christiane Maaß. 2016. *Leichte Sprache: Theoretische Grundlagen. Orientierung für die Praxis.* Bibliographisches Institut. Berlin, Germany.

Agnieszka Bojko. 2005. Eye Tracking in User Experience Testing: How to Make the Most of It. *Proceedings of the 14th Annual Conference of the Usability Professionals' Association (UPA).* Montréal, Canada.

Bettina M. Bock. 2019. *„Leichte Sprache" – Kein Regelwerk: Sprachwissenschaftliche Ergebnisse und Praxisempfehlungen aus dem LeiSA-Projekt. Frank & Timme, Berlin, Germany.* Available at: https://ul.qucosa.de/api/qucosa%3A31959/attachment/ATT-0/ (Accessed: February 22, 2022)Robert Dale and Jette Viethen. 2021. The automated writing assistance landscape in 2021. *Natural Language Engineering,* 27(4): 511-518. https://doi.org/10.1017/S1351324921000164

Melissa Dawe. 2006. Desperately Seeking Simplicity. *Proceedings of the 2006 Conference on Human Factors in Computing Systems (SIGCHI 2006).* Montréal, QC, Canada, pages 1143–1152. https://doi.org/10.1145/1124772.1124943

Sarah Ebling, Alessia Battisti, Marek Kostrzewa, Dominik Pfütze, Anette Rios, Andreas Säuberli, Nicolas Spring. 2022. Automatic Text Simplification for German. *Frontiers in Communication,* 7. https://doi.org/10.3389/fcomm.2022.706718

Susan Fager, Karen Hux, David R. Beukelman and Renee Karantounis. 2006. Augmentative and Alternative Communication use and acceptance by adults with Traumatic Brain Injury. *Augmentative and Alternative Communication,* 22: 37–47. https://doi.org/10.1080/07434610500243990

Vincent Fortuin, Romann Weber, Sasha Schriber, Diana Wotruba and Markus Gross. 2018. InspireMe: Learning Sequence Models for Stories. *Proceedings of the 32nd AAAI Conference on Artificial Intelligence,* 32(1). https://ojs.aaai.org/index.php/AAAI/article/view/11407

Anke Grotlüschen, Klaus Buddeberg, Klaus, Gregor Dutz, Lisanne Heilmann, and Christopher Stammer. 2020. Low literacy in Germany: Results from the second German literacy survey. *European Journal for Research on the Education and Learning of Adults,* 11: 127-143. https://10.3384/rela.2000-7426.rela9147.

Anke Grotlüschen and Klaus Buddeberg. 2020. *LEO 2018 - Leben mit geringer Literalität, wbv Media, Bielefeld,* Germany

Léon Gulikers, Gilbert Rattnik, and Richard Piepenbrock. 1995. *German Linguistic Guide of the CELEX lexical database.* Tech. rep., Linguistic Data Consortium, Philadelphia, MA, USA

Marianne Hirschberg and Christian Lindmeier. 2013. *Der Begriff „Inklusion" - Ein Grundsatz der Menschenrechte und seine Bedeutung für die Erwachsenenbildung.* In: Burtscher, Reinhard, Ditschek, Eduard Jan, Ackermann, Karl-Ernst, Kil, Monika, and Kronauer, Martin (eds.): Zugänge zu Inklusion. Erwachsenenbildung, Behinderten-pädagogik und Soziologie im Dialog. Bertelsmann, Bielefeld, Germany. https://doi.org/10.25656/01:8573

Karin Harbusch and Gerard Kempen. 2002. A Quantitative Model of Word Order and Movement in English, Dutch and German Complement Constructions. In *Proceedings of the 19th International Conference on Computational Linguistics – Volume 1 (COLING '02), Taipei, Taiwan*, pp. 1–7.

Karin Harbusch and Gerard Kempen. 2011. Automatic Online Writing Support for L2 Learners of German Through Output Monitoring by a Natural-Language Paraphrase Generator. In *WorldCALL - International Perspectives on Computer-Assisted Language Learning.* Routledge/Taylor&Francis Group, New York, NY, USA, pp. 128–143.

Karin Harbusch and Ina Steinmetz. 2022. A Computer-Assisted Writing Tool for an Extended Variety of Leichte Sprache (Easy-to-Read German). *Frontiers in Communication,* 6. https://doi.org/10.3389/fcomm.2021.689009

Shawn Lawton Henry. 2007. Just Ask: Integrating Accessibility Throughout Design. Madison, WI: Shawn Lawton Henry. Available at: http://www.uiaccess.com/JustAsk/ (Accessed February 24, 2022)

Andreas Holzinger. 2005. Usability Engineering Methods for Software Developers. *Communica-*

tions of the ACM, 48 (1): 71-74. http://dx.doi.org/10.1145/1039539.1039541

Eduard H. Hovy. 1988. Planning Coherent Multisentential Text. In *Proceedings of the 26th Annual Meeting of the Association for Computational Linguistics (ACL 88),* New York, NY, USA, pp. 163–169. https://doi.org/10.3115/982023.982043

Gerard Kempen and Karin Harbusch. 2002. Performance Grammar: A Declarative Definition. *Language and Computers,* 45: 148–162. https://doi.org/10.1163/9789004334038_013

Gerard Kempen and Karin Harbusch. 2016. Verb-second Word Order After German Weil 'Because': Psycholinguistic Theory From Corpus-Linguistic Data. *Glossa: a journal of general linguistics*, 1(1): 1–32. https://doi.org/10.5334/gjgl.46

Inclusion Europe. 2009. Informationen für alle – Europäische Regeln, wie man Informationen leicht lesbar und leicht verständlich macht. *Inclusion Europe*, Brussels, Belgium. Available at: https://www.inclusion-europe.eu/wp-content/uploads/2017/06/DE_Information_for_all.pdf (Accessed February 21, 2022).

David McNaughton, Tracy Rackensperger, Elizabeth Benedek-Wood, Carole Krezman, Michael B. Williams and Janice Light. 2008."A child needs to be given a chance to succeed": Parents of individuals who use AAC describe the benefits and challenges of learning AAC technologies. *Augmentative and Alternative Communication*, 24(1): 43-55. https://doi.org/10.1080/07434610701421007

Netzwerk Leichte Sprache. 2013. Die Regeln für Leichte Sprache. Available at: https://www.leichte-sprache.org/wp-content/uploads/2017/11/Regeln_Leichte_Sprache.pdf (Accessed February 21, 2022).

Giulio E. Lancioni, Nirbhay N. Singh, Mark F. O'Reilly and Gloria Alberti. 2019. Assistive Technology to Support Communication in Individuals with Neurodevelopmental Disorders. *Current Developmental Disorders Reports*, 6(3): 126-130. https://doi.org/10.1007/s40474-019-00165-x

Jonathan Lazar, Jinjuan H. Feng and Harry Hochheiser. 2017. *Research Methods in Human Computer Interaction.* 2nd Edition, Morgan Kaufmann, Cambridge, MA, USA, an imprint of Elsevier. http://dx.doi.org/10.1016/B978-0-12-805390-4.00016-9

Janice Light, David McNaughton, David Beukelman, Susan Koch Fager, Melanie Fried-Oken, Thomas Jakobs and Erik Jakobs. 2019. Challenges and opportunities in augmentative and alternative communication: Research and technology development to enhance communication and participation for individuals with complex communication needs. *Augmentative and alternative communication*, 35(1): 1-12. https://doi.org/10.1080/07434618.2018.1556732

Janice Light. 1988. Interaction involving individuals using augmentative and alternative communication systems: State of the art and future directions. *Augmentative and alternative communication*, 4(2): 66-82. https://doi.org/10.1080/07434618812331274657

Stephanie Lukin and Marylin A. Walker. 2019. A Narrative Sentence Planner and Structurer for Domain Independent, Parameterizable Storytelling. *Dialogue & Discourse,* 10: 34-86. https://doi.org/10.5087/dad.2019.103

William C. Mann and Sandra A. Thompson. 1988. Rhetorical Structure Theory: Toward a Functional Theory of Text Organization. *Interdiscip. J. Study Discourse,* 8 (3): 243–281. https://doi.org/10.1515/text.1.1988.8.3.243

Julius T. Nganji and Shawulu H. Nggada. 2011. Disability-Aware Software Engineering for Improved System Accessibility and Usability. *International Journal of Software Engineering and Its Applications*, 5: 47-62.

Alan F. Newell and Peter Gregor. 2000. User sensitive inclusive design — in search of a new paradigm. In *Proceedings of the 2000 conference on Universal Usability*. Arlington, Virginia, USA, pp. 39-44. https://doi.org/10.1145/355460.355470

James W. Ney. 1980. A Short History of Sentence Combining: Its Limitations and Use. English Education, 11 (3): 169–177. http://www.jstor.org/stable/40172300

Jakob Nielsen. 1989. Usability Engineering at a Discount. In *Proceedings of the Third International Conference on Human-Computer Interaction on Designing and Using Human-Computer Interfaces and Knowledge Based Systems*, Boston, MA, USA, pp. 394–401. https://dl.acm.org/doi/10.5555/92449.92499

Richard Nordquist. 2018. An Introduction to Sentence Combining. *ThoughtCo*. Available at: https://www.thoughtco.com/an-introduction-to-sentence-combining-1692421 (Accessed February 18, 2022).

Marga Reis. 2013. „Weil-V2"-Sätze und (k)ein Ende? Anmerkungen zur Analyse von Antomo & Steinbach (2010). *Z. für Sprachwissenschaft.* 32: 221–262. https://doi.org/10.1515/zfs-2013-0008

Daniel W Otter, Julian R Medina and Jugal K. Kalita. 2021. A Survey of the Usages of Deep Learning for Natural Language Processing. *IEEE Transactions on Neural Networks and Learning Systems,* 32 (2): 604-624. https://doi.org/10.1109/TNNLS.2020.2979670

Helen Portal, Gerlinde Schmidt, Rita Crespo Fernández, Bárbara Marcondes, Milan Šveřepa, Valentina Dragičević, V. and David Lysaght. 2021. Neglect and Discrimination. Multiplied. How Covid-19 Affected the Rights of People With Intellectual Disabilities and Their Families. *Inclusion Europe.* Available at: https://www.inclusion-europe.eu/wp-content/uploads/2020/11/COVID-report-Final.pdf (Accessed February 09, 2022).

Anke Reichardt, Norbert Kruse and Frank Lipowsky. 2014. Textüberarbeitung mit Schreibkonferenz oder Textlupe. Zum Einfluss der Schreibumgebung auf die Qualität von Schülertexten. *Didaktik Deutsch,* 19: 64–85. https://nbn-resolving.org/urn:nbn:de:0111-pedocs-172071

Robert Reid, Torri Ortiz Lienemann, and Jessica L. Hagaman. 2013. *Strategy instruction for students with learning disabilities.* Guilford Press, New York, NY, USA.

Peter Rödler. 2020. Totale Institution. *Behindertenpädagogik,* 59: 345–358. https://doi.org/10.30820/0341-7301-2020-4-345

Bruce Saddler and Jennifer Preschern. 2007. Improving Sentence Writing Ability Through Sentence Combining Practice. *Teaching Exceptional Children,* 29: 6–11. http://dx.doi.org/10.1177/004005990703900301

Sean J. Smith, K. Alisa Lowrey, Amber L. Rowland and Bruce Frey. 2020. Effective Technology Supported Writing Strategies for Learners With Disabilities. *Inclusion,* 8 (1): 58–73. https://doi.org/10.1352/2326-6988-8.1.58

Ina Steinmetz and Karin Harbusch. 2020. Enabling Fast and Correct Typing in 'Leichte Sprache' (Easy Language). In *Proceedings of The Fourth Widening Natural Language Processing Workshop (WINLP 4),* Seattle, CA, USA. 64–67. http://dx.doi.org/10.18653/v1/2020.winlp-1.17

Ina Steinmetz and Karin Harbusch. 2021a. EasyTalk: A Digital Writer's Workshop for Leichte Sprache (Easy-To-Read German). *The European Conference on Education 2021: Official Conference Proceedings.* https://doi.org/10.22492/issn.2188-1162.2021.32

Ina Steinmetz and Karin Harbusch. 2021b. *EasyTalk: An assistive text-writing system* for Leichte Sprache (Easy-to-Read German). In *Proceedings of Communication Matters International AAC Conference,* Leeds, UK.

Annalu Waller. 2019. Telling Tales: Unlocking the Potential of AAC Technologies. *Int. J. Lang. Commun. Disord,* 54: 159–169. http://dx.doi.org/10.1111/1460-6984.12449

Language Models as Context-sensitive Word Search Engines

Matti Wiegmann and **Michael Völske** and **Benno Stein**
Bauhaus-Universität Weimar
{matti.wiegmann,michael.voelske,benno.stein}@uni-weimar.de

Martin Potthast
Leipzig University
martin.potthast@uni-leipzig.de

Abstract

Context-sensitive word search engines are writing assistants that support word choice, phrasing, and idiomatic language use by indexing large-scale n-gram collections and implementing a wildcard search. However, search results become unreliable with increasing context size (e.g., $n \geq 5$), when observations become sparse. This paper proposes two strategies for word search with larger n, based on masked and conditional language modeling. We build such search engines using BERT and BART and compare their capabilities in answering English context queries with those of the n-gram-based word search engine Netspeak. Our proposed strategies score within 5 percentage points MRR of n-gram collections while answering up to 5 times as many queries.[1]

1 Introduction

A wide range of computer tools has been developed to support the writing process, including both active and passive ones. Active tools automatically paraphrase a text as it is written, if the text is highly likely to be incorrect or stylistically inappropriate. Passive tools suggest either spelling, grammar, and style corrections or how to continue a sentence. Passive tools that are less integrated into word processors are context-free and context-sensitive word search engines. Context-free search engines include searchable dictionaries, thesauri, and collections of idioms in which queries are made about a known word or phrase for which alternatives are sought. In the absence of context, their search results are usually sorted alphabetically. Context-sensitive word search engines allow their users to formulate cloze-style queries to search for an unknown word or phrase, ranking the search results according to their frequency of use.

A conventional context-sensitive word search engine, as shown in Figure 1, answers a cloze

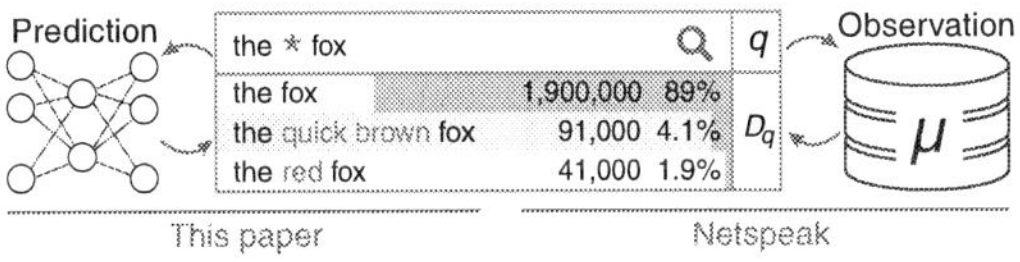

Figure 1: A context query q with result set D_q as retrieved from an index μ of observed n-grams (right), and as predicted from, e.g., a language model (left).

query $q = \texttt{the * fox}$ asking for words or phrases commonly written between 'the' and 'fox' by retrieving the appropriate subset $D_q \subseteq D$ from a collection of n-grams D. Formally, the index $\mu : Q \rightarrow \mathcal{P}(D)$ maps the set of cloze queries Q to the power set $\mathcal{P}(D)$, which is implemented as wildcard retrieval, and the results $\mu(q) = D_q$ are ordered by their occurrence frequency in a large text corpus, which approximates the frequency of use. Assuming a sufficiently large text corpus is available such that each n-gram matching a given cloze query q has been observed sufficiently often, ranking these n-grams by their frequency satisfies the probability ranking principle (Robertson, 1977). In other words, if one asks a sufficiently large number of people to answer a cloze query, the frequency distribution of the answers would correlate with that of the n-grams found. The main limitations of this approach are, (1) that the number of context words in each cloze query is limited by n, with more context reducing the size of the cloze accordingly, and, (2) that the size of the text corpus required to observe q sufficiently often increases exponentially with n, so that in practice $n < 10$.

In this work, these two limitations are addressed by using transformer-based language models to predict phrases corresponding to a query, rather than retrieving them from an n-gram index. In particular, we propose a masked language model and an autoregressive model for conditional generation to answer cloze queries (Section 3). These models are compared to Netspeak, a state-of-the-art

[1]Our code is available at Github and our data is available at Zenodo.

Proceedings of the First Workshop on Intelligent and Interactive Writing Assistants (In2Writing 2022), pages 39 - 45
May 26, 2022 ©2022 Association for Computational Linguistics

Netspeak	dBERT	dBERT$_{ft}$	BART	BART$_{ft}$
(1) *this chinese <folk>*				
new	wikipedia	force	guy	language
restaurant	language	government	girl	word
custom	translation	had	man	translation
company	dictionary	language	is	style
–	pronunciation	culture	lady	medicine
(2) *became <fascinated> with*				
acquainted	**synonymous**	involved	friends	**acquainted**
associated	**acquainted**	popular	**involved**	**involved**
involved	pregnant	**associated**	more	**associated**
familiar	friends	concerned	a	**familiar**
synonymous	affiliated	known	popular	friends
(3) *<where> people live*				
where	these	**the**	**where**	**million**
the	most	which	how	that
many	**many**	all	live	of
million	here	some	t	most
which	**where**	**where**	w	**the**
(4) *he was <cast> in the*				
not	**buried**	**involved**	a	**born**
born	interred	**buried**	also	killed
buried	**involved**	raised	**involved**	**not**
involved	killed	appointed	killed	placed
still	instrumental	placed	the	**involved**

Table 1: Selected context queries with the <original token> and the top 5 results of all models. The original token in the results is underlined, the overlap with `Netspeak`'s results is boldface.

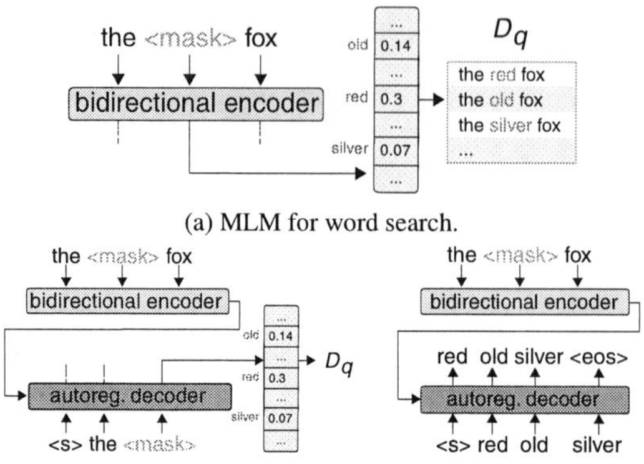

(a) MLM for word search.

(b) Denoising for word search.

(c) Infilling finetuning.

Figure 2: Context-sensitive word search can be learned using masked (MLM) or conditional language modeling (CDLM) with denoising or infilling. The result set D_q for MLM and denoising is the output at the mask's position sorted by likelihood. For infilling, D_q is the generation target. Our proposed MLM is trained and finetuned as usual; Our CDLM is trained by denoising and finetuned by infilling, but predicts via denoising.

context-sensitive word search engine based on an index of Google n-grams (Section 4). Based on the cloze test corpus CLOTH (Xie et al., 2018) and Wikitext (Merity et al., 2016), both of our proposed language models achieve an MRR near their theoretical maximum, falling short of Netspeak's only between 0.03–0.07, and they exceed a mean nDCG of 0.3 in predicting Netspeak's D_q (Section 5).

2 Related Work

In general, context-sensitive word search engines are supportive writing assistants targeting the editing phase of the writing process (Rohman, 1965; Seow, 2002). Supportive writing assistants take the form of online dictionaries, thesauri, concordancers (like WriteBetter (Bellino and Bascuñán, 2020)), or other resources offering definitions, synonyms, and translations. More advanced assistants provide a tailored query language that allows for searching words matching a pattern (`OneLook.com`), words that rhyme (`Rhymezone.com`), or words that fit a given context (e.g., Netspeak (Stein et al., 2010), Google n-gram viewer (Michel et al., 2011), Linggle (Boisson et al., 2013), and `Phrasefinder.io`). Context-sensitive word search is related to several foundational NLP tasks like lexical substitution (McCarthy and Navigli, 2007; Lee et al., 2021), word sense disambiguation, paraphrasing, and phrase-level substitution (Madnani and Dorr, 2010), although these tasks usually require a known word or phrase.

Expression matching and corpus-based statistics form the basis for writing assistants, while language models, mostly based on the transformer architecture (Vaswani et al., 2017), often take on the heavy lifting (Alikaniotis et al., 2019). Transformer-encoder models, like BERT (Devlin et al., 2019), are often pre-trained by masked language modeling, which is highly similar to wildcard word search but knows only one correct target. Encoder models are frequently applied to solve cloze tests (Gonçalo Oliveira, 2021) and its related foundational tasks. Autoregressive language models, like GPT (Radford et al., 2019), are used for infilling (Donahue et al., 2020), which is similar to mask prediction but generates arbitrary-length sequences. Conditional language models (autoencoders) are used in phrase-level substitution tasks like denoising (Lewis et al., 2019).

3 Language Modeling for Word Search

In this work, we formulate context-sensitive word search with language models as learning a distribution $p(w_q \mid q)$, where $q = q_l \; ? \; q_r$ consists of left and right side contexts q_l and q_r and a wildcard token ?. Either q_l or q_r can be empty. The result set D_q consist of all n-grams $q_l w_{q,i} q_l$ for all $w_{q,i} \in w_q$, in

	Source	Original Token		Ranked Answers		
		n	size	n	size	answers
train	Wikitext	3–9	10 M	3–5	10 M	4.2
dev	Wikitext	3–9	2.2 M	3–5	114.313	4.2
test	Wikitext	3	329.497	3	233.723	21.0
		5	383.067	5	86.435	4.3
	CLOTH	3	240.279	3	296.860	26.3
		5	318.082	5	69.915	6.0

Table 2: The original token (OT) dataset consists of n-gram queries extracted from Wikitext-103 and CLOTH and lists the original token as the single answer. The ranked answers (RA) dataset is extracted from OT by replacing the answer with the ranked results retrieved from Netspeak, discarding all unanswered queries.

Model	Wikitext				CLOTH				
	3		5		3		5		
	NA	all	NA	all	NA	all	NA	all	Time
Netspeak	0.33	–	0.46	–	0.10	–	0.22	–	5.34 ms
dBERT	0.15	0.14	0.33	0.28	0.06	0.06	**0.17**	**0.15**	–
$\mathtt{dBERT}_{\mathrm{ft}}$	**0.30**	**0.29**	0.42	**0.35**	0.05	0.05	0.10	0.08	5.05 ms
BART	0.19	0.18	0.37	0.31	0.05	0.05	0.15	0.12	–
$\mathtt{BART}_{\mathrm{ft}}$	0.29	0.28	**0.43**	0.34	**0.07**	**0.07**	**0.17**	0.12	11.27 ms
Ratio	90 %		18 %		97 %		27 %		

Table 3: The average MRR of the original token for **all** queries in the OT test datasets, split by source and query length. NA $\subseteq$ OT only considers queries that Netspeak could answer and Ratio indicates the subset size. Time indicates the average response time for one query.

descending order of likelihood. We propose two strategies to learn $p(w_q \mid q)$: via masked language modeling and via conditional language modeling with an adapted fine-tuning strategy.

Masked Language Modeling Masked language modeling (MLM) is equivalent to context-sensitive word search with only a single token as the answer. Since large language models based on transformer-encoders solve MLM by learning $p(w_q \mid q)$ and scoring all options in the vocabulary, the scored vocabulary can be used to extract D_q. As shown in Figure 2a, we use a bidirectional transformer-encoder (BERT) model, pre-trained with MLM, to estimate $p(w_q \mid q)$. We extract the 30 tokens with the highest score from the output logits of the language modeling head as D_q. We fine-tune the model with a specialized masked language modeling task, using individual n-grams as input. Although any BERT variant can be used, we choose DistilBERT for its size and speed, since context-sensitive word search is a real-time search task.

Conditional Language Modeling Conditional language modeling (CDLM) is causal (or generative) language modeling given a condition. Context-sensitive word search can be formulated as CDLM with two strategies: denoising (see Figure 2b) and infilling (see Figure 2c). Denoising takes the query as the condition and generates the original sequence, where D_q can be extracted from the output logits at the mask's position, as with an MLM. Infilling takes the query as condition and generates D_q. We use a sequence-to-sequence model for conditional generation (BART) and predict D_q with denoising, extracting the 30 tokens with the highest score. We fine-tune BART using infilling, but use denoising to predict D_q after the fine-tuning.

4 Experimental Setup

We implemented both strategies of learning context-sensitive word search using the Huggingface (Wolf et al., 2020) implementation of DistilBERT for MLM and BART for CDLM. We evaluate the pre-trained and the fine-tuned models against the two datasets with word search queries shown in Table 2.

Data We constructed two datasets with word search queries. The original token (OT) dataset offers as the single answer the token chosen by the author of the source text. The ranked answers (RA) dataset offers multiple, ordered answers with relevance judgments for each query.

The original token dataset consists of queries extracted from Wikitext-103 (Merity et al., 2016), which consists of good or featured English Wikipedia articles, and CLOTH (Xie et al., 2018), which consists of middle and high school learner's English cloze-tests. For Wikitext, we constructed n queries for each 3-to-9-gram by replacing the token at each position in the n-gram with a wildcard and adding the original token as the answer. We discarded all newlines, headlines starting with a =, n-grams with non-letter tokens to not cross sentence boundaries or quotations, and queries with proper nouns as answers. For CLOTH, we constructed a query for each 3 and 5-gram that overlapped with a cloze-gap in the dataset and added the teacher's preferred answer as the original token answer. We discarded all n-grams with non-letter tokens and proper nouns as answers. Each wildcard was assigned one of 5 word classes based on Spacy's POS annotations of the source sentences: verbs and auxiliaries, nouns, determiners and pronouns, adjectives and adverbs, and conjunctions and particles. Verb and noun classes were marked

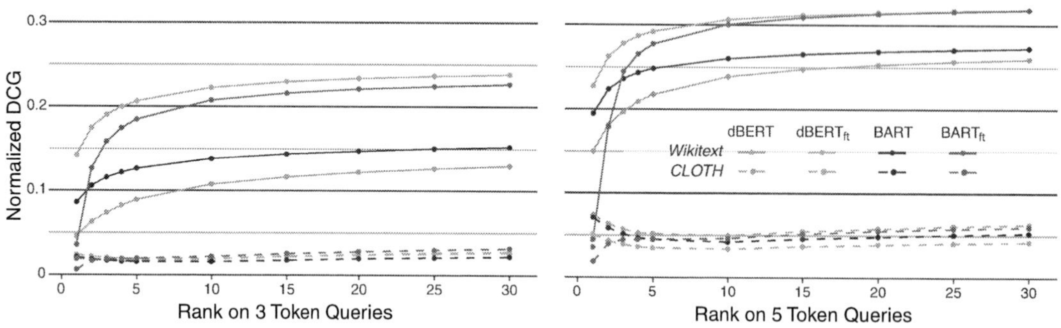

Figure 3: The nDCG of the ranked results between the models on the *ranked results* test datasets. The relevance judgments were determined via Netspeak's ranking, which is equivalent to the frequencies in Google n-grams.

if the query contains another verb or noun, respectively. As the training set, we selected the first 10 million queries from the training split of Wikitext. As the dev set, we selected all queries extracted from Wikitext's dev split. As the test set, we used all 3 and 5-gram queries from Wikitext's test split and all CLOTH splits.

The ranked answers datasets consist of the queries from the original token dataset, but all answers were replaced by the top 30 results retrieved from `Netspeak`, which is equivalent to the most frequent observations in Google n-grams. We assigned a relevance score to each result based on its absolute frequency: above 100K we assigned a high (3) score, above 10K a medium (2) score, with any occurrence a low (1), and otherwise a zero (0) relevance score. We discarded all queries with an empty result set. We determined the splits analogously to the original token dataset.

Model Configuration For the MLM strategy, we fine-tune Huggingface's implementation of DistilBERTForMaskedLM on the original token dataset, using the pre-trained `distilbert-base-uncased` checkpoint. We only exposed one n-gram as input at a time. We train the model using the standard training routine with default parameters, although we doubled the masking probability to 30 %, twice the rate used for BERT (Devlin et al., 2019), and adapted the initial learning rate to 2e-5 and the weight decay to 0.01. We evaluate the performance once with the pre-trained checkpoint as dBERT and once after fine-tuning as dBERT$_{ft}$.

For the CDLM strategy, we fine-tune Huggingface's implementation of BARTForConditionalGeneration for infilling on the *ranked answers* dataset using the pre-trained `facebook/bart-base` checkpoint. We only exposed one n-gram as input at a time and used the same hyperparameters as with the MLM strategy, except that masking was done manually. We evaluate the performance with the pre-trained checkpoint as `BART` and after fine-tuning as `BART`$_{ft}$.

5 Evaluation

We quantitatively evaluate our proposed methods using the mean reciprocal rank (MRR) and the normalized discounted cumulative gain (nDCG) (Järvelin and Kekäläinen, 2002).

System Performance We evaluate the system performance using the MRR of the author's chosen word, shown in Table 3, assuming that the author's chosen word in the source text is also a good answer to the cloze query. Therefore, the better word search engine should rank the author's choice higher on average over many queries. Table 3 shows the MRR for the four models compared to `Netspeak`, once over all queries in the test datasets, and once for the shared subset of queries where `Netspeak` returned non-empty results.

The MRR results allow three conclusions. First, our proposed fine-tuning strategy improves the pre-trained baseline's performance consistently for `BART` and on queries from Wikitext for `dBERT`. Second, on queries from RA, the best models already perform close to `Netspeak`. Third, both fine-tuned models can answer 4-5 times as many queries than `Netspeak`, which can be observed from the ratio between RA and OT datasets. Since the OT dataset contains up to 82% uncommon queries, which have no support in the Google n-grams indexed by Netspeak, the language models

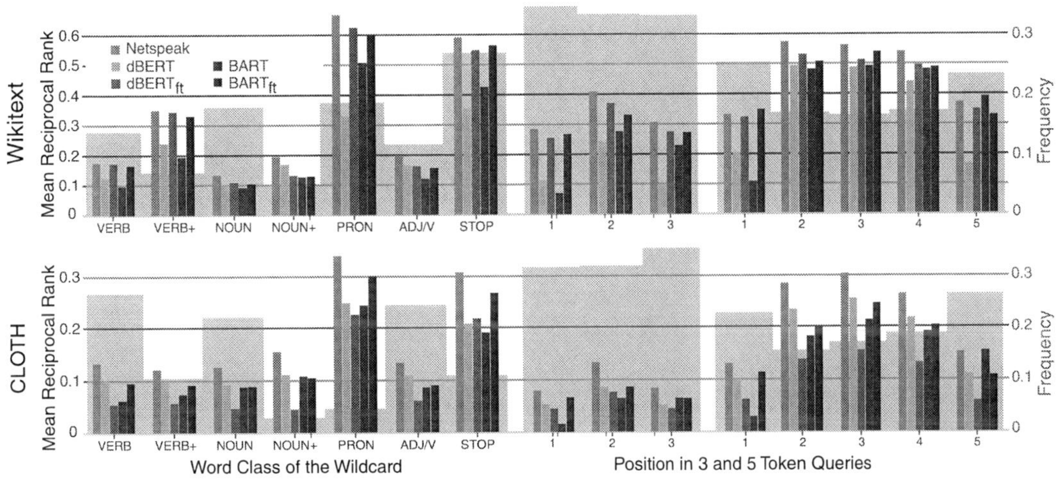

Figure 4: The MRR by word class (left) and wildcard position (center and right) of Netspeak and the four Models on the *Original Token* test dataset. Queries that Netspeak could not answer were ignored. The gray bars indicate the relative frequency.

score up to 9 percentage points lower than on RA. The MRR increases with increasing context size since additional context can only reduce the set of potentially matching answers.

Ranking We evaluate the ranking of the results using the nDCG as shown in Figure 3. Consistent with the MRR results, the fine-tuned models outperform their pre-trained counterpart, dBERT profits more from fine-tuning and performs best. Most of the relevant results are in the top ranks since the nDCG scores only marginally improve past rank 10.

Position and Word Class We evaluate further query attributes besides size and genre, wildcard position, and wildcard word class, using the MRR as shown in Figure 4. These results show that a large part of the performance gain when fine-tuning can be attributed to gains in the closed-class words. The MRR is lower for open-class words since there are more plausible options for each query and the original token is on a lower rank more often. Fine-tuning has only a marginal impact on open-class words. dBERT scores the lowest when the wildcard is either at the beginning or at the end of the query, while BART scores the lowest for wildcards at the beginning. Fine-tuning significantly improves the performance in these cases, with only marginal improving queries with wildcards in the center positions.

The performance difference between closed and open-class words also partially explains the substantially lower MRR and nDCG scores over CLOTH queries for all models: The answers to cloth-queries more often belong to lower scoring open classes, the answers to Wikitext-queries more frequently belong to the high scoring closed classes.

Runtime We compare the runtime performance by measuring the average time to answer a query (see Table 3) over all queries in the *ranked answers* test dataset. Netspeak and dBERT are equally fast with 5 ms per query, while BART takes twice as long. In practice, both language models are fast enough for context-sensitive word search. We measured the performance of the language models with sequential, non-batched queries on GPU. We measured the performance of Netspeak with a local Netspeak instance and a local index, queried through Netspeak's GRPC API. All systems were tested in identical containers with 4 AMD EPYC 7F72 CPU cores, 32 GB of RAM, and one A100 GPU.

6 Conclusion

This paper investigates whether state-of-the-art language models can mitigate the shortcomings of n-gram indices in context-sensitive word search engines. We present strategies to fine-tune masked and conditional language models so that they can answer word search queries. Our evaluation shows that our proposed methods can answer short queries (3 tokens) nearly as well as by observing actual n-gram frequencies in a large text corpus. Furthermore, our fine-tuned models perform well when supporting observations are scarce so that n-gram indices provide no results. Since this already is the dominant case for $n = 5$, we can conclude that language models, fine-tuned for word search queries, are a suitable extension to context-sensitive word search engines.

Impact Statement

Context-sensitive word search engines provide easier access to language resources and our work extends this to data from language models. This implies an increased risk of leaking sensible data contained in the source data. We avoided training models to predict proper nouns to avoid that a model can be used to search for personal information.

We use and combine data from Wikitext (i.e. Wikipedia), CLOTH, and the Google Web and Books n-grams, obtained from publicly available and appropriately acknowledged sources and according to their terms and conditions. Our derived systems and evaluation procedure may be susceptible to biases inherent in the data we used. We took no extra steps to de-bias the models or data used.

References

Dimitris Alikaniotis, Vipul Raheja, and Joel R. Tetreault. 2019. The unreasonable effectiveness of transformer language models in grammatical error correction. In *Proceedings of the Fourteenth Workshop on Innovative Use of NLP for Building Educational Applications, BEA@ACL 2019*. Association for Computational Linguistics.

Alessio Bellino and Daniela Bascuñán. 2020. Design and evaluation of writebetter: A corpus-based writing assistant. *IEEE Access*, 8:70216–70233.

Joanne Boisson, Ting-Hui Kao, Jian-Cheng Wu, Tzu-Hsi Yen, and Jason S. Chang. 2013. Linggle: A Web-scale Linguistic Search Engine for Words in Context. In *Proceedings of the 51st Annual Meeting of the Association for Computational Linguistics: System Demonstrations*, pages 139–144, Sofia, Bulgaria. Association for Computational Linguistics.

Jacob Devlin, Ming-Wei Chang, Kenton Lee, and Kristina Toutanova. 2019. BERT: Pre-training of deep bidirectional transformers for language understanding. In *Proceedings of the 2019 Conference of the North American Chapter of the Association for Computational Linguistics: Human Language Technologies, Volume 1 Long and Short Papers)*, pages 4171–4186, Minneapolis, Minnesota. Association for Computational Linguistics.

Chris Donahue, Mina Lee, and Percy Liang. 2020. Enabling language models to fill in the blanks. In *Proceedings of the 58th Annual Meeting of the Association for Computational Linguistics*, pages 2492–2501, Online. Association for Computational Linguistics.

Hugo Gonçalo Oliveira. 2021. Answering fill-in-the-blank questions in portuguese with transformer language models. In *Progress in Artificial Intelligence*, pages 739–751, Cham. Springer International Publishing.

Kalervo Järvelin and Jaana Kekäläinen. 2002. Cumulated gain-based evaluation of ir techniques. *ACM Trans. Inf. Syst.*, 20(4):422?446.

Mina Lee, Chris Donahue, Robin Jia, Alexander Iyabor, and Percy Liang. 2021. Swords: A benchmark for lexical substitution with improved data coverage and quality. In *Proceedings of the 2021 Conference of the North American Chapter of the Association for Computational Linguistics: Human Language Technologies*, pages 4362–4379, Online. Association for Computational Linguistics.

Mike Lewis, Yinhan Liu, Naman Goyal, Marjan Ghazvininejad, Abdelrahman Mohamed, Omer Levy, Ves Stoyanov, and Luke Zettlemoyer. 2019. Bart: Denoising sequence-to-sequence pre-training for natural language generation, translation, and comprehension. *arXiv preprint arXiv:1910.13461*.

Nitin Madnani and Bonnie J. Dorr. 2010. Generating phrasal and sentential paraphrases: A survey of data-driven methods. *Computational Linguistics*, 36(3):341–387.

Diana McCarthy and Roberto Navigli. 2007. SemEval-2007 task 10: English lexical substitution task. In *Proceedings of the Fourth International Workshop on Semantic Evaluations (SemEval-2007)*, pages 48–53, Prague, Czech Republic. Association for Computational Linguistics.

Stephen Merity, Caiming Xiong, James Bradbury, and Richard Socher. 2016. Pointer sentinel mixture models. *CoRR*, abs/1609.07843.

Jean-Baptiste Michel, Yuan Kui Shen, Aviva Presser Aiden, Adrian Veres, Matthew K. Gray, null null, Joseph P. Pickett, Dale Hoiberg, Dan Clancy, Peter Norvig, Jon Orwant, Steven Pinker, Martin A. Nowak, and Erez Lieberman Aiden. 2011. Quantitative analysis of culture using millions of digitized books. *Science*, 331(6014):176–182.

Alec Radford, Jeffrey Wu, Rewon Child, David Luan, Dario Amodei, and Ilya Sutskever. 2019. Language models are unsupervised multitask learners.

Stephen E Robertson. 1977. The probability ranking principle in ir. *Journal of documentation*.

D Gordon Rohman. 1965. Pre-writing the stage of discovery in the writing process. *College composition and communication*, 16(2):106–112.

Anthony Seow. 2002. The writing process and process writing. *Methodology in language teaching: An anthology of current practice*, pages 315–320.

Benno Stein, Martin Potthast, and Martin Trenkmann. 2010. Retrieving Customary Web Language to Assist Writers. In *Advances in Information Retrieval. 32nd European Conference on Information Retrieval (ECIR 2010)*, volume 5993 of *Lecture Notes in Computer Science*, pages 631–635, Berlin Heidelberg New York. Springer.

Ashish Vaswani, Noam Shazeer, Niki Parmar, Jakob Uszkoreit, Llion Jones, Aidan N Gomez, Łukasz Kaiser, and Illia Polosukhin. 2017. Attention is all you need. In *Advances in neural information processing systems*, pages 5998–6008.

Thomas Wolf, Lysandre Debut, Victor Sanh, Julien Chaumond, Clement Delangue, Anthony Moi, Perric Cistac, Clara Ma, Yacine Jernite, Julien Plu, Canwen Xu, Teven Scao, Sylvain Gugger, Mariama Drame, Quentin Lhoest, and Alexander M. Rush. 2020. Transformers: State-of-the-Art Natural Language Processing.

Qizhe Xie, Guokun Lai, Zihang Dai, and Eduard H. Hovy. 2018. Large-scale cloze test dataset created by teachers. In *Proceedings of the 2018 Conference on Empirical Methods in Natural Language Processing*, pages 2344–2356, Brussels, Belgium. Association for Computational Linguistics.

Plug-and-Play Controller for Story Completion: A Pilot Study toward Emotion-aware Story Writing Assistance

Yusuke Mori[1] and **Hiroaki Yamane**[2,1] and **Ryohei Shimizu**[1] and **Tatsuya Harada**[1,2]
[1]The University of Tokyo
[2]RIKEN
{mori, yamane, shimizu, harada}@mi.t.u-tokyo.ac.jp

Abstract

Emotions are essential for storytelling and narrative generation, and as such, the relationship between stories and emotions has been extensively studied. The authors of this paper, including a professional novelist, have examined the use of natural language processing to address the problems of novelists from the perspective of practical creative writing. In particular, the story completion task, which requires understanding the existing unfinished context, was studied from the perspective of creative support for human writers, to generate appropriate content to complete the unfinished parts. It was found that unsupervised pre-trained large neural models of the sequence-to-sequence type are useful for this task. Furthermore, based on the plug-and-play module for controllable text generation using GPT-2, an additional module was implemented to consider emotions. Although this is a preliminary study, and the results leave room for improvement before incorporating the model into a practical system, this effort is an important step in complementing the emotional trajectory of the story.

1 Introduction

In this study, the authors, one of whom is a professional novelist, examined the use of natural language processing to solve the problems faced by novelists from the perspective of practical creative writing. Among the diverse topics related to automatic storytelling and human creativity, **"emotion"** should be emphasized as an important keyword. The relationship between stories and emotions has been an essential part of the research in the field of humanities, especially in the cognitive and affective science of literature (Hogan, 2006; Pandit and Hogan, 2006; Johnson-Laird and Oatley, 2008; Hogan, 2010, 2019).

In providing practical knowledge for authors, creative techniques emphasize the importance of being conscious of readers' emotions (Field, 2006; Snyder, 2005). The theory of the **emotional arc**, which states that a good story can be typified by emotional movement, is well known from the introduction by a popular American novelist, Vonnegut (1995). As presented in Reagan et al. (2016), studies have been conducted to reveal the close relationship between emotions and stories.

Ackerman and Puglisi (2012) insisted that a key component of every character is emotion. In the context of serious storytelling, Lugmayr et al. (2017) insisted that a fundamental aspect of storytelling is emotions, that is, the cognitive aspects that the story evokes in its audience. Numerous efforts have been made to disclose the mystery of the relationship between emotions and stories (Anderson and McMaster, 1982; Strapparava and Mihalcea, 2008; Abdul-Mageed and Ungar, 2017; Kim and Klinger, 2018, 2019a,b; Zad and Finlayson, 2020).

This study focuses on introducing emotions into a story completion (SC) task. The basic task setting in SC is shown in Figure 1.[1] In the field of story generation and understanding, Wang and Wan (2019) proposed SC. We believe that the artificial intelligence (AI) ability to solve SC tasks is important in the context of providing creative support. If writers cannot complete a story and do not know how to proceed with a plot, a suitable model can provide them with appropriate support.

The main contributions of this study are as follows:

- The importance of emotion in stories was confirmed from the perspective of a professional writer, based on which, the possibility of incorporating emotions into SC tasks is discussed for creative support, and a specific method is proposed to accomplish this.

[1]The original story in this figure is from ROCStories (storyid: 0bb3f8b6-117c-45d0-861f-d9953ccc7ddb; storytitle: Dancing).

Proceedings of the First Workshop on Intelligent and Interactive Writing Assistants (In2Writing 2022), pages 46 - 57
May 26, 2022

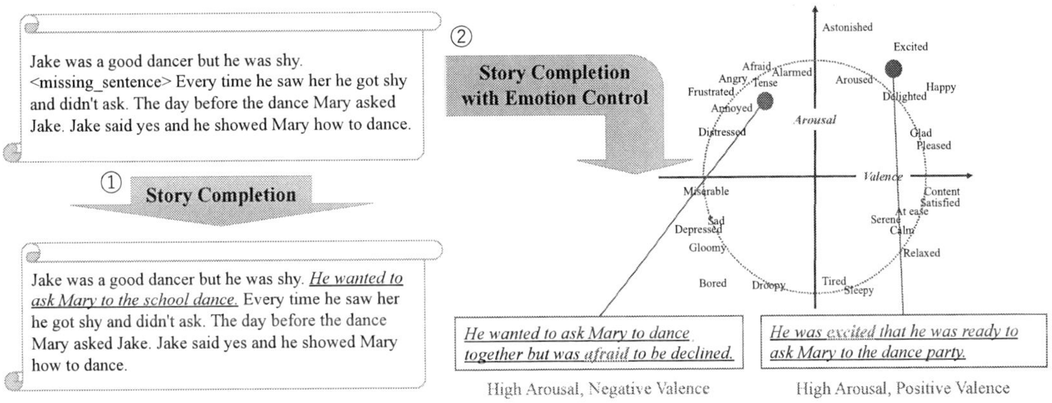

Figure 1: Conceptual diagram of the functionality this study aims for. ① Overview of the story completion task. To address the <missing_position> token in an incomplete story, unsupervised pre-trained large neural models are used. ② PPLM is used to control the emotions of the generative text. The representation of the emotions in this figure was reconstructed from an image by Russell (1980).

- Control of SC was examined through our implementation using the plug-and-play language model (PPLM) (Dathathri et al., 2020), whereby the application of the PPLM, which is originally limited, was expanded.

This study is a preliminary study, and the results should be improved before incorporating the model into a practical system. However, we believe that this effort is an important step toward complementing the emotional trajectory of the story and worth discussing for future directions.

As a complementary contribution to this study, we would like to note that a professional writer researched how to use natural language processing (NLP) technology to reflect the viewpoints of writers and researchers. We expect that this work will contribute to building a bridge toward collaborative work between professional writers and researchers in NLP and human computer interface (HCI) to accelerate research in the field of story writing assistance.

2 Related Work

2.1 Story Completion

In the field of story generation and understanding, Wang and Wan (2019) proposed SC. Given any four sentences in a five-sentence story, the objective of the task is to generate a sentence that is not provided (missing plot), to complete the story. In addition to this, research on text infilling has been actively conducted in recent years (Ippolito et al., 2019; Donahue et al., 2020; Huang et al., 2020; Wang et al., 2020). We pointed out that the ability to solve an SC task is essential from the viewpoint of creative support for writers (Mori et al., 2020). If writers cannot complete a story and do not know how to proceed with the plot, AI can provide appropriate support for filling in the blanks.

In this study, controlled text generation with emotion awareness is applied to SC. Focusing on stories, a method is proposed to handle this task in a simple manner by including a special token, specific to the task. By organizing the task in a simple manner, it becomes possible to solve it in a similar way with various models.

2.2 Emotion-aware Storytelling

Some studies have attempted to control story generation by considering emotions (Chandu et al., 2019; Luo et al., 2019; Brahman and Chaturvedi, 2020; Dathathri et al., 2020; Xu et al., 2020). The study closest to ours is that of Brahman and Chaturvedi (2020). They insisted that their study was the first to model the emotional trajectory of the protagonist in neural storytelling. There are significant differences between their study and ours with respect to task setting and the approach taken.

First, Brahman and Chaturvedi (2020) attempted to generate an entire story from the task, while our focus is on the SC task that a model reads to understand what is written in the original context. In this study, dimensional emotions (valence and arousal) were used instead of categorical emotions (four basic emotions in addition to neutral). Dividing emotions into categories is easy to understand, but for precise control, it is desirable to handle emotions as continuous values. Luo et al. (2019) tackled fine-grained emotion control of story generation, but their objective was story ending rather than completion. Moreover, the controlled emotion was restricted to one dimension (positive-negative). The interest in this study is the control of more diverse two-dimensional emotions based on Russell's circumplex model (Russell, 1980).

2.3 Controllable text generation with Transformer

There are some works in unsupervised pre-trained large neural models for control text generation. Keskar et al. (2019) proposed CTRL to control specific aspects of text generation in large-scale language models. Based on the large-scale language model MEGATRON (Shoeybi et al., 2020) and knowledge-enhanced story generation (Guan et al., 2020), Xu et al. (2020) proposed MEGATRON-CNTRL. In other studies, Rashkin et al. (2020) proposed the task of outline-conditioned story generation, whereby the input only provided a rough sketch of the plot. Therefore, models must generate a story by interweaving the key points provided in the outline. Inspired by plug-and-play generative networks (PPGN) (Nguyen et al., 2017) in computer vision, Dathathri et al. (2020) proposed PPLM, an alternative approach for controlled text generation. Their approach uses attachment models for pre-trained GPT-2 (Radford et al., 2019) to control the word probability distribution during the word-by-word generation process. Optimization is performed ex post facto in the activation space; therefore, no retraining or fine-tuning of the core language model is required. Following this approach, methods have been presented to control the output by adding modules for output control without modifying the core model, such as DELOREAN (DEcoding for nonmonotonic LOgical REAsoNing) (Qin et al., 2020), side-tuning (Zhang et al., 2020a), auxiliary tuning (Zeldes et al., 2020), and GeDi (Krause et al., 2021).

In this study, PPLM, which is a well-designed, simple, and powerful method, is applied for emotion-controllable story generation. Dathathri et al. (2020) explored controlled generation for assistive story writing, demonstrating the usefulness of PPLM in this area. However, they conducted an exploration of open-ended story generation, not SC.

3 Methods

This section describes the proposed method in detail, emphasizing the ingenuity of its implementation. The proposed model has a novel architecture composed of two main parts for SC tasks.

- Fine-tuning unsupervised pre-trained large neural models for the SC task.
- Emotion-aware controlling of fine-tuned models using PPLM.

Studies on applying unsupervised pre-trained large neural models for text infilling have been actively conducted recently (Ippolito et al., 2019; Donahue et al., 2020; Huang et al., 2020; Wang et al., 2020). The first part of our method follows this trend and is verified using various models.

In Subsection 3.2, a modified version of PPLM (Dathathri et al., 2020) is proposed for emotion-aware SC. PPLM, given a prompt (user input text), generates subsequent sentences, as it uses GPT-2 as a base model and tiny attribute models. In this study, the PPLM model was expanded through concatenation with other models.

The model code was implemented using PyTorch (Paszke et al., 2019), which is an open-source machine-learning framework provided as a Python library.[2] To make use of unsupervised pre-trained large neural models, our code was also based on Huggingface Transformers (Wolf et al., 2020), which provide general-purpose architectures for natural language understanding (NLU) and natural language generation (NLG).

The focus here is mainly on Seq2Seq language models (Seq2SeqLMs). For Seq2SeqLMs and its variants, the models below were used.

- BART (Lewis et al., 2020) - BART base, BART large
- T5 (Raffel et al., 2020) - T5 base, T5 large
- PEGASUS (Zhang et al., 2020b) - PEGASUS large
- ProphetNet (Qi et al., 2020) - XLM-ProphetNet large [3]

[2] `https://pytorch.org/`

[3] We used XLM-ProphetNet because only "uncased" models of ProphetNet were available for pre-trained models. Hence, XLM-ProphetNet, specifically, "microsoft/xprophetnet-large-wiki100-cased," which is a cased version, was used.

Model		#layers	#hidden units	#multi-attention heads
BART (Lewis et al., 2020)	base	6	768	12
	large	12	1024	16
T5 (Raffel et al., 2020)	base	6	768	12
	large	12	1024	16
PEGASUS	large	16	1024	16
ProphetNet	XLM-ProphetNet large	12	1024	16

Table 1: Details of pre-trained models. The Seq2SeqLM in this study consists of encoders and decoders, both having the same number of layers, as indicated in the table for each.

Causal language models (CLMs), which have a left-to-right architecture, do not seem to perform well on SC because they were originally designed for the generation of a continuation of the given prompt and not for completing the missing part, by considering the before and after of the missing part. However, Donahue et al. (2020) proposed the infilling by language modeling (ILM), an approach that enables CLMs to leverage the entire context for text infilling. We left it for future work to apply CLMs to controllable story completion with our proposed method.

PyTorch version 1.11.0, and HuggingFace Transformers version 4.18.0 were used.[4] The details of pre-trained models are displayed in Table 1.

3.1 No-emotion-aware baselines

Initially, models for SC that do not consider emotions should be trained for plug-and-play control. In this study, these methods are referred to as "No-emotion-aware baselines." As shown in Figure 1, a special token was defined for the SC task: "<missing_position>". A special token is inserted into the missing position k, such that the input to the model becomes $S' = \{s_1, ..., s_{k-1}$, <missing_position>, $s_{k+1}, ..., s_n\}$. s stands for a sentence, and the subscript number indicates the position of the sentence in the entire text. Subsequently, the model outputs s_k, as defined in the task.

For Seq2SeqLMs, the S' are concatenated into one text and fed to the encoder. The encoder then passes the calculated embeddings to the decoder and generates text. The output is expected to be a single sentence; however, it was also explored if the model could learn from fine-tuning, including "generate only one sentence," constraints.

[4]We plan to make our code publicly available at `https://github.com/mil-tokyo/controllable-story-completion-pilot-study`.

3.2 Emotion Controlling Methods

In this study, PPLM was updated for use in emotion control during story completion. PPLM was originally implemented as an additional module for GPT-2 (the default model was GPT2-medium). Adapting PPLM to Seq2SeqLMs required some implementation ingenuities. PPLM was originally designed to generate the continuation of a given text using a decoder-only model. In contrast, in this study, the given text is first processed with the encoder, and then the resulting tensor is used to generate sentences with the decoder.

PPLM has two types of attribute models: bag-of-words (PPLM-BoW) and discriminator (PPLM-Discrim). Originally, PPLM-BoW did not include an emotion control set. PPLM-Discrim has a pre-trained model for sentiment control, but it is positive–negative. In this study, the focus was on PPLM-BoW because it can function by preparing a list of words without additional learning. Thus, the original word list provided in PPLM can be used, but this does not consider valence and arousal. Hence, the NRC valence, arousal, and dominance lexicon (Mohammad, 2018) (NRC-VAD lexicon) was used to obtain the word list annotated with dimensional emotion values, which was subsequently fed into PPLM-BoW. Instead of using the entire NRC-VAD lexicon as is, in our implementation, a range of values can be specified for valence and arousal (and dominance) at runtime to obtain a subset within that range.

4 Experimental Setup

4.1 Dataset

In this pilot study, the proposed method was trained and evaluated using ROCStories (Mostafazadeh et al., 2016). As shown in Table 2, the dataset was randomly split in a ratio of 8:1:1 to obtain training, development, and test sets. One sentence was removed from the five-sentence story. The missing position k was randomly determined based on a

set	#stories	how to give k
Training	78,528	randomly during training
dev	9,816	when creating a dataset
Test	9,817	when creating a dataset
total	98,161	

Table 2: Overview of the dataset used.

discrete uniform distribution. For the development and test sets, the removal procedure was performed when creating the dataset to improve reproducibility. For the training set, the original five-sentence story was retained in the dataset and a sentence was randomly removed while reading the data during training. This setting followed that of our previous study (Mori et al., 2020).

4.2 Training Details

For training, the AdamW (Loshchilov and Hutter, 2019) optimizer was used with parameters $\beta_1 = 0.9, \beta_2 = 0.999, and \epsilon = 1e - 08$. The initial learning rate was set to $3e - 05$ and linearly decreased thereafter from the initial point to 0 to avoid overfitting. The model was fine-tuned using NVIDIA Tesla V100 GPUs and the size of the training batch was set to 8.

We use two sets of training parameters. One is task-specific parameters, defined for each model based on with reference to its use for the summarization task. The other is common parameters for all models.

Seq2SeqLMs significantly improved the performance compared to conventional models in text-to-text tasks, especially in summarization and translation. Of these two well-worked tasks, we hypothesized that the training settings for summarization are closer to what we need for SC. SC requires methods to understand the context, to generate appropriate sentences for completion. The given context is typically longer than a sentence for completion. In summary, methods are required to understand the entire text, to generate shorter sentences to represent it. Although there are two types of approaches, extractive summarization and abstractive summarization, the basic objective is the same. On the other hand, in translation tasks, although it is also important to understand the input content, the output length is not significantly different from the input length (note that there is a difference related to the nature of each language). There are also application examples, such as paraphrasing in one language, but the input and output are generally in different languages during translation.

What varies from model to model is the setting such as length penalty and max length of input and output sequence. The length penalty places a constraint on the length of the generated sentences, prompting the generation of longer sentences if it is greater than 1.0, and shorter sentences if it is less than 1.0. As mentioned above, task-specific parameters prepared for summarization were used in this study. This was done to ensure the fairness of the settings by unifying the parameters in "solving SC by directly applying the settings of the summarization task." [5] For this reason, the length penalty was set to 2.0 for T5 in this experiment, 1.0 for BART, and 0.8 for PEGASUS. For XLM-ProphetNet, the penalty was 2.0.

For a different sense of fairness, we provided another setting that uses a common length penalty. In this setting, the length penalty is 1.0.

4.3 Evaluation Metrics

It is necessary to evaluate a large number of models and their variants (model parameters, training parameters, tasks that are fine-tuned beforehand, etc.). Thus, automatic evaluation metrics were employed instead of human evaluation. Stories entertain the reader (or evoke other emotions); therefore, human evaluation is important. However, there is a huge cost involved in terms of time and money for evaluating various parameters in many models. In addition, there are factors such as age, gender, and regional trends in texts, particularly in stories. The problem is that stories liked by someone are not always liked by others. In this section, the focus is on automatic evaluation metrics for a large number of models. The human evaluation of a narrowed-down list of promising candidate models is left for future work.

The following metrics were used for the evaluation: BLEU (Papineni et al., 2002), ROUGE (Lin, 2004), METEOR (Banerjee and Lavie, 2005), BERTScore (Zhang* et al., 2020),[6] and BLEURT (Sellam et al., 2020).[7] The Python library HuggingFace Datasets was used for certain metrics;

[5]There is no generic parameter for the "summarization task" for PEGASUS, so the parameter for summarization of the XSUM dataset was used.

[6]https://github.com/Tiiiger/bert_score

[7]https://github.com/google-research/bleurt

'sacrebleu' as BLEU, ROUGE and METEOR.[8] For each of BERTScore and BLEURT, the original implementation of each paper was used.

5 Results

5.1 No-emotion-aware baselines

First, experiments were conducted using no-emotion-aware baselines. Table 3 lists the test set results of Seq2SeqLMs evaluated using automatic evaluation metrics. In this comparison, the entire story was not compared; however, the generated complementary sentence was compared with the original sentence (the missing sentence). The value of F1 was used for ROUGE and BERTScore. In addition, for BERTScore, the authors obtained an average when evaluating the models.[9] BLEURT was treated in a similar manner.

The results indicated that BART large exhibited the highest scores for every metric. For a deeper analysis of the metric results, Table 4 was created for average generation length and runtime. In BART base, BART large, and PEGASUS, the two training settings didn't have a significant impact. On the other hand, for T5 base, T5 large, and XLM-ProphetNet, better results were obtained when using task-specific parameters. The result suggests that the parameters for summarization work well for story completion, especially when the model requires a large length penalty for summarization tasks.

Table 5 and 6 display the examples generated.

5.2 Emotion Controlling Method

The Seq2SeqLM + PPLM-BoW results are presented in Table 7. As BART large displayed the best result in the no-emotion-aware baseline experiment, BART large was used as the first step of Emotion-aware SC with Seq2SeqLM + PPLM.

In the examples shown in Table 7, the ranges of valence and arousal were set to $0.0 <= valence <= 0.3$ and $0.7 <= arousal <= 1.0$, respectively. As valence is negative and arousal is high, negative and excited emotions are expected to emerge. The results of an uncontrolled trial (unperturbed) and three controlled trials (perturbed) are presented as examples. Perturbed 1 seems to be controlled by "negative and excited." In the context of careful driving, it is not unnatural for events related to the car to occur, and on top of that, the expression that the car gets stuck is negative. We showed an example where the generation of emotion-controlled sentences worked well. However, the adjustment of the parameters to generate a sequence was very severe. PPLM provides parameters to manipulate the generated results, but it is very difficult to adjust these parameters, at least in combination with Seq2SeqLM.

We should note that the BART large model used here was trained with an older version of PyTorch and Transformers. Unfortunately, the version trained with PyTorch 1.11.0 and Transformers 4.18.0 used in this Seq2SeqLM Story Completion did not produce good results with the same generation parameters. Although we could run the modified PPLM with the libraries of the newer version, the choice of the fine-tuned model is also severe.

PPLM was originally designed for use with GPT-2, but in this study, it was modified and applied to Seq2SeqLM. Specifically, it was confirmed that PPLM works on BART. However, when we used the Seq2SeqLM model which was fine-tuned for no-emotion-aware SC to generate sentences controlled with PPLM, we found that the sentences tended to be shorter than those generated without PPLM.

6 Discussion

The no-emotion-aware baseline results indicate that BART large exhibited the highest scores for every metric. In this study, we used two sets of training parameters: one is based on summarization task-specific parameters and the other is common parameters. The result showed that the parameters for summarization work well for story completion, compared to common parameters that do not account for differences between models. Future studies should search for specific parameters for each model that are more suitable for SC.

In this study, PPLM was extended and combined with BART, a representative model of Seq2SeqLMs. In addition, by combining PPLM with the NRC-VAD lexicon, a basis was created for SC to consider valence and arousal. However, there is still a lot of room for improvement in the results.

In text generation, it is important to control the behavior of the model using parameters such as

[8] https://github.com/huggingface/datasets

[9] https://github.com/Tiiiger/bert_score/blob/master/example/Demo.ipynb

	BLEU	ROUGE-1	ROUGE-2	ROUGE-L	METEOR	BERTScore	BLEURT
BART base w/ specific param	5.352848	0.265496	0.082603	0.245470	0.254414	0.909720	-0.432042
BART large w/ specific param	7.390772	0.291679	0.106530	0.271545	0.279876	0.914704	-0.373194
PEGASUS large w/ specific param	5.401445	0.265151	0.085482	0.243784	0.266451	0.909168	-0.443984
T5 base w/ specific param	4.390108	0.253425	0.070985	0.232174	0.244871	0.907397	-0.473313
T5 large w/ specific param	6.249401	0.282742	0.095236	0.259644	0.276074	0.912142	-0.404434
XLM-ProphetNet large w/ specific param	0.116252	0.159532	0.010753	0.148529	0.065040	0.853637	-0.821382
BART base	5.352848	0.265651	0.082704	0.245416	0.254414	0.909720	-0.432042
BART large	7.390772	0.291414	0.106375	0.271576	0.279876	0.914704	-0.373194
20220410_003_pegasus_large	5.401445	0.265209	0.085513	0.243719	0.266451	0.909168	-0.443984
T5 base	2.330794	0.257133	0.074025	0.241255	0.194306	0.900627	-0.911796
T5 large	2.332709	0.288103	0.098576	0.270357	0.225574	0.903646	-0.912072
XLM-ProphetNet large	0.071638	0.158260	0.009964	0.146465	0.064679	0.852067	-0.798809

Table 3: The result of no-emotion-aware Seq2SeqLMs evaluated with automatic evaluation metrics.

	BLEU	generated length	runtime	samples/sec
BART base w/ specific param	5.3528	14.5	344.5440	-0.003
BART large w/ specific param	7.3907	15.0	546.4531	-0.002
PEGASUS large w/ specific param	5.4014	13.6	890.2809	-0.001
T5 base w/ specific param	4.3901	14.9	595.7259	-0.002
T5 large w/ specific param	6.2494	14.7	1031.0659	-0.001
XLM-ProphetNet large w/ specific param	0.1163	10.8	960.6619	-0.001
BART base	5.3528	14.5	352.5765	-0.003
BART large	7.3907	15.0	556.1080	-0.002
20220410_003_pegasus_large	5.4014	13.6	893.2609	-0.001
T5 base	2.3308	13.8	487.8538	-0.002
T5 large	2.3327	13.6	866.5806	-0.001
XLM-ProphetNet large[10]	0.0716	9.0	11589.1036	-0.000

Table 4: The mean generated length and the runtime of no-emotion-aware Seq2SeqLMs. "w/ specific param" indicates that the model is trained using the task-specific parameters of each model.

storyid	dc36af5e-a65f-4193-8f3c-5162c8af6755
context	<missing_position> I wanted to take out some fish. But then the lady was not using gloves. I was disgusted. I ended up walking out.
missing_id	0
GT	I went to a restaurant yesterday.
BART base	I went to the fish market with my friends.
BART large	I went to the fish market yesterday.
PEGASUS large	I went to the fish market today for the first time.
T5 base	I went to a fish market one day. I was very hungry.
T5 large	I went to a fish market one day with my friends.
XLM-ProphetNet large	She was to to the....
GT completed story	I went to a restaurant yesterday. I wanted to take out some fish. But then the lady was not using gloves. I was disgusted. I ended up walking out.
BART base completed story	I went to the fish market with my friends. I wanted to take out some fish. But then the lady was not using gloves. I was disgusted. I ended up walking out.
BART large completed story	I went to the fish market yesterday. I wanted to take out some fish. But then the lady was not using gloves. I was disgusted. I ended up walking out.
PEGASUS large completed story	I went to the fish market today for the first time. I wanted to take out some fish. But then the lady was not using gloves. I was disgusted. I ended up walking out.
T5 base completed story	I went to a fish market one day. I was very hungry. I wanted to take out some fish. But then the lady was not using gloves. I was disgusted. I ended up walking out.
T5 large completed story	I went to a fish market one day with my friends. I wanted to take out some fish. But then the lady was not using gloves. I was disgusted. I ended up walking out.
XLM-ProphetNet large completed story	She was to to the.... I wanted to take out some fish. But then the lady was not using gloves. I was disgusted. I ended up walking out.

Table 5: Examples of contexts and completion sentences generated by no-emotion-aware Seq2SeqLMs. In this case, the task-specific parameters for each model were used.

the length penalty. Two types of parameters were experimented with in this study, but further effort is required to determine the best parameter. The optimal hyperparameters seem to be naturally different for each model. It is not realistic to check all outputs using the human eye while adjusting hyperparameters within a wide range of values for many models. Therefore, an automatic evaluation

storyid	f2a013bd-852f-43f4-9012-4db8ae44c64e
context	Jane had a very sick dog. Her dog was old and couldn't run anymore. So that he still felt young, Jane used to walk her dog in a pram. <missing_position> Jane didn't care as she knew she was making him feel better.
missing_id	3
GT	This would look strange to the public.
BART base	One day, her dog fell down and broke his leg.
BART large	Her dog got very sick and couldn't run anymore.
PEGASUS large	One day, her dog got sick and had to be put down.
T5 base	One day, she noticed that her dog was very sick.
T5 large	One day, her dog got sick and couldn't walk.
XLM-ProphetNet large	He was to to the the..
GT completed story	Jane had a very sick dog. Her dog was old and couldn't run anymore. So that he still felt young, Jane used to walk her dog in a pram. This would look strange to the public. Jane didn't care as she knew she was making him feel better.
BART base completed story	Jane had a very sick dog. Her dog was old and couldn't run anymore. So that he still felt young, Jane used to walk her dog in a pram. One day, her dog fell down and broke his leg. Jane didn't care as she knew she was making him feel better.
BART large completed story	Jane had a very sick dog. Her dog was old and couldn't run anymore. So that he still felt young, Jane used to walk her dog in a pram. Her dog got very sick and couldn't run anymore. Jane didn't care as she knew she was making him feel better.
PEGASUS large completed story	Jane had a very sick dog. Her dog was old and couldn't run anymore. So that he still felt young, Jane used to walk her dog in a pram. One day, her dog got sick and had to be put down. Jane didn't care as she knew she was making him feel better.
T5 base completed story	Jane had a very sick dog. Her dog was old and couldn't run anymore. So that he still felt young, Jane used to walk her dog in a pram. One day, she noticed that her dog was very sick. Jane didn't care as she knew she was making him feel better.
T5 large completed story	Jane had a very sick dog. Her dog was old and couldn't run anymore. So that he still felt young, Jane used to walk her dog in a pram. One day, her dog got sick and couldn't walk. Jane didn't care as she knew she was making him feel better.
XLM-ProphetNet large completed story	Jane had a very sick dog. Her dog was old and couldn't run anymore. So that he still felt young, Jane used to walk her dog in a pram. He was to to the the.. Jane didn't care as she knew she was making him feel better.

Table 6: Examples of contexts and completion sentences generated by no-emotion-aware Seq2SeqLMs. In this case, the same hyperparameters were used for length penalty and max length.

Context	I got a call from the hospital. My doctor told me to stop everything I'm doing and come to her. Although I was nervous, I tried to drive calmly. <missing_sentence> The doctor diagnosed me with leukemia.
missing sentence	The front desk worker sent me to an office.
Unperturbed	However, my blood.ItItMy
Perturbed 0	However, the car..
Perturbed 1	My car got stuck...
Perturbed 2	......

Table 7: An example of emotion-controlled SC with BART large + PPLM-BoW (0.0 <= Valence <= 0.3 and 0.7 <= Arousal <= 1.0).

mechanism is required.

The application of these methods to other datasets is left for future work. As a representative example, the WritingPrompts dataset (Fan et al., 2018) was considered. Stories in WritingPrompts vary in terms of length; therefore, the importance of a single sentence varies from one story to the other. With very long stories, generally trimming is used to retain a predetermined number of words from the start while truncating the rest. Hence, this dataset was not considered to be suitable for the SC tasks for now. Thus, as a starting point, ROCStories was adopted.

7 Considerations by a Professional Writer

As noted in the Introduction, one of the authors of this study was a professional novelist. This work is a collaborative effort between researchers and a professional creative writer. More precisely, the first author of this paper is a professional Japanese novelist as well as a researcher in the field of story understanding and generation.

In Section 6, the viewpoint of the researchers is discussed. In this section, the positioning and prospects of this study are discussed from the novelist's perspective.

In an experiment conducted separately from this study, four professional creative writers were asked to evaluate a creative writing support system.[11] The results of that experiment confirmed that there might be a negative perception of the system's ability to control the output if there are parameters with which the user is not familiar. Although it would be desirable for users to have the freedom to adjust the outcome, too many parameters make them lost. They do not know what to do, resulting in confusion on the user's part in using the system and in a negative impression.

As previously mentioned, our modified PPLM for controllable SC addressed in this study is difficult to adjust. Moreover, in its current state, users are required to understand what "valence" and "arousal" mean. We believe that treating both dimensions rather than one dimension (positive-negative) would be important for future directions in this area, but this idea is not yet widespread. Hence, it is difficult for this approach to provide professional writers with the desired results for now. At this point, there was concern that other professional writers would have a negative impression of the "creative writing support system that controls the emotions of the generated text" as a whole. That is why no human evaluation was conducted on this study, except by the novelist author.

For practitioners, the extent to which AI could replace their own work is an important issue; there is also concern that it could trigger a sense of avoidance toward AI. Prudence is needed in conducting research, and professional evaluations, which are important topics of discussion.

Some professional novelists write from beginning to end in order, while others come up with certain parts but cannot come up with the correct sentences to fill in the gaps. SC is an important task in helping the latter. From the creative writer's perspective, it is helpful to have a system that understands the meaning of one's own writing and then fills in the missing parts. Furthermore, as the importance of the emotional arc in a story becomes increasingly apparent, a system that controls the output of the emotions desired by the user as well as an evaluation index that considers emotions would be helpful.

[11]The details of the human evaluation consist the part of the doctoral dissertation of the first author. The dissertation will be publicly available in the UTokyo Repository, `https://repository.dl.itc.u-tokyo.ac.jp/`.

8 Conclusion

In this study, the SC task was considered for various emotions. Previous studies on emotion-aware story generation have restricted emotions to one dimension (positive-negative) or categorical ones. Our aim was to control more diverse emotions, so the issue of two-dimensional control was addressed based on Russell's circumplex model.

Our implementation made it possible to control SC using PPLM. This expands the application of PPLM, which was originally limited to the task of "generating the continuation of a prompt." Although the goal of controlling emotions was accomplished, it was difficult to adjust the parameters. Whether this difficulty in coordination can be improved through innovative implementation or demands a completely different approach requires further examination.

Acknowledgements

We would like to thank Yusuke Mukuta for the helpful discussions. This work was partially supported by JST AIP Acceleration Research JPMJCR20U3, Moonshot R&D Grant Number JPMJPS2011, JSPS KAKENHI Grant Number JP19H01115, and JP20H05556 and Basic Research Grant (Super AI) of Institute for AI and Beyond of the University of Tokyo.

References

Muhammad Abdul-Mageed and Lyle Ungar. 2017. Emonet: Fine-grained emotion detection with gated recurrent neural networks. In *Proceedings of the 55th Annual Meeting of the Association for Computational Linguistics (Volume 1: Long Papers)*, pages 718–728, Vancouver, Canada. Association for Computational Linguistics.

Angela Ackerman and Becca Puglisi. 2012. *The Emotion Thesaurus: A Writer's Guide to Character Expression.* JADD Publishing.

C. W. Anderson and G. E. McMaster. 1982. Computer assisted modeling of affective tone in written documents. *Computers and the Humanities*, 16(1):1–9.

Satanjeev Banerjee and Alon Lavie. 2005. METEOR: An automatic metric for MT evaluation with improved correlation with human judgments. In *Proceedings of the ACL Workshop on Intrinsic and Ex-*

trinsic Evaluation Measures for Machine Translation and/or Summarization, pages 65–72, Ann Arbor, Michigan. Association for Computational Linguistics.

Faeze Brahman and Snigdha Chaturvedi. 2020. Modeling protagonist emotions for emotion-aware storytelling. In *Proceedings of the 2020 Conference on Empirical Methods in Natural Language Processing*, Punta Cana, Dominican Republic. Association for Computational Linguistics.

Khyathi Chandu, Shrimai Prabhumoye, Ruslan Salakhutdinov, and Alan W Black. 2019. "my way of telling a story": Persona based grounded story generation. In *Proceedings of the Second Workshop on Storytelling*, pages 11–21, Florence, Italy. Association for Computational Linguistics.

Sumanth Dathathri, Andrea Madotto, Janice Lan, Jane Hung, Eric Frank, Piero Molino, Jason Yosinski, and Rosanne Liu. 2020. Plug and play language models: A simple approach to controlled text generation. In *International Conference on Learning Representations*.

Chris Donahue, Mina Lee, and Percy Liang. 2020. Enabling language models to fill in the blanks. In *Proceedings of the 58th Annual Meeting of the Association for Computational Linguistics*, pages 2492–2501, Online. Association for Computational Linguistics.

Angela Fan, Mike Lewis, and Yann Dauphin. 2018. Hierarchical neural story generation. In *Proceedings of the 56th Annual Meeting of the Association for Computational Linguistics (Volume 1: Long Papers)*, pages 889–898, Melbourne, Australia. Association for Computational Linguistics.

Syd Field. 2006. *The Screenwriter's Workbook, Revised Edition*. Delta Trade Paperbacks.

Jian Guan, Fei Huang, Zhihao Zhao, Xiaoyan Zhu, and Minlie Huang. 2020. A knowledge-enhanced pretraining model for commonsense story generation. *Transactions of the Association for Computational Linguistics*, 8:93–108.

Patrick Colm Hogan. 2006. Narrative universals, heroic tragi-comedy, and shakespeare's political ambivalence. *College Literature*, 33(1):34–66.

Patrick Colm Hogan. 2010. A passion for plot: Prolegomena to affective narratology. *symplokē*, 18(1-2):65–81.

Patrick Colm Hogan. 2019. Description, explanation, and the meanings of "narrative". *Evolutionary Studies in Imaginative Culture*, 3:45+. 1, 45, Critical essay.

Yichen Huang, Yizhe Zhang, Oussama Elachqar, and Yu Cheng. 2020. INSET: Sentence infilling with INter-SEntential transformer. In *Proceedings of the 58th Annual Meeting of the Association for Computational Linguistics*, pages 2502–2515, Online. Association for Computational Linguistics.

Daphne Ippolito, David Grangier, Chris Callison-Burch, and Douglas Eck. 2019. Unsupervised hierarchical story infilling. In *Proceedings of the First Workshop on Narrative Understanding*, pages 37–43, Minneapolis, Minnesota. Association for Computational Linguistics.

R. N. Johnson-Laird and Keith Oatley. 2008. *Emotions, music, and literature.*, Handbook of emotions, 3rd ed., pages 102–113. The Guilford Press, New York, NY, US.

Nitish Shirish Keskar, Bryan McCann, Lav R Varshney, Caiming Xiong, and Richard Socher. 2019. Ctrl: A conditional transformer language model for controllable generation. *arXiv preprint arXiv:1909.05858*.

Evgeny Kim and Roman Klinger. 2018. Who feels what and why? annotation of a literature corpus with semantic roles of emotions. In *Proceedings of the 27th International Conference on Computational Linguistics*, pages 1345–1359, Santa Fe, New Mexico, USA. Association for Computational Linguistics.

Evgeny Kim and Roman Klinger. 2019a. An analysis of emotion communication channels in fan-fiction: Towards emotional storytelling. In *Proceedings of the Second Workshop on Storytelling*, pages 56–64, Florence, Italy. Association for Computational Linguistics.

Evgeny Kim and Roman Klinger. 2019b. Frowning Frodo, wincing Leia, and a seriously great friendship: Learning to classify emotional relationships of fictional characters. In *Proceedings of the 2019 Conference of the North American Chapter of the Association for Computational Linguistics: Human Language Technologies, Volume 1 (Long and Short Papers)*, pages 647–653, Minneapolis, Minnesota. Association for Computational Linguistics.

Ben Krause, Akhilesh Deepak Gotmare, Bryan McCann, Nitish Shirish Keskar, Shafiq Joty, richard socher, and Nazneen Rajani. 2021. Gedi: Generative discriminator guided sequence generation.

Mike Lewis, Yinhan Liu, Naman Goyal, Marjan Ghazvininejad, Abdelrahman Mohamed, Omer Levy, Veselin Stoyanov, and Luke Zettlemoyer. 2020. BART: Denoising sequence-to-sequence pre-training for natural language generation, translation, and comprehension. In *Proceedings of the 58th Annual Meeting of the Association for Computational Linguistics*, pages 7871–7880, Online. Association for Computational Linguistics.

Chin-Yew Lin. 2004. ROUGE: A package for automatic evaluation of summaries. In *Text Summarization Branches Out*, pages 74–81, Barcelona, Spain. Association for Computational Linguistics.

Ilya Loshchilov and Frank Hutter. 2019. Decoupled weight decay regularization. In *International Conference on Learning Representations*.

Artur Lugmayr, Erkki Sutinen, Jarkko Suhonen, Carolina Islas Sedano, Helmut Hlavacs, and Calkin Suero Montero. 2017. Serious storytelling - a first definition and review. *Multimedia Tools and Applications*, 76:15707–15733.

Fuli Luo, Damai Dai, Pengcheng Yang, Tianyu Liu, Baobao Chang, Zhifang Sui, and Xu Sun. 2019. Learning to control the fine-grained sentiment for story ending generation. In *Proceedings of the 57th Annual Meeting of the Association for Computational Linguistics*, pages 6020–6026, Florence, Italy. Association for Computational Linguistics.

Saif Mohammad. 2018. Obtaining reliable human ratings of valence, arousal, and dominance for 20,000 English words. In *Proceedings of the 56th Annual Meeting of the Association for Computational Linguistics (Volume 1: Long Papers)*, pages 174–184, Melbourne, Australia. Association for Computational Linguistics.

Yusuke Mori, Hiroaki Yamane, Yusuke Mukuta, and Tatsuya Harada. 2020. Finding and generating a missing part for story completion. In *Proceedings of the The 4th Joint SIGHUM Workshop on Computational Linguistics for Cultural Heritage, Social Sciences, Humanities and Literature*, pages 156–166, Online. International Committee on Computational Linguistics.

Nasrin Mostafazadeh, Nathanael Chambers, Xiaodong He, Devi Parikh, Dhruv Batra, Lucy Vanderwende, Pushmeet Kohli, and James Allen. 2016. A corpus and cloze evaluation for deeper understanding of commonsense stories. In *Proceedings of the 2016 Conference of the North American Chapter of the Association for Computational Linguistics: Human Language Technologies*, pages 839–849, San Diego, California. Association for Computational Linguistics.

Anh Nguyen, Jeff Clune, Yoshua Bengio, Alexey Dosovitskiy, and Jason Yosinski. 2017. Plug & play generative networks: Conditional iterative generation of images in latent space. In *Proceedings of the IEEE Conference on Computer Vision and Pattern Recognition*. IEEE.

Lalita Pandit and Patrick Colm Hogan. 2006. Introduction: morsels and modules: on embodying cognition in shakespeare's plays (1). *College Literature*, 33:1+. 1, Article.

Kishore Papineni, Salim Roukos, Todd Ward, and Wei-Jing Zhu. 2002. BLEU: A method for automatic evaluation of machine translation. In *Proceedings of the 40th Annual Meeting on Association for Computational Linguistics*, pages 311–318, Stroudsburg, PA, USA. Association for Computational Linguistics.

Adam Paszke, Sam Gross, Francisco Massa, Adam Lerer, James Bradbury, Gregory Chanan, Trevor Killeen, Zeming Lin, Natalia Gimelshein, Luca Antiga, Alban Desmaison, Andreas Kopf, Edward Yang, Zachary DeVito, Martin Raison, Alykhan Tejani, Sasank Chilamkurthy, Benoit Steiner, Lu Fang, Junjie Bai, and Soumith Chintala. 2019. Pytorch: An imperative style, high-performance deep learning library. In H. Wallach, H. Larochelle, A. Beygelzimer, F. d'Alché-Buc, E. Fox, and R. Garnett, editors, *Advances in Neural Information Processing Systems 32*, pages 8024–8035. Curran Associates, Inc.

Weizhen Qi, Yu Yan, Yeyun Gong, Dayiheng Liu, Nan Duan, Jiusheng Chen, Ruofei Zhang, and Ming Zhou. 2020. Prophetnet: Predicting future n-gram for sequence-to-sequence pre-training. In *Proceedings of the 2020 Conference on Empirical Methods in Natural Language Processing*, Punta Cana, Dominican Republic. Association for Computational Linguistics.

Lianhui Qin, Vered Shwartz, Peter West, Chandra Bhagavatula, Jena D. Hwang, Ronan Le Bras, Antoine Bosselut, and Yejin Choi. 2020. Back to the future: Unsupervised backprop-based decoding for counterfactual and abductive commonsense reasoning. In *Proceedings of the 2020 Conference on Empirical Methods in Natural Language Processing (EMNLP)*, pages 794–805, Online. Association for Computational Linguistics.

Alec Radford, Jeff Wu, Rewon Child, David Luan, Dario Amodei, and Ilya Sutskever. 2019. Language models are unsupervised multitask learners.

Colin Raffel, Noam Shazeer, Adam Roberts, Katherine Lee, Sharan Narang, Michael Matena, Yanqi Zhou, Wei Li, and Peter J. Liu. 2020. Exploring the limits of transfer learning with a unified text-to-text transformer. *Journal of Machine Learning Research*, 21(140):1–67.

Hannah Rashkin, Asli Celikyilmaz, Yejin Choi, and Jianfeng Gao. 2020. Plotmachines: Outline-conditioned generation with dynamic plot state tracking.

Andrew J. Reagan, Lewis Mitchell, Dilan Kiley, Christopher M. Danforth, and Peter Sheridan Dodds. 2016. The emotional arcs of stories are dominated by six basic shapes. *EPJ Data Science*, 5(1):31.

James A. Russell. 1980. A circumplex model of affect. *Journal of personality and social psychology*, 39:1161–1178.

Thibault Sellam, Dipanjan Das, and Ankur Parikh. 2020. BLEURT: Learning robust metrics for text generation. In *Proceedings of the 58th Annual Meeting of the Association for Computational Linguistics*, pages 7881–7892, Online. Association for Computational Linguistics.

Mohammad Shoeybi, Mostofa Patwary, Raul Puri, Patrick LeGresley, Jared Casper, and Bryan Catanzaro. 2020. Megatron-lm: Training multi-billion parameter language models using model parallelism.

Blake Snyder. 2005. *SAVE THE CAT! The Last Book on Screenwriting You'll Ever Need.* Michael Wiese Productions.

Carlo Strapparava and Rada Mihalcea. 2008. Learning to identify emotions in text. In *Proceedings of the 2008 ACM Symposium on Applied Computing*, SAC '08, pages 1556–1560, New York, NY, USA. ACM.

Kurt Vonnegut. 1995. Kurt vonnegut on the shapes of stories. https://www.youtube.com/watch?v=oP3c1h8v2ZQ. Video. Accessed: October 17, 2020.

Su Wang, Greg Durrett, and Katrin Erk. 2020. Narrative interpolation for generating and understanding stories.

Tianming Wang and Xiaojun Wan. 2019. T-CVAE: Transformer-based conditioned variational autoencoder for story completion. In *Proceedings of the Twenty-Eighth International Joint Conference on Artificial Intelligence*, pages 5233–5239. International Joint Conferences on Artificial Intelligence Organization.

Thomas Wolf, Lysandre Debut, Victor Sanh, Julien Chaumond, Clement Delangue, Anthony Moi, Pierric Cistac, Tim Rault, Remi Louf, Morgan Funtowicz, Joe Davison, Sam Shleifer, Patrick von Platen, Clara Ma, Yacine Jernite, Julien Plu, Canwen Xu, Teven Le Scao, Sylvain Gugger, Mariama Drame, Quentin Lhoest, and Alexander Rush. 2020. Transformers: State-of-the-art natural language processing. In *Proceedings of the 2020 Conference on Empirical Methods in Natural Language Processing: System Demonstrations*, pages 38–45, Online. Association for Computational Linguistics.

Peng Xu, Mostofa Patwary, Mohammad Shoeybi, Raul Puri, Pascale Fung, Anima Anandkumar, and Bryan Catanzaro. 2020. Megatron-cntrl: Controllable story generation with external knowledge using large-scale language models. In *Proceedings of the 2020 Conference on Empirical Methods in Natural Language Processing*, Punta Cana, Dominican Republic. Association for Computational Linguistics.

Samira Zad and Mark Finlayson. 2020. Systematic evaluation of a framework for unsupervised emotion recognition for narrative text. In *Proceedings of the First Joint Workshop on Narrative Understanding, Storylines, and Events*, pages 26–37, Online. Association for Computational Linguistics.

Yoel Zeldes, Dan Padnos, Or Sharir, and Barak Peleg. 2020. Technical report: Auxiliary tuning and its application to conditional text generation.

Jeffrey O. Zhang, Alexander Sax, Amir Zamir, Leonidas Guibas, and Jitendra Malik. 2020a. Side-tuning: A baseline for network adaptation via additive side networks. In *Computer Vision – ECCV 2020*, pages 698–714, Cham. Springer International Publishing.

Jingqing Zhang, Yao Zhao, Mohammad Saleh, and Peter Liu. 2020b. PEGASUS: Pre-training with extracted gap-sentences for abstractive summarization. In *Proceedings of the 37th International Conference on Machine Learning*, volume 119 of *Proceedings of Machine Learning Research*, pages 11328–11339. PMLR.

Tianyi Zhang*, Varsha Kishore*, Felix Wu*, Kilian Q. Weinberger, and Yoav Artzi. 2020. Bertscore: Evaluating text generation with bert. In *International Conference on Learning Representations*.

Text Revision by On-the-Fly Representation Optimization

Jingjing Li[1], Zichao Li[2], Tao Ge[3], Irwin King[1], Michael R. Lyu[1]
[1] The Chinese University of Hong Kong
[2] McGill University [3] Microsoft Research Asia
llee.jingjing@gmail.com zichao.li@mail.mcgill.ca
tage@microsoft.com {king, lyu}@cse.cuhk.edu.hk

Abstract

Text revision refers to a family of natural language generation tasks, where the source and target sequences share moderate resemblance in surface form but differentiate in attributes, such as text style transfer (Shen et al., 2017), text simplification (Xu et al., 2016), counterfactual debiasing (Zmigrod et al., 2019), grammar error correction (Sun et al., 2022) and sentence fusion (Malmi et al., 2019).

As the most popular solution, sequence-to-sequence (seq2seq) learning achieves state-of-the-art results on many text revision tasks today. However, it becomes less applicable when there is no large-scale annotated parallel data for training.

With recent breakthroughs in self-supervised learning have enabled the pre-trained Transformer models (Vaswani et al., 2017), such as BERT (Devlin et al., 2018), RoBERTa (Liu et al., 2019) and GPT (Radford et al., 2020), to learn sufficient distributed representation of natural language, which is universally transferable to a wide range of downstream tasks even without labeled data (Tenney et al., 2019; Zhang et al., 2019; Wu et al., 2020). In this work, we borrow the power of a pre-trained Transformer for text revision without any parallel data.

In this paper, we propose OREO, a method of On-the-fly REpresentation Optimization for text revision. Instead of generating an entire sequence of tokens from scratch, OREO first detects partial text span to be edited, then conducts in-place span revision:

Step 1: Representation optimization Given an input sentence $X^{(i)}$ at the i-th iteration, RoBERTa parameterized by θ transforms it to a sequence of hidden states $H^{(i)}$, conditioned on which the attribute head estimates the probability of target attribute $P_{W_{\text{Att}}}(z^*|H^{(i)})$. Then, for each revision, we find a small local perturbation on $H^{(i)}$ that maximally increases the likelihood of target attribute. As such, the update rule of hidden states is:

$$H^{(i+1)} = H^{(i)} - \lambda \frac{\nabla_{H^{(i)}}\mathcal{L}}{\|\nabla_{H^{(i)}}\mathcal{L}\|_2}, \quad (1)$$

where λ is a hyper-parameter that controls the norm of perturbation, and

$$\mathcal{L} = -\log P_{W_{\text{Att}}}(z^*|H^{(i)}). \quad (2)$$

Step 2: Span replacement After hidden states are updated, OREO conducts span replacement. We calculate magnitude of $\nabla_{H^{(i)}}\mathcal{L}$ for i-th token, where $\mathcal{L}$ is calculated with (2), and select the span with largest magnitude. The selected span $X^{(i)}_{t:t+N}$ of length N is replaced by `[LM-MASK]` tokens. RoBERTa takes as input the masked sequence, and predicts a new span autoregressively with the previously updated hidden states.

The training for OREO is simple: we fine-tune the RoBERTa model with masked language modeling and attribute classification jointly. The first objective forces RoBERTa to infill a span consistent with the semantics and attributes represented by hidden states, while the latter one steers the hidden states towards a desired attribute.

We experiment with two fundamental revision tasks, text simplification and formalization. In text simplification, our method surpassed the supervised baseline by 4.2 SARI score and unsupervised baseline 5.3 SARI score on Newsela-turk (Maddela et al., 2020). In text formalization, our approach outperforms all of the unsupervised baseline models in terms of content preservation and formality on GYAFC-fr (Rao and Tetreault, 2018). Ablation study is conducted to validate the design of each component in the model, through which we have following key findings: (1) representation optimization is essential to formality metrics; (2) infilling conditioned on hidden states helps preserve content; (3) our gradient-guided span selection contributes to both of them.[1]

[1]This paper was originally published at AAAI 2022. Access the full version here.

Proceedings of the First Workshop on Intelligent and Interactive Writing Assistants (In2Writing 2022), pages 58 - 59
May 26, 2022 ©2022 Association for Computational Linguistics

References

Jacob Devlin, Ming-Wei Chang, Kenton Lee, and Kristina Toutanova. 2018. Bert: Pre-training of deep bidirectional transformers for language understanding. *arXiv preprint arXiv:1810.04805*.

Yinhan Liu, Myle Ott, Naman Goyal, Jingfei Du, Mandar Joshi, Danqi Chen, Omer Levy, Mike Lewis, Luke Zettlemoyer, and Veselin Stoyanov. 2019. Roberta: A robustly optimized bert pretraining approach. *arXiv preprint arXiv:1907.11692*.

Mounica Maddela, Fernando Alva-Manchego, and Wei Xu. 2020. Controllable text simplification with explicit paraphrasing. *arXiv preprint arXiv:2010.11004*.

Eric Malmi, Sebastian Krause, Sascha Rothe, Daniil Mirylenka, and Aliaksei Severyn. 2019. Encode, tag, realize: High-precision text editing. In *Proceedings of the 2019 Conference on Empirical Methods in Natural Language Processing and the 9th International Joint Conference on Natural Language Processing (EMNLP-IJCNLP)*, pages 5057–5068.

Alec Radford, Karthik Narasimhan, Tim Salimans, and Ilya Sutskever. 2020. Improving language understanding by generative pre-training.

Sudha Rao and Joel R. Tetreault. 2018. Dear sir or madam, may i introduce the gyafc dataset: Corpus, benchmarks and metrics for formality style transfer. In *NAACL-HLT*.

Tianxiao Shen, Tao Lei, Regina Barzilay, and Tommi Jaakkola. 2017. Style transfer from non-parallel text by cross-alignment. In *NIPS*, pages 6830–6841.

Xin Sun, Tao Ge, Shuming Ma, Jingjing Li, Furu Wei, and Houfeng Wang. 2022. A unified strategy for multilingual grammatical error correction with pretrained cross-lingual language model. *arXiv preprint arXiv:2201.10707*.

Ian Tenney, Dipanjan Das, and Ellie Pavlick. 2019. Bert rediscovers the classical nlp pipeline. In *ACL*, pages 4593–4601.

Ashish Vaswani, Noam Shazeer, Niki Parmar, Jakob Uszkoreit, Llion Jones, Aidan N Gomez, Lukasz Kaiser, and Illia Polosukhin. 2017. Attention is all you need. In *NIPS*.

Zhiyong Wu, Yun Chen, Ben Kao, and Qun Liu. 2020. Perturbed masking: Parameter-free probing for analyzing and interpreting bert. In *ACL*, pages 4166–4176.

Wei Xu, Courtney Napoles, Ellie Pavlick, Quanze Chen, and Chris Callison-Burch. 2016. Optimizing statistical machine translation for text simplification. *TACL*, 4:401–415.

Tianyi Zhang, Varsha Kishore, Felix Wu, Kilian Q. Weinberger, and Yoav Artzi. 2019. Bertscore: Evaluating text generation with bert. *ArXiv*, abs/1904.09675.

Ran Zmigrod, Sabrina J. Mielke, Hanna Wallach, and Ryan Cotterell. 2019. Counterfactual data augmentation for mitigating gender stereotypes in languages with rich morphology. In *ACL*, pages 1651–1661.

The Pure Poet: How Good is the Subjective Credibility and Stylistic Quality of Literary Short Texts Written with an Artificial Intelligence Tool as Compared to Texts Written by Human Authors?*

Vivian Emily Gunser[1], Steffen Gottschling[1], Birgit Brucker[1], Sandra Richter[2], Dîlan Canan Çakir[2], and Peter Gerjets[1]

[1] Leibniz-Institut fuer Wissensmedien, Schleichstr. 6, 72076 Tuebingen, Germany
{v.gunser, s.gottschling, b.brucker, p.gerjets}@iwm-tuebingen.de

[2] Deutsches Literaturarchiv Marbach, Schillerhoehe 8-10, 71672 Marbach am Neckar, Germany
{sandra.richter, dilan.cakir,}@dla-marbach.de

Abstract

The application of artificial intelligence (AI) for text generation in creative domains raises questions regarding the credibility of AI-generated content. In two studies, we explored if readers can differentiate between AI-based and human-written texts (generated based on the first line of texts and poems of classic authors) and how the stylistic qualities of these texts are rated. Participants read 9 AI-based continuations and either 9 human-written continuations (Study 1, *N*=120) or 9 original continuations (Study 2, *N*=302). Participants' task was to decide whether a continuation was written with an AI-tool or not, to indicate their confidence in each decision, and to assess the stylistic text quality. Results showed that participants generally had low accuracy for differentiating between text types but were overconfident in their decisions. Regarding the assessment of stylistic quality, AI-continuations were perceived as less well-written, inspiring, fascinating, interesting, and aesthetic than both human-written and original continuations.

1 Introduction

Artificial intelligence (AI) is increasingly used to provide support in creative domains such as the composition of emotional film trailers (Smith et al., 2017) or the ideation in fashion design (Jeon et al., 2021). As part of this trend, advanced tools for human-AI co-creative processes have been developed in recent years. For instance, in a visual arts context, an empathic AI-tool has been developed that provides help in portrait drawing by means of embodied conversational interaction (Yalçın, Abukhodair & DiPaola, 2020). Another example from the field of music composition is an AI-tool enabling computational melodic harmonization (CHAMELEON) that has been developed by Zacharakis et al. (2021). When evaluating this tool with experienced and inexperienced music composers engaging in human-AI co-creative processes it turned out that this tool was particularly helpful for less experienced students to better express their ideas.

In this paper we will focus on using AI-tools in an even more complex creative domain then music, namely the production of literary texts such as short stories or poems. This domain can be seen as providing harder challenges than music composition or drawing due to the complexity of its underlying semantic structure and the embodied grounding of the symbols used to express it (cf. Barsalou, 1999, 2008; Fischer & Zwaan, 2008; Lakoff & Johnson, 1980, 1999; Scherer & Wallbott, 1994).

* this paper was published previously by Proceedings of CogSci 2022 (44st Annual Meeting of the Cognitive Science Society)

Proceedings of the First Workshop on Intelligent and Interactive Writing Assistants (In2Writing 2022), pages 60 - 61
May 26, 2022 ©2022 Association for Computational Linguistics

References

Barsalou, L. W. (1999). Perceptual symbol systems. *Behavioral and Brain Sciences*, 22 (04), 577–660.

Barsalou, L. W. (2008). Grounded cognition. *Annual Review of Psychology*, 59, 617– 645.Bringsjord, S., & Ferrucci, D. (1999). *Artificial intelligence and literary creativity: Inside the mind of brutus, a storytelling machine.* Mahwah, NJ: Lawrence Erlbaum Associates.

Fischer, M. H., & Zwaan, R. A. (2008). Embodied language: A review of the role of the motor system in language comprehension. *Quarterly journal of experimental psychology*, *61*(6), 825-850.

Jeon, Y., Jin, S., Shih, P. C., & Han, K. (2021, May). FashionQ: An AI-Driven Creativity Support Tool for Facilitating Ideation in Fashion Design. *Proceedings of the 2021 CHI Conference on Human Factors in Computing Systems* (pp. 1-18). New York, NY: Association for Computing Machinery.

Lakoff, G. & Johnson, M. (1980). Metaphors we live by. Chicago. The University of Chicago Press.

Lakoff, G. & Johnson, M. (1999). Philosophy in the flesh: The embodied mind and its challenge to western thought. New York: Basic Books.

Scherer, K. R. & Wallbott, G. H. (1994). Evidence for universality and cultural variation of differential emotion response patterning. Journal of Personality and Social Psychology, 66, 310.

Smith, J. R., Joshi, D., Huet, B., Hsu, W., & Cota, J. (2017). Harnessing AI for augmenting creativity: Application to movie trailer creation. *Proceedings of the 25th ACM international conference on Multimedia* (pp. 1799-1808). New York, NY: Association for Computing Machinery.

Yalçın, Ö. N., Abukhodair, N., & DiPaola, S. (2020). Empathic AI Painter: A Computational Creativity System with Embodied Conversational Interaction. *Proceedings of the NeurIPS 2019 Competition and Demonstration Track, Vancouver: CA, 123* (pp. 131-141).

Zacharakis, A., Kaliakatsos-Papakostas, M., Kalaitzidou, S., & Cambouropoulos, E. (2021). Evaluating Human-Computer Co-creative Processes in Music: A Case Study on the CHAMELEON Melodic Harmonizer. *Frontiers in Psychology*, 12, 1-16.

Interactive Children's Story Rewriting Through Parent-Children Interaction

Yoonjoo Lee[a] **Tae Soo Kim**[a] **Minsuk Chang**[b] **Juho Kim**[a]
[a]School of Computing, KAIST [b]NAVER AI Lab
{yoonjoo.lee, taesoo.kim}@kaist.ac.kr
minsuk.chang@navercorp.com
juhokim@kaist.ac.kr

Abstract

Storytelling in early childhood provides significant benefits in language and literacy development, relationship building, and entertainment. To maximize these benefits, it is important to empower children with more agency. Interactive story rewriting through parent-children interaction can boost children's agency and help build the relationship between parent and child as they collaboratively create changes to an original story. However, for children with limited proficiency in reading and writing, parents must carry out multiple tasks to guide the rewriting process, which can incur high cognitive load. In this work, we introduce an interface design that aims to support children and parents to rewrite stories together with the help of AI techniques. We describe three design goals determined by a review of prior literature in interactive storytelling and existing educational activities. We also propose a preliminary prompt-based pipeline that uses GPT-3 to realize the design goals and enable the interface.

1 Introduction

Storytelling in early childhood can enhance language and literacy development and contribute to improved oracy, listening, reading, and writing skills later in life (Mello, 2001; Peck, 1989). When interaction is added to the storytelling experience—for example, a storyteller asking a child a question—the attention of the child can be maintained. Enhancing the children's engagement can increase the educational benefits of interactive storytelling (Ligthart et al., 2020; Kotaman, 2020). Therefore, researchers have developed a number of technologies to support interactive storytelling for young children, which range from letting children record and playback stories (Cassell and Ryokai, 2001; Budd et al., 2007) to asking children to answer comprehension-based questions (Zhang et al., 2022) or illustrate stories (Rubegni and Landoni, 2014).

In engaging children with interactive storytelling, three aspects of agency are important: autonomy, competence, and effectance (Roth and Koenitz, 2016; Murray, 2017). Children feel more engaged if they feel more autonomous and competent in their decision-making (Ryan et al., 2006). Also, it is important to make children feel their decisions have an immediate (local effectance) and overall (global effectance) effect on the narrative (Klimmt et al., 2007). As an example of interactive stories that support these aspects of agency, *"pick-a-path"* or *"choose your own adventure"* stories can maintain children's engagement by providing different plots that children can explore depending on their choices about the plot (Green and Jenkins, 2014).

Like "pick-a-path" stories, story rewriting can be one of the activities to support children's agency in interactive storytelling in that a child makes decisions (autonomous and competent) and the story changes according to this decision (effectance). Though it is well known that story rewriting activities are helpful for developing storytelling and reading comprehension skills (Lin et al., 2021), it is challenging to provide the rewriting activities to children with limited proficiency in reading and writing. As children may struggle to rewrite stories by themselves, parents could help them by participating in this activity. Based on existing rewriting activities and literature on scaffolding children's story writing and constraints from younger children's lack of proficiency in reading and writing (Spycher, 2017; House&Museum, 2020), parent-children story rewriting can be composed of the following processes: (1) changing the setting and finding what to change in the story, (2) parents asking questions to their children about how they might want to change the story, and (3) rewriting the story based on the children's decisions. However, it is difficult for parents to carry out these processes alone, because parents have been shown to struggle in similar multitasking scenarios such as provid-

Proceedings of the First Workshop on Intelligent and Interactive Writing Assistants (In2Writing 2022), pages 62 - 71
May 26, 2022 ©2022 Association for Computational Linguistics

ing story-relevant questions while storytelling due to the high cognitive load incurred (Zhang et al., 2022).

Instead of burdening parents, a viable solution for parent-children story rewriting can be to adopt a human-AI collaborative approach. AI models can quickly and automatically perform tasks that can be tedious for humans, while allowing children and parents to focus on the tasks that increase the children's agency and build parent-child relationships. Specifically, entity extraction, question generation, and text generation techniques from recent natural language-based AI technologies can reduce the load on parents in the aforementioned processes of story rewriting, allowing them to focus more on the interactions with their children. Therefore, in this work, we introduce design sketches of our interface that supports children to rewrite the story through parent-children interaction with the help of AI techniques. Specifically, the system can help parents using a three-step pipeline: (1) finding entities in the story that could be changed based on a set of pre-defined dimensions from literature, (2) generating questions that a parent can ask their child to decide on how to rewrite, and (3) rewriting stories based on the child's decisions while keeping coherency with prior context.

2 Design Goals

This work focuses on supporting interactive rewriting of children's stories through parent-child interaction to provide children with agency in storytelling experiences. Since children's reading skills are very different from age to age and it is important to provide support that fits their age, we set the target age range of our potential users to be three to eight years old, including the pre-reading stage and early-reading stage (Hoien and Lundberg, 1988; Norman and Malicky, 1987). This work aims to allow children in these stages in reading development to make decisions on story elements by answering to their parents' questions and experience rewritten stories based on these interactions with their parents. Our review of the previous literature on interactive storytelling and story writing, as well as existing educational activities for story writing, led to three high-level goals that informed our design of a human-AI system for interactive story rewriting.

2.1 Provide candidate dimensions to be changed by parents and children

As a first step in teaching how to rewrite, existing activities help students learn which dimensions (e.g., point-of-view, characters, setting) a story consists of and what each dimension means. After that, students are asked to mark up the story with everything they would need to change while considering the dimensions learned (House&Museum, 2020). However, since children in the pre-reading stage cannot read and the aforementioned task might be hard for those in the early-reading stage (Hoien and Lundberg, 1988; Norman and Malicky, 1987), figuring out these dimensions would be challenging for children. Although finding all these elements would be easy for parents, they may also feel aversion to this tedious task (Lin et al., 2021). Therefore, to help parents identify the elements to change in the story, we first identified six dimensions that compose a story by referring to existing taxonomies, which range from general dimensions of stories (Adolfo et al., 2017; Carbonell, 1980) to a schema of children's story understanding (Paris and Paris, 2003). These were the identified dimensions:

- **Character**: the people in a story, primary and secondary, protagonists and antagonists.
- **Setting**: where and when a story takes place, and the interaction between those elements.
  - **Time**: time of day, date, month, year, season, and point in history—past, present, or future.
  - **Place**: town/state/region/country, geography, natural environment, built environment (roads and buildings, rooms and furnishings).
- **Description of the character**: adjectives or complements describing the character.
- **Feeling/emotion**: description of how characters feel.
- **Action**: what characters do and how they do it.

Based on these findings, our prototype provides candidate entities in the original story corresponding to each dimension to help parents notice what to change so that they can ask their children about how they want to rewrite it.

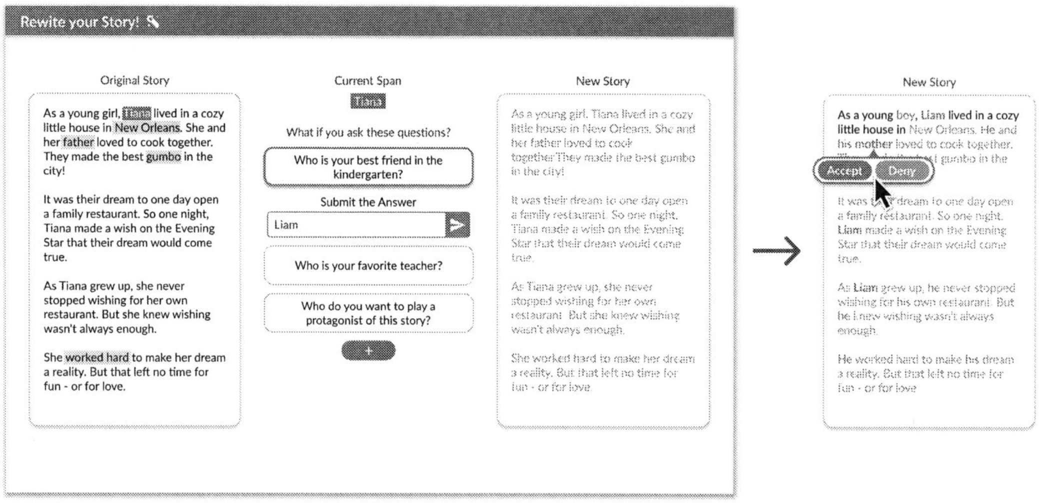

Figure 1: The design for the interactive story rewriting interface shows that (1) the parent has chosen the first question to ask their child, (2) the child answered with "Liam" as a name to replace "Tiana" (i.e., the main character's name), (3) the story has been rewritten based on this entity change, and (4) the user can accept or deny additional changes by clicking on them in the rewritten story.

2.2 Support building relationships between parents and children through question answering about how to rewrite

Rewriting activities have been designed to help students with reading and writing proficiency to rewrite stories by themselves (Calkins, 1980; House&Museum, 2020), however, children in our target age range lack proficiency in reading or writing and may need external guidance to decide on how to change chosen entities. One way to do so is for parents to explicitly ask their children questions to elicit these preferences and decisions. Moreover, dialogic reading theory (Zevenbergen and Whitehurst, 2003) emphasizes the educational benefits (e.g., language development) of parents asking questions to children during storytelling. This theory also encourages parents to ask follow-up questions that align with their child's interest (even when it is less related to the story's content) instead of simply reading all the words in the book. Therefore, we aim to support parents to ask questions about how to change the story to allow younger children to make a change in the story while also helping to build the relationship between parents and children.

2.3 Present rewritten stories based on the child's decisions

When children decide to change a story and believe that their changes will have meaningful outcomes on the story, they feel agency in the process (Riedl and Bulitko, 2013). Based on prior work, key elements towards fulfilling children's agency are autonomy and effectance (Murray, 1998; Roth and Koenitz, 2016). Thus, it is important to change the text according to the children's choices while also considering the following points. First, changing additional spans that are relevant to the entities that the children chose to change allows the children to recognize the effect of their choices. For example, if a child changes the setting from "New Orleans" to "Seoul," then changing the food "Gumbo" accordingly would make the child feel that their choices have more impact beyond just changing the name of the city. Also, changing "Gumbo" would be more meaningful for them than changing "little house", for example, due to the relevancy of these entities with the setting "New Orleans". The second point is that effectance (i.e., the effect a chosen entity has on the story) should be applied in moderation—too many automatic changes can take away opportunities for children to make their own changes. Although it depends on the child's literacy and comprehension of the story, it is important for parents to be able to control how many additional spans the system changes. Finally, if the character is changed, there could be linguistic elements like pronouns that might also have to be changed in subsequent parts of the story. Therefore, even for parents with prior story-rewriting experiences, it can be hard to rewrite an entire story according to their children's choices as they should consider the three points described above to support children's agency.

3 System

Based on the design goals, we envision an interface that supports parent-AI-child interaction for interactive story rewriting. In this section, we describe the interface and a preliminary prompt-based pipeline that uses GPT-3 (Brown et al., 2020) to enable such an interface.

3.1 Interface

The interface, shown in Figure 1, consists of three main components: original story component (left), Q&A component (middle), and rewritten story component (right).

Through the original story component, the parent user can see the original story as well as potential spans that can be changed while reading the story. Here, spans refers to *"within-sentence phrases (up to a threshold length) in the document"* (Wadden et al., 2019). The changeable spans are highlighted and are prompted to be changed in the order that they appear in the story, with the current span to change is highlighted with more contrast. These highlights allow the parent to get an overview of what parts of the story will be changed before they start reading the story to their child. As seen from the figure, the first span to change in the story is the name of the main character, "Tiana".

To start asking their child how they would want to change the current span, the parent can refer to the Q&A component. The Q&A component presents a set of AI-generated suggested questions that the parent could ask their child to elicit answers that could be used to replace the current span. In the example, the current span is the main character's name so the suggested questions are worded such that they prompt the child to answer with names. Additionally, to help parents understand their children better and build their relationship, the suggested questions ask about the child's preferences, feelings, and/or daily lives. If they are not satisfied with the suggested questions, parents can click on the "+" button to generate more suggested questions.

From the Q&A component, the parent can select a question they like, ask it to their child, and then enter the answer that their child gave into the interface. With the answer submitted, the parent can then see how the story has been rewritten: the current span has changed to the submitted answer (e.g., "Tiana" changed to "Liam") and other parts of the story have also been changed accordingly (e.g., "girl" changed to "boy"). Rewritten parts of the story are colored to help parents notice them more easily to encourage parents to talk about them with their child. For these additional rewrites based on the change that the child requested, the parent can accept or deny them by clicking on that part of the text. Finally, the interface indicates the parts of the story that the parent can now read to their child by making them more salient.

3.2 Pipeline

As an initial step to investigate how such an interactive story rewriting system could be realized, we leveraged the few-shot capabilities of a large language model (LLM), in this case GPT-3, to develop a preliminary pipeline for the interface using prompt engineering.

3.2.1 Span extraction

Our pipeline extracts spans in the story based on a set of pre-defined dimensions in Section 2.1. As mentioned before, the dimensions were: character, setting (time and place), description of character, feeling/emotion, and action. We designed prompts to extract spans corresponding to each dimension above in the original story, as shown in Figure 2. For each sentence in the original story, the interface extracts spans to be changed.

3.2.2 Question generation

Our interface provides questions that parents can ask their child to decide how to rewrite a span. To generate these questions, we design prompts that contain pairs of spans and questions, where the questions could be answered by the span. In the case of characters, when the original span is added to the prompt as the given word ("Cinderella" in Fig. 2), the model generates questions that children can answer with names. The prompts include few-shot examples such that generated questions ask about children's preferences, daily lives, and ideas as writers of this story. For example, the pipeline provides questions like *"Who is your favorite person to play with?"*, as well as *"Who do you want to make a protagonist of this book?"*. In case of action-related questions, the generated questions ask children what they would do or what they had

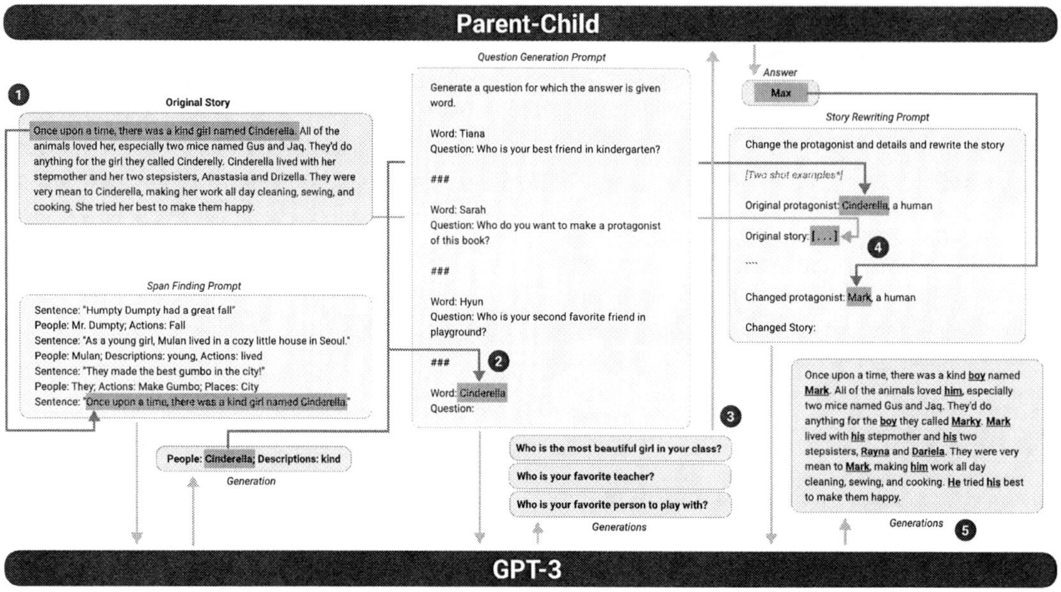

Figure 2: The prompt-based pipeline: (1) a span finding prompt is used to elicit the model to extract spans from the sentences in the original story, (2) questions are then generated with the extracted span and a question generation prompt, (3) several questions are generated which the parent can then ask their child to get an answer span, (4) the answer is combined with the original span and paragraph with the story rewriting prompt template (*full prompt template in Appendix A), and (5) the model is prompted to rewrite the paragraph (changed spans are underlined).

done in previous experiences similar to the given situation in the story.

3.2.3 Story Rewriting

To rewrite story paragraphs based on the child's decisions while keeping coherency with prior context, we designed two rules for rewriting based on our design goals in Section 2: (1) change spans according to the children's answers, (2) additionally change semantically relevant spans (e.g., pronouns, objects), (3) control how many additional changes are made to the story text by the LLM according to the parents' choices. Based on these rules, we designed two-shot examples of how to change an original story paragraph into a changed one with the relevant spans modified. A prompt is constructed with these examples, the original spans, the original story paragraph, and the changed spans (i.e., the child's answers to the parent's questions entered into the interface). This prompt is passed to the model to generate the rewritten story. We checked whether children's choices are reflected in the changed text (i.e., all instances of the original span have been changed), if not, we generate again until the choices are reflected. For the original span targeted to change (like "Cinderella" in Fig. 2), we used coreference resolution techniques (Clark and Manning, 2015) to find mentions of the same entity in the original paragraph to exclude them from spans to change so that the same entity is not asked to be changed again. To ensure coherency of the paragraph, the same technique is also used to check whether the generated text changes relevant linguistic elements, such as pronouns, appropriately based on changes in specific spans. Finally, to let parents have more control on additional changes, the system initially allows parents to accept or dismiss the additional entity changes generated by LMs. After multiple steps, the pipeline can construct a prompt with examples from previous steps: rewritten stories with additional changes that the parent accepted. With this prompt, the pipeline can generate additional changes that are more adapted to the parent and more likely to be accepted.

4 Evaluation Plan

We describe plans for evaluating our system, including the technical evaluation and human evaluation for each tasks in the pipeline, and a user study.

4.1 Plan for Technical Evaluation

In order to evaluate our entity extraction pipeline, we plan to collect a dataset that includes annotations for story-based entities allocated to each of our dimensions and coreference clusters. These annotations will be added to the 278 fairytales in the FAIRYTALE QA dataset (Xu et al., 2022). Following the convention established in this line of work, an entity prediction is considered correct if its type label and head region match those of the gold entity (Luan et al., 2018). We can compare our pipeline with a baseline such as DyGIE++ (Wadden et al., 2019), a state-of-the-art end-to-end IE model which extracts entities and relations jointly, on our dataset.

4.2 Plan for Human Evaluation

The purpose of question generation is to ask how to change these story dimensions and to build relationships between parents and children. Therefore, based on the literature (Xu et al., 2021; Yao et al., 2021) and our goal of asking children about how to change the dimensions, we will invite experts with degrees in related fields (e.g., education) or substantial experience in parenting and dialogic reading. These experts will then be asked to score the questions generated according to the following criteria.

- **Readability**: The generated QA pair is in readable English grammar and words.
- **Question-Answer Relevancy**: How the generated question is relevant to the answer.
- **Question Diversity**: Richness and diversity in content to prompt varied dialogues between parents and children.

To assess how well the rewritten story addresses the particular change being requested, we plan to conduct human evaluation adapted from how Qin et al. (Qin et al., 2019) assessed the quality of rewritten endings in counterfactual story generation tasks. We will present crowdworkers from Amazon Mechanical Turk with one paragraph from the original story, the seed change (i.e., the initial change that determines how the story will be rewritten), and the rewritten story. Then, we will ask workers to answer the following questions on a 5-point Likert scale: (1) Does the rewritten story respect the changes induced by the seed change?, (2) Does the rewritten story keep coherence with details in the prior context of the rewritten story?, and (3) Is the plot of the rewritten story relevant to the plot of the original story? Moreover, inspired by Lee et al.'s work (Lee et al., 2022) that measured how helpful LM generations are to writers, we will also ask workers to accept or dismiss our pipeline's suggestions for additional changes, and calculate the rewriting performance by using the following metric: (the number of accepted suggestions) / (the number of total suggestions).

4.3 Plan for User Study

To explore how interactively rewriting stories through our system affects children's agency and how parents and children use our system, we plan to run a user study where participants (i.e., parent-child pairs) will use our system to interactively rewrite one story. We plan to answer the following questions through this study.

1. Could our interactive story rewriting system enhance children's agency?
2. How do parents and children interact while using our system? Can parents successfully use our system to create interactive story rewriting experiences for their children?
3. Do parents find our system usable, useful, and enjoyable?

To examine whether our system provides children with choices and allows them to tailor the story content to their own needs or preferences, we will provide a questionnaire that asks about two dimensions that determine agency: autonomy (freedom to choose from a large set of options without feeling pushed in one direction) and effectance (how meaningful children's choices are for the story progression). These questions are based on the literature (Roth and Koenitz, 2016; Kucirkova, 2022) that studied how to evaluate interactive systems designed to support children's agency. After the collaborative story rewriting activity, the children will be asked to rate their experience using the Smileyometer instrument (Read and MacFarlane, 2006), which communicates the idea of the Likert scale using smiley faces.

To understand how parents and children used our system, we plan to observe user behaviors during the user study. Our aim is to answer the following questions:

- How did the parents decide which entity to change among the potential entities recommended by the system? What kinds of entities did parents ask their children to change?

- How did parents ask questions? What kinds of questions, among the generated questions, did parents ask their children?

- How did parents read the rewritten stories?

Based on these questions, we plan to make a list of behaviors of interest, which can be objectively identified and with little room for subjective interpretation. For example, behaviors such as *asking a generated question*, *asking a question of their own*, or *asking a generated question as follow up questions* can be annotated.

We plan to ask parents to answer a post-study usability questionnaire to collect and analyze their assessment of our system, including the perceived usefulness of the key features, the perceived difficulty of use, and their willingness to use the system in their real life. We will design this questionnaire following how previous work has made questionnaires to evaluate AI-enabled task automation and creativity tools (Zhang et al., 2022; Li et al., 2019).

5 Future Work

In this work, we presented a preliminary pipeline for human-AI story rewriting that uses prompts and the few-shot capabilities of GPT-3. In future work, finding well-performing models for each subtask in the pipeline and conducting evaluation of such models are our immediate next steps. For entity extraction, we are planning to experiment with extraction methods that prior work adopted, such as leveraging QA models to extract story dimensions (Ammanabrolu et al., 2020) and extracting candidate spans through heuristics designed based on a pedagogical framework (Yao et al., 2021). In the case of question generation, it is necessary to identify more concrete types of questions that parents would need to build meaningful relationships with their children. We have a plan to conduct formative interviews and an extensive literature survey to identify them. We then plan to use LLMs to generate diverse sets of questions based on these question types. To engage children more in the parent-child interaction, asking multi-turn questions might be a better solution than asking independent questions in separate rounds (Zevenbergen and Whitehurst, 2003). Moreover, through multi-turn questions, children can be elicited for choices on multiple spans. By passing multiple span changes to the model at once, additional semantically relevant spans can be found and rewritten by considering the post context of stories. For story rewriting, although our system lets users accept or dismiss the additional entity changes generated by LMs, it is necessary to identify what people expect for how much a story should change based on seed changes. A preliminary study to identify and meet users' expectations can serve as a first step toward understanding how to rewrite stories. Moreover, rewritten stories made by a generative model could propagate and may even amplify various biases (e.g., gender, race, and culture) found in text corpora, which can cause negative outcomes like reinforcing gender stereotypes or building narrow understandings of normative behavior. As a first step to prevent this, our system can apply various NLP techniques for recognizing and mitigating biases (Sun et al., 2019) and warn users that a given generation might have a specific bias and help them deal with this bias.

Acknowledgements

This work was partly supported by the KAIST-NAVER Hypercreative AI Center.

References

Bianca Trish Adolfo, Jerson Lao, Joanna Pauline Rivera, John Zem Talens, and Ethel Chua Joy Ong. 2017. Generating children's stories from character and event models. In *International Workshop on Multi-disciplinary Trends in Artificial Intelligence*, pages 266–280. Springer.

Prithviraj Ammanabrolu, Wesley Cheung, Dan Tu, William Broniec, and Mark Riedl. 2020. Bringing stories alive: Generating interactive fiction worlds. In *Proceedings of the AAAI Conference on Artificial Intelligence and Interactive Digital Entertainment*, volume 16, pages 3–9.

Tom Brown, Benjamin Mann, Nick Ryder, Melanie Subbiah, Jared D Kaplan, Prafulla Dhariwal, Arvind Neelakantan, Pranav Shyam, Girish Sastry, Amanda Askell, Sandhini Agarwal, Ariel Herbert-Voss, Gretchen Krueger, Tom Henighan, Rewon Child, Aditya Ramesh, Daniel Ziegler, Jeffrey Wu, Clemens Winter, Chris Hesse, Mark Chen, Eric Sigler, Mateusz Litwin, Scott Gray, Benjamin Chess, Jack Clark, Christopher Berner, Sam McCandlish, Alec Radford, Ilya Sutskever, and Dario Amodei. 2020. Language models are few-shot learners. In *Advances in Neural Information Processing Systems*, volume 33, pages 1877–1901. Curran Associates, Inc.

Jim Budd, Krystina Madej, Jenna Stephens-Wells, Janice de Jong, Ehren Katzur, and Laura Mulligan. 2007. Pagecraft: Learning in context a tangible interactive storytelling platform to support early narrative development for young children. In *Proceedings of the 6th International Conference on Interaction Design and Children*, IDC '07, page 97–100, New York, NY, USA. Association for Computing Machinery.

Lucy McCormick Calkins. 1980. Children'a rewriting strategies. *Research in the Teaching of English*, 14(4):331–341.

Jaime G Carbonell. 1980. Towards a process model of human personality traits. *Artificial Intelligence*, 15(1-2):49–74.

J. Cassell and K. Ryokai. 2001. Making space for voice: Technologies to support children's fantasy and storytelling. *Personal Ubiquitous Comput.*, 5(3):169–190.

Kevin Clark and Christopher D. Manning. 2015. Entity-centric coreference resolution with model stacking. In *Proceedings of the 53rd Annual Meeting of the Association for Computational Linguistics and the 7th International Joint Conference on Natural Language Processing (Volume 1: Long Papers)*, pages 1405–1415, Beijing, China. Association for Computational Linguistics.

Melanie C Green and Keenan M Jenkins. 2014. Interactive narratives: Processes and outcomes in user-directed stories. *Journal of Communication*, 64(3):479–500.

Torleiv Hoien and Ingvar Lundberg. 1988. Stages of word recognition in early reading development. *Scandinavian Journal of Educational Research*, 32(4):163–182.

MarkTwain House&Museum. 2020. Creative writing through rewriting.

Christoph Klimmt, Tilo Hartmann, and Andreas Frey. 2007. Effectance and control as determinants of video game enjoyment. *Cyberpsychology & behavior*, 10(6):845–848.

Huseyin Kotaman. 2020. Impacts of dialogical storybook reading on young children's reading attitudes and vocabulary development. *Reading Improvement*, 57(1):40–45.

Natalia Kucirkova. 2022. Children's agency and reading with story-apps: considerations of design, behavioural and social dimensions. *Qualitative Research in Psychology*, 19(1):66–90.

Mina Lee, Percy Liang, and Qian Yang. 2022. Coauthor: Designing a human-ai collaborative writing dataset for exploring language model capabilities. *arXiv preprint arXiv:2201.06796*.

Toby Jia-Jun Li, Marissa Radensky, Justin Jia, Kirielle Singarajah, Tom M. Mitchell, and Brad A. Myers. 2019. Pumice: A multi-modal agent that learns concepts and conditionals from natural language and demonstrations. In *Proceedings of the 32nd Annual ACM Symposium on User Interface Software and Technology*, UIST '19, page 577–589, New York, NY, USA. Association for Computing Machinery.

Mike EU Ligthart, Mark A Neerincx, and Koen V Hindriks. 2020. Design patterns for an interactive storytelling robot to support children's engagement and agency. In *Proceedings of the 2020 ACM/IEEE International Conference on Human-Robot Interaction*, pages 409–418.

Chaolan Lin, Selma Šabanović, Lynn Dombrowski, Andrew D Miller, Erin Brady, and Karl F MacDorman. 2021. Parental acceptance of children's storytelling robots: A projection of the uncanny valley of ai. *Frontiers in Robotics and AI*, 8:49.

Yi Luan, Luheng He, Mari Ostendorf, and Hannaneh Hajishirzi. 2018. Multi-task identification of entities, relations, and coreference for scientific knowledge graph construction. In *Proceedings of the 2018 Conference on Empirical Methods in Natural Language Processing*, pages 3219–3232, Brussels, Belgium. Association for Computational Linguistics.

Robin A. Mello. 2001. Building bridges: How storytelling influences teacher/student relationships.

Janet H Murray. 1998. *Hamlet on the Holodeck, updated edition: The Future of Narrative in Cyberspace*. JSTOR.

Janet H Murray. 2017. *Hamlet on the Holodeck, updated edition: The Future of Narrative in Cyberspace*. MIT press.

Charles A Norman and Grace Malicky. 1987. Stages in the reading development of adults. *Journal of Reading*, 30(4):302–307.

Alison H Paris and Scott G Paris. 2003. Assessing narrative comprehension in young children. *Reading Research Quarterly*, 38(1):36–76.

Jackie Peck. 1989. Using storytelling to promote language and literacy development. *The Reading Teacher*, 43(2):138–141.

Lianhui Qin, Antoine Bosselut, Ari Holtzman, Chandra Bhagavatula, Elizabeth Clark, and Yejin Choi. 2019. Counterfactual story reasoning and generation. In *Proceedings of the 2019 Conference on Empirical Methods in Natural Language Processing and the 9th International Joint Conference on Natural Language Processing (EMNLP-IJCNLP)*, pages 5043–5053, Hong Kong, China. Association for Computational Linguistics.

Janet C. Read and Stuart MacFarlane. 2006. Using the fun toolkit and other survey methods to gather opinions in child computer interaction. In *Proceedings of the 2006 Conference on Interaction Design and Children*, IDC '06, page 81–88, New York, NY, USA. Association for Computing Machinery.

Mark O. Riedl and Vadim Bulitko. 2013. Interactive narrative: An intelligent systems approach. *AI Mag.*, 34(1):67–77.

Christian Roth and Hartmut Koenitz. 2016. Evaluating the user experience of interactive digital narrative. In *Proceedings of the 1st International Workshop on Multimedia Alternate Realities*, AltMM '16, page 31–36, New York, NY, USA. Association for Computing Machinery.

Elisa Rubegni and Monica Landoni. 2014. Fiabot! design and evaluation of a mobile storytelling application for schools. In *Proceedings of the 2014 conference on Interaction design and children*, pages 165–174.

Richard M Ryan, C Scott Rigby, and Andrew Przybylski. 2006. The motivational pull of video games: A self-determination theory approach. *Motivation and emotion*, 30(4):344–360.

Pamela Spycher. 2017. *Scaffolding Writing Through the" Teaching and Learning Cycle"*. WestEd.

Tony Sun, Andrew Gaut, Shirlyn Tang, Yuxin Huang, Mai ElSherief, Jieyu Zhao, Diba Mirza, Elizabeth Belding, Kai-Wei Chang, and William Yang Wang. 2019. Mitigating gender bias in natural language processing: Literature review. In *Proceedings of the 57th Annual Meeting of the Association for Computational Linguistics*, pages 1630–1640, Florence, Italy. Association for Computational Linguistics.

David Wadden, Ulme Wennberg, Yi Luan, and Hannaneh Hajishirzi. 2019. Entity, relation, and event extraction with contextualized span representations. In *Proceedings of the 2019 Conference on Empirical Methods in Natural Language Processing and the 9th International Joint Conference on Natural Language Processing (EMNLP-IJCNLP)*, pages 5784–5789, Hong Kong, China. Association for Computational Linguistics.

Ying Xu, Stacy Branham, Xinwei Deng, Penelope Collins, and Mark Warschauer. 2021. Are current voice interfaces designed to support children's language development? In *Proceedings of the 2021 CHI Conference on Human Factors in Computing Systems*, CHI '21, New York, NY, USA. Association for Computing Machinery.

Ying Xu, Dakuo Wang, Mo Yu, Daniel Ritchie, Bingsheng Yao, Tongshuang Wu, Zheng Zhang, Toby Jia-Jun Li, Nora Bradford, Branda Sun, Tran Bao Hoang, Yisi Sang, Yufang Hou, Xiaojuan Ma, Diyi Yang, Nanyun Peng, Zhou Yu, and Mark Warschauer. 2022. Fantastic questions and where to find them: Fairytaleqa – an authentic dataset for narrative comprehension.

Bingsheng Yao, Dakuo Wang, Tongshuang Wu, Tran Hoang, Branda Sun, Toby Jia-Jun Li, Mo Yu, and Ying Xu. 2021. It is ai's turn to ask human a question: Question and answer pair generation for children storybooks in fairytaleqa dataset. *arXiv preprint arXiv:2109.03423*.

Andrea A Zevenbergen and Grover J Whitehurst. 2003. Dialogic reading: A shared picture book reading intervention for preschoolers. *On reading books to children: Parents and teachers*, pages 177–200.

Zheng Zhang, Ying Xu, Yanhao Wang, Bingsheng Yao, Daniel E. Ritchie, Tongshuang Sherry Wu, Mo Yu, Dakuo Wang, and Toby Jia-Jun Li. 2022. Storybuddy: A human-ai collaborative chatbot for parent-child interactive storytelling with flexible parental involvement. *ArXiv*, abs/2202.06205.

A Story rewriting prompt template

```
Change the protagonist and
details and rewrite the story

Original protagonist: Merida, a
human
Details:
1. cake
2. bear

Original story: Back at the
castle, Merida presented the
cake to her mother. She watched
closely as Elinor took a bite.
At first, nothing happened. But
then, Elinor began to feel sick.
Merida helped Elinor into bed.
The next thing Merida knew, a
huge, furry shape was rising
from the sheets! The Witch's cake
had turned Elinor into a bear!
Worried her mother was in danger,
Merida sneaked her out of the
castle.

''''

Changed protagonist: Lucy, a dog
Details:
1. candy
2. fish

Changed story: Back at the
castle, Lucy presented the candy
to her owner. She watched closely
as Bill took a bite. At first,
nothing happened. But then, Bill
began to feel sick. Lucy helped
Bill into bed. The next thing
Lucy knew, a huge, scales shape
was rising from the sheets! The
Witch's candy had turned her
owner into a fish! Worried her
owner was in danger, Lucy sneaked
him out of the castle.

Original protagonist: Mulan, a
human
Details:
1. China
2. dog

Original story: Thousands of
years ago in ancient China, there
lived a beautiful young woman
named Mulan. She lived with her
parents and a dog named Little
Brother. Mulan's father had once
been a great warrior, but his
leg had been injured in battle.
As an only child, Mulan felt
responsible for upholding the
family honor. One day, a man
arrived with terrible news from
the Emperor. The Huns, China's
enemy, had invaded.

''''

Changed protagonist: Julian, a
tiger
Details:
1. Tigerland
2. mouse

Changed story: Thousands of
years ago in ancient Tigerland,
there lived a beautiful young
tiger named Julian. It lived
with parents and a mouse named
Little Mousy. Julian's father had
once been a great warrior, but
he had been injured in Tiger-Lion
battle. As an only child, Julian
felt responsible for upholding
the family honor. One day, a
white-furred tiger arrived with
terrible news from the King tiger.
The Lions, Tigerland's enemy, had
invaded.
```

News Article Retrieval in Context for Event-centric Narrative Creation

Nikos Voskarides[1*] **Edgar Meij**[2] **Sabrina Sauer**[3] **Maarten de Rijke**[4]
[1] Amazon, Barcelona, Spain
[2] Bloomberg, London, United Kingdom
[3] University of Groningen, Groningen, The Netherlands
[4] University of Amsterdam, Amsterdam, The Netherlands
nvvoskar@amazon.com, emeij@bloomberg.net
s.c.sauer@rug.nl, m.derijke@uva.nl

Abstract

Writers such as journalists often use automatic tools to find relevant content to include in their narratives. In this paper, we focus on supporting writers in the news domain to develop event-centric narratives. Given an incomplete narrative that specifies a main event and a context, we aim to retrieve news articles that discuss relevant events that would enable the continuation of the narrative. We formally define this task and propose a retrieval dataset construction procedure that relies on existing news articles to simulate incomplete narratives and relevant articles. Experiments on two datasets derived from this procedure show that state-of-the-art lexical and semantic rankers are not sufficient for this task. We show that combining those with a ranker that ranks articles by reverse chronological order outperforms those rankers alone. We also perform analysis of the results that sheds light on the characteristics of this task.[1]

1 Introduction

Professional writers such as journalists generate narratives centered around specific events or topics. As shown in recent studies, such writers envision automatic systems that suggest material relevant to the narrative they are creating (Diakopoulos, 2019). This material may provide background information or connections that can help writers generate new angles on the narrative and thus help engage the reader (Kirkpatrick, 2015).

Writers in the news domain often develop narratives around a single main event, and refer to other, related events that can serve different functions in relation to the narrative (van Dijk, 1988). These include explaining the cause or the context of the main event or providing supporting information (Choubey et al., 2020). Recent work has focused on automatically profiling news article content (i.e., paragraphs or sentences) in relation to their discourse function (Yarlott et al., 2018).

In this paper, instead of profiling existing narratives, we consider a scenario where a writer has generated an incomplete narrative about a specific event up to a certain point, and aims to explore other news articles that discuss relevant events to include in their narrative. A news article that discusses a different event from the past is relevant to the writer's incomplete narrative if it relates to the narrative's main event and to the *narrative's context*. Relevance to the narrative's main event is topical in nature but, importantly, relevance to the narrative's context is not only topical: to be relevant to the narrative's context, a news article should enable the continuation of the narrative by expanding the narrative discourse (Caswell and Dörr, 2018).

We model the problem of finding a relevant news article given an incomplete narrative as a retrieval task where the query is an incomplete narrative and the unit of retrieval is a news article. We automatically generate retrieval datasets for this task by harvesting links from existing narratives manually created by journalists. Using the generated datasets, we analyze the characteristics of this task and study the performance of different rankers on this task. We find that state-of-the-art lexical and semantic rankers are not sufficient for this task and that combining those with a ranker that ranks articles by their reverse chronological order outperforms those rankers alone.

Our main contributions are: (i) we propose the task of news article retrieval in context for event–centric narrative creation; (ii) we propose an automatic retrieval dataset construction procedure for this task; and (iii) we empirically evaluate the performance of different rankers on this task and perform an in-depth analysis of the results to better understand the characteristics of this task.

* Research conducted when the first author was at the University of Amsterdam.

[1]This is an extended abstract of a paper published at ACM ICTIR 2021: https://dl.acm.org/doi/10.1145/3471158.3472247.

Proceedings of the First Workshop on Intelligent and Interactive Writing Assistants (In2Writing 2022), pages 72 - 73
May 26, 2022 ©2022 Association for Computational Linguistics

References

David Caswell and Konstantin Dörr. 2018. Automated Journalism 2.0: Event-driven narratives. *Journalism Practice*, 12(4).

Prafulla Kumar Choubey, Aaron Lee, Ruihong Huang, and Lu Wang. 2020. Discourse as a Function of Event: Profiling Discourse Structure in News Articles around the Main Event. In *ACL*. ACL.

Nicholas Diakopoulos. 2019. *Automating the News: How Algorithms Are Rewriting the Media*. Harvard University Press.

Keith Kirkpatrick. 2015. Putting the Data Science into Journalism. *Commun. ACM*, 58(5).

Teun A. van Dijk. 1988. *News as Discourse*. University of Groningen.

W. Victor Yarlott, Cristina Cornelio, Tian Gao, and Mark Finlayson. 2018. Identifying the Discourse Function of News Article Paragraphs. In *Workshop on Events and Stories in the News 2018*. ACL.

Unmet Creativity Support Needs in Computationally Supported Creative Writing

Max Kreminski
University of California, Santa Cruz
mkremins@ucsc.edu

Chris Martens
North Carolina State University
martens@csc.ncsu.edu

Abstract

Large language models (LLMs) enabled by the datasets and computing power of the last decade have recently gained popularity for their capacity to generate plausible natural language text from human-provided prompts. This ability makes them appealing to fiction writers as prospective co-creative agents, addressing the common challenge of writer's block, or *getting unstuck*. However, creative writers face additional challenges, including maintaining narrative consistency, developing plot structure, architecting reader experience, and refining their expressive intent, which are not well-addressed by current LLM-backed tools. In this paper, we define these needs by grounding them in cognitive and theoretical literature, then survey previous computational narrative research that holds promise for supporting each of them in a co-creative setting.

1 Introduction

Mixed-initiative co-creative (Liapis et al., 2016; Deterding et al., 2017) creativity support tools (Shneiderman, 2007) for creative writing have recently seen a surge of interest in research communities, coinciding with the introduction of large language models (LLMs) such as GPT-3 (Brown et al., 2020) that can provide coherent suggestions for the continuation of human-written text. Several recent efforts have been made to understand the experiences of writers who work with these tools to produce texts (Manjavacas et al., 2017; Roemmele and Gordon, 2018; Calderwood et al., 2020). However, less attention has been paid to the development of systems that can provide forms of creative writing support beyond short-term suggestions for textual continuation.

Meanwhile, recent efforts to understand the playful creative writing communities that have emerged around interactive emergent narrative games (Kreminski et al., 2019b; Kreminski and Wardrip-Fruin, 2019) and to provide computational support for playful creative writing at the plot-structure level (Kreminski et al., 2020a) have revealed a preliminary inventory of several distinct but interrelated creativity support needs among creative writers, including:

- Getting unstuck
- Maintaining consistency
- Constructing a satisfying overall story arc, including a conclusion/resolution
- Managing reader experience
- Refining and iterating on expressive intent

Current large language models are good at addressing the first of these needs, *getting unstuck*, via short-term suggestions that can prompt writers to take their stories in unexpected new directions. However, they do not directly address consistency maintenance, longer-term plot structure, management of reader experience, or the challenge of refining high-level expressive intent, and some novelists even suggest that LLMs may actively work against the construction of coherent plot structure due to the highly divergent nature of LLM suggestions (Calderwood et al., 2020). Some recent work aims to improve LLMs in ways that could enable them to meet these needs: for instance, work in long text generation (Hua and Wang, 2020; Guan et al., 2021; Tan et al., 2021) could assist users with consistency maintenance; work on hierarchical concept-driven language models (Wang et al., 2021) could help to maintain plot structure in generated text; and work in diverse decoding methods (Ippolito et al., 2019; See et al., 2019) could help users refine their intent by selecting from among diverse potential completions of the same text. However, the possibility of supporting these needs through other forms of technology may also be worth investigating.

Proceedings of the First Workshop on Intelligent and Interactive Writing Assistants (In2Writing 2022), pages 74 - 82
May 26, 2022 ©2022 Association for Computational Linguistics

In this paper, we describe each of these creative writing support needs in more detail, then survey previous research from communities outside of NLP/computational linguistics that have either been shown capable of addressing, or that show potential for supporting these creative needs. Our aim with this paper is to create a bridge between the ACL community and AI/digital games research community that may yield productive insight towards synthesizing these approaches that have evolved in parallel.

We limit the scope of our discussion primarily to narrative fiction, particularly in the form of short stories, novels, and game writing/interactive storytelling, so the suggestions made here may not all be applicable to other forms of creative writing (such as poetry). However, we attempt to avoid limiting ourselves to purely text-based storytelling in which only the written word is used to convey meaning; we are also interested in forms of narrative fiction that target visual, audio, and hybrid renderings of fictional events, such as film and game narrative, since many technologies capable of reasoning about plot structure are readily applicable to these domains.

2 Creative Writing Support Needs

2.1 Getting Unstuck

One common source of difficulty in creative writing is the prevalence of *writer's block*, or the sense that one has become "stuck" and cannot think of any obvious way for the story to proceed. Because writer's block is frequently experienced by writers and difficult to escape, it is often discussed in guides for writers, along with descriptions of exercises and practices that can help prevent writers from becoming blocked or enable them to become unblocked (Lamott, 2007). These exercises and practices take many forms, but they often involve the use of genre-typical plot devices to advance the action in lieu of any more natural continuation (e.g., Raymond Chandler's oft-cited description of a genre-typical move in hardboiled detective fiction: "When in doubt have a man come through the door with a gun in his hand" (Chandler, 1950)) and the use of unfiltered stream-of-consciousness writing for a fixed amount of time (e.g., one hour each day) to help writers continue working through a block (Goldberg, 2005).

It is in helping writers get unstuck that the strengths of large language models are especially apparent. Language model continuations of human-written text tend to be syntactically valid and relevant to storyworld entities or situations that were described in the immediately preceding text, enabling them to function as viable short-term suggestions for what might happen next in a written story. This is true even though these suggestions may sometimes take the story in unexpected or unwanted directions: regardless of whether users accept the suggestions that are provided, co-writing with a language model can shift the user's task from the wholesale invention of a new direction for the story to take (the precise thing that it is difficult to do when blocked) toward the acceptance or rejection of computer-provided suggestions. The latter task can be subjectively easier to perform (Smith, 2012, p. 57), and once a desirable continuation is located, further plot events may occur to the user naturally even without ongoing computational support.

2.2 Maintaining Consistency

When constructing a work of fiction, the author aims to convey a mental model of an underlying *story world*: a set of characters, settings, objects, and relationships between all of these things that change over the course of narrative events according to certain logics that may or may not rely on real-world, non-fictional analogs. Practicing novelists often maintain (and advise beginning writers to maintain) "story bibles" or other collections of extradiegetic "storywork" apart from the narrative text itself that serve to document story world information (Ousby, 2009). The use of story world documentation points to a need to *maintain consistency* in works of fiction. As stories and their casts of characters grow in size, and more of the fictional timeline is filled in, the author runs increasing risk of introducing inconsistencies (conflicting factual assertions or implications), plot holes, or unexplained situations that may break the reader's ability to suspend disbelief.

In order to reason about consistency, authors need to reason about narrative material at a level more abstract than narrative text (including storyboards, scene scripts, etc). It can be useful to reason about the story world and its logic—the *represented* phenomena—separately from the story artifact itself—the *representation of* those phenomena. This distinction basically aligns with the classical Russian narratologists' distinction between

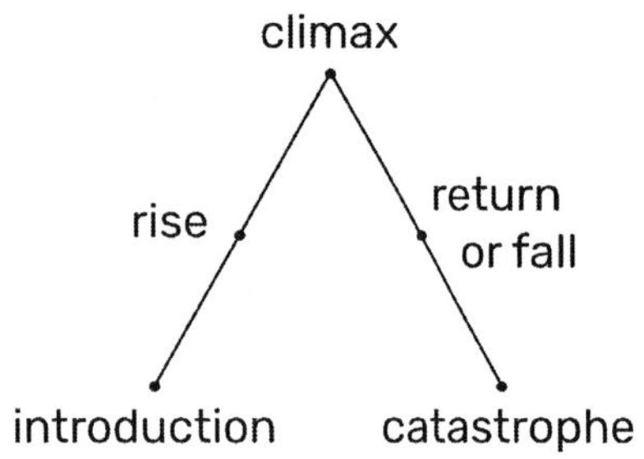

Figure 1: Freytag's pyramid

fabula and *syuzhet* (Gorman, 2018), or its adaptation in anglophone narratology as *story* versus *discourse* (Chatman, 1980). Correspondingly, cognitive linguists have long recognized the presence of *situation models* as knowledge structures that readers create to interpret the semantic relationships between referents in natural language sequences (Zwaan and Radvansky, 1998). The ability to directly author and manipulate knowledge corresponding to a situation model (or similar) is central to a fiction author's task.

2.3 Plot Structure

When writers think about *plot structure*, they may have in mind a set of "acts" (as in "3-act structure") or a continuous curve describing the dramatic tension of the story over time, as in Freytag's pyramid (Freytag, 1894). Although the notion of conflict is not universal (Hunter, 2016), usually, a plot follows a sequence of identifiable *beats* that include establishment of an initial situation, and inciting incident or a need that spurs characters to action, a series of events in which the characters attempt to address the inciting incident, an emotional peak that resolves it, and a denouement or resolution that describes the aftermath (see Figure 1). A number of conceptual models have been proposed and used for describing plot structure, such as the Freytag pyramid, the Monomyth or Hero's Journey (Campbell, 2008), and Dan Harmon's Story Circle (O'Meara, 2015).

Importantly, plot structures describe global rather than local features of a text, and they have more to do with the underlying world model (see previous section) than they do with the specific actions or events that are inferable from lexical properties of the text. Cohn and colleagues have established that readers make sense of stories in a "grammatical" way akin to parsing sentences: they expect certain structures that parse the entire story into something story-like, and in the absence of these structures, comprehension falters (Cohn, 2020).

2.4 Reader Experience

The movement of "human-centered design" proposes that designers benefit when they make an effort to empathize with users: by understanding the experience of the people who will experience and interact with the designed work, we can more intentionally shape those experiences. Likewise, a written work has an experiential impact on its readers, and understanding the levers that affect that impact is a key part of narrative intelligence.

Three examples of reader experience are **pacing**, **tension**, and **surprise**. Pacing refers to the amount of time that a reader spends with each segment, scene, or act of the overall plot (see previous section on plot structure). Poor pacing can cause a reader to get bored or overwhelmed with the story and fail to connect with the characters or the underlying message that the writer is attempting to convey. Tension refers to elements of conflict, threat, or suspense, that cause discomfort in the reader and evoke a sense of wanting the tension to resolve, pushing them forward in the story to feel relief. Surprise refers to encountering unexpected narrative events that shift the reader's mental model of the story and, if done well, increase the reader's curiosity to reconcile their failure to predict what would happen.

Reasoning about reader experience requires a good understanding of how stories work at a cognitive level: e.g., that readers work as *problem solvers* when processing narrative text, working to stay one step ahead of the story to make sense of what has happened so far and predict what will happen next (Gerrig and Bernardo, 1994). If story authors strategically *withhold* information, they can *elicit inferences* on the part of readers to fill in the gaps in ways that can evoke humor, shock, or horror understanding (Cohn, 2019).

2.5 Refining Expressive Intent

One difficulty in creative work is that the creator themselves may not know exactly what they are trying to express, and the expressive intent may shift as the creator's understanding of the work evolves. This is particularly true in storytelling: for instance, a writer's understanding of a particular character's personality may shift (often becoming more nuanced over time) as the writer develops a deeper backstory for the character and places them in plot situations that allow different aspects of the character's personality to come to the forefront. Similarly, the originally intended ending for a story may come to feel inconsistent with the author's better understanding of the story's intended themes partway through the writing process. Divergent suggestions provided by computational support tools may exacerbate these difficulties, making it harder (rather than easier) for writers to "find the heart" of what they are trying to express.

Consequently, it may be helpful for computational support tools to explicitly ask the user about their high-level expressive intent; provide them with a place to write down and edit their intent, perhaps in a machine-understandable form; infer expressive goals from what the user has already written, perhaps allowing them to accept or reject suggestions as to what high-level goals they were trying to accomplish with a particular span of text; and try to provide suggestions that are consistent with the user's high-level expressive goals. Several design patterns for "reflective creators" (Kreminski and Mateas, 2021)—a particular genre of creativity support tools that aim to help users refine their intent—may be of use in this context.

3 Technologies and Approaches

In this section, we overview technologies that have shown promise for addressing the needs outlined in the previous section.

3.1 Maintaining Consistency

The key technological tool for maintaining consistency is a *world model*, or a computational representation of the diegetic phenomena that a story aims to fictionalize. These phenomena include characters (and potentially their interior phenomena such as their personalities and beliefs), settings, character relationships, and narrative actions or events that can modify the world. By representing a world model in its own right, one can specify consistency constraints as (e.g.) first-order logic formulas whose constituent predicates refer to the world model.

World models appear in a number of computational narrative tools. For example, the *stories as plans* approach began as an observation that generating consistent narratives could be cast as an automated planning problem, for which there exist efficient solvers (Young, 1999). Given a description of narrative action schema in terms of their preconditions and effects, and a description of an initial and target story world state, planners generate sequences of narrative actions that are *consistent* in the sense that each action's preconditions are met by the implied world state following the prefix of the sequence leading up to it. Figure 2 shows an example story generation problem set up in this manner, alongside a planner's output. This observation has led to a long history of plan-based approaches to narrative generation (Porteous et al., 2010; Riedl and Young, 2010; Ware and Young, 2011; Young et al., 2013) as well as ongoing research that aims to incorporate more robust models of character intention and belief (Eger and Martens, 2017; Shirvani et al., 2017, 2018; Wadsley and Ryan, 2013).

The *stories as proofs* approach is closely related to planning in that it also relies on a solver to generate logical sequences of events that can be interpreted as consistent stories (Bosser et al., 2010; Martens et al., 2013, 2014); the solver in this case is a linear logic theorem prover (or logic programming language) that can be run in a non-goal-directed (forward chaining) mode, leading to increased solution diversity. The forward-chaining mode also enables a natural introduction of user interaction, allowing a human to "steer" the search process by selecting from among all possible actions (whose preconditions are met in the current world state). This approach suggests opportunities for incorporating world models into a human-centered writing practice, affording levers for authors to express and enforce story consistency.

3.2 Plot Structure

Machine-learned language models are good at capturing local coherence, but tend to struggle with the global constraints implied by plot structure. In direct mappings from text corpora to text output, these structures are at best latent properties of edge weights in a neural network, rather than rules that can be inspected and modified with authorial control.

By contrast, symbolic representation techniques like context-free grammars and logic programming provide a high degree of expressive control. For instance, Gervas (Gervás, 2013) encodes Vladimir Propp's narratological functions as a BNF gram-

Domain

dig(?char,?item)

Precons: ?char alive.
?item buried.
?char knows ?item.

Effects: ?char has ?item.
¬ ?item buried.

Consent: ?char

open(?char)

Precons: ?char alive.
?char has ?item.

Effects: R opened.
¬ ?char alive.

Consent: ?char

give(?gvr,?item,?rcvr)

Precons: ?gvr alive.
?gvr has ?item.
?rcvr alive.

Effects: ?rcvr has ?item.
¬ ?gvr has ?item.

Consent: ?gvr ?rcvr

take(?thief,?item,?char)

Precons: ?thief alive.
?char has ?item.
¬ ?char alive OR
?thief armed.

Effects: ?thief has ?item.
¬ ?char has ?item.

Consent: ?thief

Problem

Initial state:

- Ark buried
- Indiana alive
- Indiana knows where the Ark is
- Indiana intends USArmy has Ark
- USArmy alive
- USArmy intends USArmy has Ark
- Nazis alive
- Nazis armed
- Nazis intend Ark opened

Goal:

- USArmy has Ark
- not (Nazis alive)

Solution

dig(Indiana, Ark)
take(Nazis, Ark, Indiana)
open(Nazis)
take(USArmy, Ark, Nazis)

Figure 2: Example planning domain and problem (input) and sample solution plan (output) courtesy of Ware and Young (Ware and Young, 2014).

mar whose expansions correspond to example plots of Russian folktales that Propp's work was designed to describe. Likewise, Cohn's grammar for the visual narrative structure of short comic strips has been implemented as a comic-generating algorithm (Martens and Cardona-Rivera, 2016).

BRUTUS (Bringsjord and Ferrucci, 1999) is an example from the 1990s in which high-level plot structure patterns, such as "one character betrays another," are specified as first-order logic rules that can be written in Prolog and over which queries can be run to generate example narratives that fit a given plot structure. More recently, answer set programming has been used to codify the narrative planning techniques discussed in the previous section, on which plot structure constraints can then be layered (Dabral and Martens, 2020).

3.3 Reader Experience

To support authors in crafting an intentional experience for their readers, computational tools need to be able to reason about (or perhaps even simulate) the reader's cognitive processes. Distinguishing between story and discourse is one promising first step for reader experience support, since it allows a narrative generation engine to retell the same story (plot-wise) in different ways (Rishes et al., 2013). When generating narrative *discourse*, it is possible to relate the told portion of the story to its underlying world model and add a layer of modeling for what the reader (or viewer) will know and infer based on what they have been shown. Jhala and Young's cinematic discourse engine does exactly this in order to plan camera shots for scenes taking place in 3D worlds (Jhala and Young, 2010)

Drama managers are another compelling tool from the interactive storytelling community that bring to bear on reader experience (Roberts and Isbell, 2007). They are conceived as storytelling agents that track player choices throughout the narrative and coordinate the characters and objects in the world to steer the player and the story toward convergent goals. They sometimes generate or select narrative content appropriate to the emergent properties of the situation, as in the breakaway interactive drama Façade (Mateas and Stern, 2003). Such tools could allow authors to tag story content with world model-relevant properties in similar ways, then work with a drama management tool to remix and recombine passages of text as they draft the scene-by-scene structure.

Finally, technologies have been created for modeling reader cognition to support reader experience effects such as pacing, tension, and surprise. The IDTension system uses a world model and the story-discourse distinction to model tension in an interactive drama setting (Szilas, 2003); the Suspenser system models the reader's inference generation process as a planning algorithm (Cheong and Young, 2006). Graesser and Franklin's QUEST model of reader understanding describes the narrative comprehension process as measured through their ability to answer questions, and describes a *knowledge structure* that encodes this question-answering ability (Graesser and Franklin, 1990), and Cardona-Rivera et al. have implemented the QUEST model as an algorithm to annotating generated story content with relevant reader inferences according to this model (Cardona-Rivera and Young, 2019).

3.4 Refining Expressive Intent

Since refinement of expressive intent has only recently been recognized as an explicit goal for creativity support tools in some contexts, relatively little work has been done to provide computational support for intent refinement in storytelling contexts. However, Writing Buddy (Samuel et al., 2016), Mimisbrunnur (Stefnisson and Thue, 2018), and *Why Are We Like This?* (Kreminski et al., 2020a,b) all address this challenge to some extent by providing explicit interfaces for the specification of *author goals*: high-level, machine-interpretable descriptions of what the human user wants to have happen in the story they are writing. These systems then use this information to provide suggestions for story events or storyworld state updates that respect the user's goals, simultaneously assisting users in reflecting on their own goals (by asking them to state these goals explicitly) and in maintaining consistency with these goals (by using goal descriptions to steer suggestions).

Additionally, *story sifting* technologies (Ryan et al., 2015; Ryan, 2018; Kreminski et al., 2019a)—which apply pattern matching to the identification of potentially compelling new plot directions in chronicles of past story events—can also be applied to the task of inferring an author's intent for the story they are writing. If an intelligent writing tool can use story sifting to discover the beginnings of a potentially interesting plot thread are discovered via story sifting, it can then explicitly ask the user whether the narrative direction implied by this plot thread is of interest to them; regardless of the user's answer, this information can be used to interactively build up an explicit model of what the user does and does not want to happen within the story they are telling.

4 Conclusion

We have presented five creative writing support needs, only one of which (getting unstuck) is meaningfully supported by current large language models, and surveyed technologies for addressing the remaining four needs that have arisen from the AI/digital games research community. These technologies are at varying levels of maturity, and most of them have only been tested in purely automated or generative forms rather than in mixed-initiative, co-creative interaction modes. An important line of future work will be to evaluate these technologies in those modes and determine interfaces and interaction protocols that amplify and foster human creativity in the writing process.

Our goal with this paper is not to assert the superiority of world-model or knowledge-engineering based approaches over LLMs, but rather to emphasize that there is a set of needs and affordances that these techniques can address and provide that are complementary to the needs addressed and affordances provided by LLMs. By bridging research communities focused (on one hand) on computing with natural language and (on the other) on simulating story worlds and reasoning about narrative structure, we hope to pave the way for hybrid and unified models that can transform the human creative writing experience—much like the neurosymbolic approaches to automated story generation (Martin, 2021) that undergird several recent advances in story generation as a field.

References

Anne-Gwenn Bosser, Marc O Cavazza, and Ronan Champagnat. 2010. Linear logic for non-linear storytelling. In *19th European Conference on Artificial Intelligence*, pages 713–718. IOS Press.

Selmer Bringsjord and David Ferrucci. 1999. *Artificial intelligence and literary creativity: Inside the mind of BRUTUS, a storytelling machine*. Psychology Press.

Tom Brown, Benjamin Mann, Nick Ryder, Melanie Subbiah, Jared D Kaplan, Prafulla Dhariwal, Arvind Neelakantan, Pranav Shyam, Girish Sastry, Amanda Askell, et al. 2020. Language models are few-shot learners. *Advances in Neural Information Processing Systems*, 33:1877–1901.

Alex Calderwood, Vivian Qiu, Katy Ilonka Gero, and Lydia B Chilton. 2020. How novelists use generative language models: An exploratory user study. In *HAI-GEN + user2agent @ IUI*.

Joseph Campbell. 2008. *The Hero with a Thousand Faces*, volume 17. New World Library.

Rogelio E. Cardona-Rivera and R. Michael Young. 2019. Desiderata for a computational model of human online narrative sensemaking. In *Working Notes of the 2019 AAAI Spring Symposium on Story-enabled Intelligence*.

Raymond Chandler. 1950. The simple art of murder. *Saturday Review of Literature*.

Seymour B. Chatman. 1980. *Story and Discourse: Narrative Structure in Fiction and Film*. Cornell University Press.

Yun-Gyung Cheong and R Michael Young. 2006. A computational model of narrative generation for suspense. In *AAAI*, pages 1906–1907.

Neil Cohn. 2019. Being explicit about the implicit: inference generating techniques in visual narrative. *Language and Cognition*, 11(1):66–97.

Neil Cohn. 2020. Your brain on comics: A cognitive model of visual narrative comprehension. *Topics in cognitive science*, 12(1):352–386.

Chinmaya Dabral and Chris Martens. 2020. Generating explorable narrative spaces with answer set programming. In *Proceedings of the AAAI Conference on Artificial Intelligence and Interactive Digital Entertainment*, volume 16, pages 45–51.

Sebastian Deterding, Jonathan Hook, Rebecca Fiebrink, Marco Gillies, Jeremy Gow, Memo Akten, Gillian Smith, Antonios Liapis, and Kate Compton. 2017. Mixed-initiative creative interfaces. In *Proceedings of the 2017 CHI Conference Extended Abstracts on Human Factors in Computing Systems*, pages 628–635.

Markus Eger and Chris Martens. 2017. Character beliefs in story generation. In *Thirteenth Artificial Intelligence and Interactive Digital Entertainment Conference*.

Gustav Freytag. 1894. *Freytag's Technique of the Drama*. Scott, Foresman.

Richard J. Gerrig and Allan B. I. Bernardo. 1994. Readers as problem-solvers in the experience of suspense. *Poetics*, 22(6):459–472.

Pablo Gervás. 2013. Propp's morphology of the folk tale as a grammar for generation. In *2013 Workshop on Computational Models of Narrative*. Schloss Dagstuhl-Leibniz-Zentrum fuer Informatik.

Natalie Goldberg. 2005. *Writing Down the Bones: Freeing the Writer Within*. Shambhala.

David Gorman. 2018. Russian formalism. *A Companion to Literary Theory*, pages 36–47.

Arthur C Graesser and Stanley P Franklin. 1990. Quest: A cognitive model of question answering. *Discourse processes*, 13(3):279–303.

Jian Guan, Xiaoxi Mao, Changjie Fan, Zitao Liu, Wenbiao Ding, and Minlie Huang. 2021. Long text generation by modeling sentence-level and discourse-level coherence. In *Proceedings of the 59th Annual Meeting of the Association for Computational Linguistics and the 11th International Joint Conference on Natural Language Processing (Volume 1: Long Papers)*, pages 6379–6393.

Xinyu Hua and Lu Wang. 2020. PAIR: Planning and iterative refinement in pre-trained transformers for long text generation. In *Proceedings of the 2020 Conference on Empirical Methods in Natural Language Processing (EMNLP)*, pages 781–793, Online. Association for Computational Linguistics.

Mead Hunter. 2016. From conflict to concord: Lessons from the mouse. *Etudes*.

Daphne Ippolito, Reno Kriz, Maria Kustikova, João Sedoc, and Chris Callison-Burch. 2019. Comparison of diverse decoding methods from conditional language models. In *Proceedings of the 57th Annual Meeting of the Association for Computational Linguistics*, pages 3752–3762.

Arnav Jhala and R. Michael Young. 2010. Cinematic visual discourse: Representation, generation, and evaluation. *IEEE Transactions on Computational Intelligence and AI in Games*, 2(2):69–81.

Max Kreminski, Melanie Dickinson, Michael Mateas, and Noah Wardrip-Fruin. 2020a. Why Are We Like This?: Exploring writing mechanics for an AI-augmented storytelling game. In *Proceedings of the 2020 Conference of the Electronic Literature Organization*.

Max Kreminski, Melanie Dickinson, Michael Mateas, and Noah Wardrip-Fruin. 2020b. Why Are We Like This?: The AI architecture of a co-creative storytelling game. In *International Conference on the Foundations of Digital Games*.

Max Kreminski, Melanie Dickinson, and Noah Wardrip-Fruin. 2019a. Felt: a simple story sifter. In *International Conference on Interactive Digital Storytelling*, pages 267–281. Springer.

Max Kreminski and Michael Mateas. 2021. Reflective creators. In *International Conference on Computational Creativity*.

Max Kreminski, Ben Samuel, Edward Melcer, and Noah Wardrip-Fruin. 2019b. Evaluating AI-based games through retellings. In *Proceedings of the AAAI Conference on Artificial Intelligence and Interactive Digital Entertainment*, volume 15, pages 45–51.

Max Kreminski and Noah Wardrip-Fruin. 2019. Generative games as storytelling partners. In *Proceedings of the 14th International Conference on the Foundations of Digital Games*.

Anne Lamott. 2007. *Bird by Bird: Some Instructions on Writing and Life*. Knopf Doubleday.

Antonios Liapis, Georgios N. Yannakakis, Constantine Alexopoulos, and Phil Lopes. 2016. Can computers foster human users' creativity? theory and praxis of mixed-initiative co-creativity. *Digital Culture & Education (DCE)*, 8(2):136–152.

Enrique Manjavacas, Folgert Karsdorp, Ben Burtenshaw, and Mike Kestemont. 2017. Synthetic literature: Writing science fiction in a co-creative process. In *Proceedings of the Workshop on Computational Creativity in Natural Language Generation (CC-NLG 2017)*, pages 29–37.

Chris Martens, Anne-Gwenn Bosser, Joao F Ferreira, and Marc Cavazza. 2013. Linear logic programming for narrative generation. In *International Conference on Logic Programming and Nonmonotonic Reasoning*, pages 427–432. Springer.

Chris Martens and Rogelio E. Cardona-Rivera. 2016. Generating abstract comics. In *Proceedings of the 10th International Conference on Interactive Digital Storytelling*, pages 168–175. Springer.

Chris Martens, Joao F Ferreira, Anne-Gwenn Bosser, and Marc Cavazza. 2014. Generative story worlds as linear logic programs. In *Seventh Intelligent Narrative Technologies Workshop*.

Lara Jean Martin. 2021. *Neurosymbolic Automated Story Generation*. Ph.D. thesis, Georgia Institute of Technology.

Michael Mateas and Andrew Stern. 2003. Façade: An experiment in building a fully-realized interactive drama. In *Game Developers Conference*, volume 2, pages 4–8.

Louise Ousby. 2009. *Whatever it takes: an exploration of writing tools and strategies for completing a novel.* Ph.D. thesis, Queensland University of Technology.

Radha O'Meara. 2015. Changing the way we think about character change in episodic television series. *Journal of Screenwriting*, 6(2):189–201.

Julie Porteous, Marc Cavazza, and Fred Charles. 2010. Applying planning to interactive storytelling: Narrative control using state constraints. *ACM Transactions on Intelligent Systems and Technology (TIST)*, 1(2):1–21.

Mark O Riedl and Robert Michael Young. 2010. Narrative planning: Balancing plot and character. *Journal of Artificial Intelligence Research*, 39:217–268.

Elena Rishes, Stephanie M Lukin, David K Elson, and Marilyn A Walker. 2013. Generating different story tellings from semantic representations of narrative. In *International Conference on Interactive Digital Storytelling*, pages 192–204. Springer.

David L Roberts and Charles L Isbell. 2007. Desiderata for managers of interactive experiences: A survey of recent advances in drama management. In *Proceedings of the First Workshop on Agent-Based Systems for Human Learning and Entertainment (ABSHLE 07)*.

Melissa Roemmele and Andrew Gordon. 2018. Linguistic features of helpfulness in automated support for creative writing. In *Proceedings of the First Workshop on Storytelling*, pages 14–19.

James Ryan. 2018. *Curating Simulated Storyworlds*. Ph.D. thesis, University of California, Santa Cruz.

James Owen Ryan, Michael Mateas, and Noah Wardrip-Fruin. 2015. Open design challenges for interactive emergent narrative. In *International Conference on Interactive Digital Storytelling*, pages 14–26. Springer.

Ben Samuel, Michael Mateas, and Noah Wardrip-Fruin. 2016. The design of writing buddy: a mixed-initiative approach towards computational story collaboration. In *International Conference on Interactive Digital Storytelling*, pages 388–396. Springer.

Abigail See, Aneesh Pappu, Rohun Saxena, Akhila Yerukola, and Christopher D. Manning. 2019. Do massively pretrained language models make better storytellers? In *Proceedings of the 23rd Conference on Computational Natural Language Learning (CoNLL)*, pages 843–861, Hong Kong, China. Association for Computational Linguistics.

Alireza Shirvani, Rachelyn Farrell, and Stephen G Ware. 2018. Combining intentionality and belief: Revisiting believable character plans. In *Fourteenth Artificial Intelligence and Interactive Digital Entertainment Conference*.

Alireza Shirvani, Stephen G. Ware, and Rachelyn Farrell. 2017. A possible worlds model of belief for state-space narrative planning. In *Proceedings of the 13th AAAI Conference on Artificial Intelligence and Interactive Digital Entertainment*.

Ben Shneiderman. 2007. Creativity support tools: Accelerating discovery and innovation. *Communications of the ACM*, 50(12):20–32.

Adam Marshall Smith. 2012. *Mechanizing Exploratory Game Design*. Ph.D. thesis, University of California, Santa Cruz.

Ingibergur Stefnisson and David Thue. 2018. Mimisbrunnur: AI-assisted authoring for interactive storytelling. In *Proceedings of the AAAI Conference on artificial Intelligence and Interactive Digital entertainment*, volume 14, pages 236–242.

Nicolas Szilas. 2003. Idtension: a narrative engine for interactive drama. In *Proceedings of the technologies for interactive digital storytelling and entertainment (TIDSE) conference*, volume 3, pages 1–11.

Bowen Tan, Zichao Yang, Maruan AI-Shedivat, Eric P Xing, and Zhiting Hu. 2021. Progressive generation of long text with pretrained language models. In *Proceedings of the 2021 Conference of the North American Chapter of the Association for Computational Linguistics: Human Language Technologies*, pages 4313–4324.

Theo Wadsley and Malcolm Ryan. 2013. A belief-desire-intention model for narrative generation. In *Ninth Artificial Intelligence and Interactive Digital Entertainment Conference*.

Yashen Wang, Huanhuan Zhang, Zhirun Liu, and Qiang Zhou. 2021. Hierarchical concept-driven language model. *ACM Transactions on Knowledge Discovery from Data (TKDD)*, 15(6):1–22.

Stephen G Ware and R Michael Young. 2011. Cpocl: A narrative planner supporting conflict. In *Seventh artificial intelligence and interactive digital entertainment conference*.

Stephen G Ware and R Michael Young. 2014. Glaive: a state-space narrative planner supporting intentionality and conflict. In *Tenth Artificial Intelligence and Interactive Digital Entertainment Conference*.

R Michael Young. 1999. Notes on the use of plan structures in the creation of interactive plot. In *AAAI fall symposium on narrative intelligence*, pages 164–167.

R. Michael Young, Stephen Ware, Brad Cassell, and Justus Robertson. 2013. Plans and Planning in Narrative Generation: A Review of Plan-Based Approaches to the Generation of Story, Discourse, and Interactivity in Narratives. *Sprache und Datenverarbeitung*, 37(1–2):67–77.

Rolf A. Zwaan and Gabriel A. Radvansky. 1998. Situation models in language comprehension and memory. *Psychological bulletin*, 123(2):162.

Sparks: Inspiration for Science Writing using Language Models

Katy Ilonka Gero and **Vivian Liu** and **Lydia B. Chilton**
Columbia University
katy@cs.columbia.edu, vl2463@columbia.edu,
chilton@cs.columbia.edu

Abstract

Large-scale language models are rapidly improving, performing well on a variety of tasks with little to no customization. In this work we investigate how language models can support science writing, a challenging writing task that is both open-ended and highly constrained. We present a system for generating "sparks", sentences related to a scientific concept intended to inspire writers. We run a user study with 13 STEM graduate students and find three main use cases of sparks—*inspiration*, *translation*, and *perspective*—each of which correlates with a unique interaction pattern. We also find that while participants were more likely to select higher quality sparks, the overall quality of sparks seen by a given participant did not correlate with their satisfaction with the tool.[1]

1 Introduction

New developments in large-scale language models have produced models that are capable of generating coherent, convincing text in a wide variety of domains (Vaswani et al., 2017; Brown et al., 2020; Adiwardana et al., 2020). Their success has spurred improvements on many tasks, from classification and summarization (Brown et al., 2020) to creative writing support (Coenen et al., 2021). These improvements demonstrate that language models have the potential to support writers in real-world, high-impact domains.

Despite their successes, language models continue to exhibit known problems, such as generic outputs (Holtzman et al., 2020), lack of diversity in their outputs (Ippolito et al., 2019), and factually false or contradictory information (Lin et al., 2021). Additionally, there remain many unknowns about how this technology will interface with people in real-world writing tasks, such as how language models can best contribute to different writing forms (Calderwood et al., 2018) and how to mitigate the bias that language models encode (Bender et al., 2021).

In this work we study how language models can be applied to a real-world, high-impact writing task: science writing. This introduces challenges different to those in traditional creative writing tasks which tend to deal with common objects and relations. Science writing requires a system to demonstrate proficiency within an area of expertise. We pose the following research question: *How can language model outputs support writers in a creative but constrained writing task?*

As a test-bed, we use a science writing form called "tweetorials" (Breu, 2020). Tweetorials are short, technical explanations of around 500 words written on Twitter for a general audience; they have a low-barrier to entry and are gaining popularity as a science writing form (Soragni and Maitra, 2019). We present a system that aims to inspire writers when writing tweetorials on a topic of their expertise. This system provides what we call "sparks": sentences generated with a language model intended to spark ideas in the writer.

We report on a study in which we have 13 graduate students from five STEM disciplines write tweetorials with our system and report on how they thought about and made use of the sparks. We make the following contributions:

- a system that generates "sparks" related to a scientific concept, including a custom decoding method for generating sparks from a pre-trained language model;
- an evaluation demonstrating that sparks are more coherent and diverse than a baseline, and approach a human gold standard;
- a user study with 13 graduate students showing three main use cases of sparks and corresponding interaction patterns, as well as an analysis on how spark quality relates to participant satisfaction.

[1]This extended abstract summarizes work published in Designing Interactive Systems (Gero et al., 2022).

Proceedings of the First Workshop on Intelligent and Interactive Writing Assistants (In2Writing 2022), pages 83 - 84
May 26, 2022 ©2022 Association for Computational Linguistics

References

Daniel Adiwardana, Minh-Thang Luong, David R. So, Jamie Hall, Noah Fiedel, Romal Thoppilan, Zi Yang, Apoorv Kulshreshtha, Gaurav Nemade, Yifeng Lu, and Quoc V. Le. 2020. Towards a Human-like Open-Domain Chatbot. *arXiv:2001.09977 [cs, stat]* (Feb. 2020). http://arxiv.org/abs/2001.09977 arXiv: 2001.09977.

Emily M. Bender, Timnit Gebru, Angelina McMillan-Major, and Shmargaret Shmitchell. 2021. On the Dangers of Stochastic Parrots: Can Language Models Be Too Big?. In *Proceedings of the 2021 ACM Conference on Fairness, Accountability, and Transparency*. ACM, Virtual Event Canada, 610–623. https://doi.org/10.1145/3442188.3445922

Anthony C. Breu. 2020. From Tweetstorm to Tweetorials: Threaded Tweets as a Tool for Medical Education and Knowledge Dissemination. *Seminars in Nephrology* 40, 3 (May 2020), 273–278. https://doi.org/10.1016/j.semnephrol.2020.04.005

Tom B. Brown, Benjamin Mann, Nick Ryder, Melanie Subbiah, Jared Kaplan, Prafulla Dhariwal, Arvind Neelakantan, Pranav Shyam, Girish Sastry, Amanda Askell, Sandhini Agarwal, Ariel Herbert-Voss, Gretchen Krueger, Tom Henighan, Rewon Child, Aditya Ramesh, Daniel M. Ziegler, Jeffrey Wu, Clemens Winter, Christopher Hesse, Mark Chen, Eric Sigler, Mateusz Litwin, Scott Gray, Benjamin Chess, Jack Clark, Christopher Berner, Sam McCandlish, Alec Radford, Ilya Sutskever, and Dario Amodei. 2020. Language Models are Few-Shot Learners. *arXiv:2005.14165 [cs]* (July 2020). http://arxiv.org/abs/2005.14165 arXiv: 2005.14165.

Alex Calderwood, Vivian Qiu, Katy Ilonka Gero, and Lydia B Chilton. 2018. How Novelists Use Generative Language Models: An Exploratory User Study. In *23rd International Conference on Intelligent User Interfaces*. ACM.

Andy Coenen, Luke Davis, Daphne Ippolito, Emily Reif, and Ann Yuan. 2021. Wordcraft: a Human-AI Collaborative Editor for Story Writing. *arXiv:2107.07430 [cs]* (July 2021). http://arxiv.org/abs/2107.07430 arXiv: 2107.07430.

Katy Ilonka Gero, Vivian Liu, and Lydia B. Chilton. 2022. Sparks: Inspiration for Science Writing using Language Models. In *Designing Interactive Systems Conference 2022*. ACM, Virtual Event USA.

Ari Holtzman, Jan Buys, Li Du, Maxwell Forbes, and Yejin Choi. 2020. The Curious Case of Neural Text Degeneration. *arXiv:1904.09751 [cs]* (Feb. 2020). http://arxiv.org/abs/1904.09751 arXiv: 1904.09751.

Daphne Ippolito, Reno Kriz, Maria Kustikova, João Sedoc, and Chris Callison-Burch. 2019. Comparison of Diverse Decoding Methods from Conditional Language Models. *arXiv:1906.06362 [cs]* (June 2019). http://arxiv.org/abs/1906.06362 arXiv: 1906.06362.

Stephanie Lin, Jacob Hilton, and Owain Evans. 2021. TruthfulQA: Measuring How Models Mimic Human Falsehoods. *arXiv preprint arXiv:2109.07958* (2021), 13. https://arxiv.org/abs/2109.07958

Alice Soragni and Anirban Maitra. 2019. Of scientists and tweets. *Nature Reviews Cancer* 19, 9 (Sept. 2019), 479–480. https://doi.org/10.1038/s41568-019-0170-4

Ashish Vaswani, Noam Shazeer, Niki Parmar, Jakob Uszkoreit, Llion Jones, Aidan N Gomez, Łukasz Kaiser, and Illia Polosukhin. 2017. Attention is All you Need. In *Advances in Neural Information Processing Systems*, Vol. 30.

ChipSong: A Controllable Lyric Generation System for Chinese Popular Song

Nayu Liu[1], Wenjing Han[1], Guangcan Liu[1], Peng Zhou[1], Ran Zhang[1], Xiaorui Wang[1], Huabin Ruan[2*]
[1] Kuaishou Technology Co., Ltd, Beijing, China
[2]School of Life Sciences, Tsinghua University, Beijing, China
{liunayu, hanwenjing, liuguangcan, zhoupeng, zhangran, wangxiaorui}@kuaishou.com, ruanhuabin@tsinghua.edu.cn

Abstract

In this work, we take a further step towards satisfying practical demands in Chinese lyric generation from musical short-video creators, in respect of the challenges on songs' format constraints, creating specific lyrics from open-ended inspiration inputs, and language rhyme grace. One representative detail in these demands is to control lyric format at word level, that is, for Chinese songs, creators even expect fix-length words on certain positions in a lyric to match a special melody, while previous methods lack such ability. Although recent lyric generation community has made gratifying progress, most methods are not comprehensive enough to simultaneously meet these demands. As a result, we propose *ChipSong*, which is an assisted lyric generation system built based on a Transformer-based autoregressive language model architecture, and generates controlled lyric paragraphs fit for musical short-video display purpose, by designing 1) a novel *Begin-Internal-End* (BIE) word-granularity embedding sequence with its guided attention mechanism for word-level length format control, and an explicit symbol set for sentence-level length format control; 2) an open-ended trigger word mechanism to guide specific lyric contents generation; 3) a paradigm of *reverse order training and shielding decoding* for rhyme control. Extensive experiments show that our ChipSong generates fluent lyrics, with assuring the high consistency to pre-determined control conditions.

1 Introduction

Lyric generation is a recent emerging topic in intelligent music research community, which has attracted increasing attention and gained progress in the past few years (Watanabe et al., 2018; Manjavacas et al., 2019; Fan et al., 2019; Li et al., 2020; Zhang et al., 2020a; Nikolov et al., 2020; Sheng et al., 2021). Meanwhile, observing a large amount of music lovers, amateurs, and professional musicians are gathering on today's fast growing Chinese short-video platforms (e.g., Kwai, TikTok, Wesee, etc.), where they create and post musical short-videos actively, with purpose to obtain more *Follows* and *Likes* from general population; we believe it is worth to customize a lyric generation system for their short-video display purpose.

Hence, in this paper, we aim to put more emphasis on assisting creators from practical short-video scenario with realistic demands. In oder to collect their real demands, a qualitative investigation with 85 potential users (ages: 18$\sim$40 years; 42 female, 43 males; 19 full-time musicians, 66 part-time musicians) is conducted at the very first stage. Here, we briefly release 4 representative demands as follow: 1) *short lyric paragraphs* are required to fit in short-video durations, mostly under 60 sec. (Zhang et al., 2020b); 2) *open-ended inspiration inputs* are desired to guide specific content generation from various creators; 3) *length format controlling at* sentence and even *word level* is expected to strictly match melody length format for flexible creation intents, where a Chinese word is generally composed of multiple characters (e.g., "爱" means *love*, "爱好" means *hobby*, "爱尔兰" means *Ireland*) and one character sounds one syllable; 4) *rich rhyme patterns* are needed for smooth song singing. Although recent progress has been made on lyric generation, previous works are not comprehensive enough to simultaneously meet these customized demands; What's more, as far as we know, none of the existing work supports word-level length format control.

Taking the above challenges in mind, we develop *ChipSong*, a lyric generation system, to assist musical short-video creators for **Chi**nese **p**opular **song** creation. As shown in Figure 1, with ChipSong, a creator is encouraged to input a group of open-ended words (which are referred to as *trigger words* in the following) to represent his/her inspiration,

*Corresponding author

Proceedings of the First Workshop on Intelligent and Interactive Writing Assistants (In2Writing 2022), pages 85 - 95
May 26, 2022 ©2022 Association for Computational Linguistics

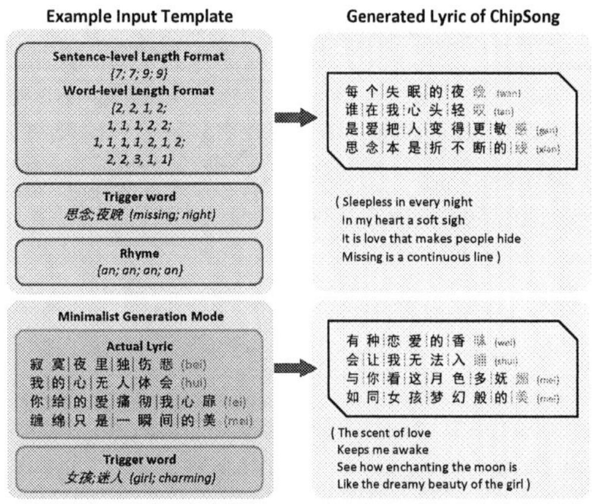

Figure 1: Our ChipSong system generates lyrics based on the preset template including length formats, trigger words, and rhymes. The blue box shows an example template, and the green box shows the generated lyrics. A minimalist generation mode of ChipSong is shown in the orange box, which extracts the format and rhyme of the actual lyric to imitatively generate a lyric. English translations of Chinese are provided in parentheses.

and a sequence of numbers to tell the length of each lyric line or even each word (a combination of Chinese characters) in a line for matching melody length. The creator can also choose rhyme for the last character in each line from Chinese 14-rhyme[1] groups. Moreover, a minimalist generation mode is provided, where the creator only has to input trigger words and an actual lyric he/she is interested in, then ChipSong will extract the lyric's format and rhyme pattern, and generate a new lyric according to the input trigger words and the extracted format and rhyme, thus fully imitating the original lyric for making a cover song version.

To ensure the relevance of generated lyrics with the above controlling attributes, following efforts are made in this paper: 1) A large corpus of $848K$ Chinese lyrics are gathered, and tailored according to proper lengths for short-video display. 2) A two-stage sampling strategy is designed to produce a large number of potential trigger words from lyrics themselves without human annotation, and an autoregressive language model is self-supervisedly trained to complete the whole lyric sequence according to partially-observed trigger words, thus stimulating users' open-ended inspiration inputs. 3) Both explicit and implicit control methods are proposed to arrange the format of sentence- and word- level length respectively, where sentence length is controlled via explicit character sets, and word length is controlled via a well-designed implicit *Begin-Internal-End* (BIE) word-granularity embedding sequence with its guided attention mechanism. 4) A strategy of *reverse order training & shielding decoding* is designed to learn a reverse language model, guaranteeing fluent text generation following rhyme control, inspired by the observation that, during lyric creation, humans usually first determine which word to use in the rhyming position of a sentence and then create the rest of that sentence based on the rhyming word. Experimentally, both automatic and human evaluations demonstrate that our ChipSong system generates fluent lyrics with high consistency to predetermined control conditions.

In summary, oriented to the actual demands of musical short-video creators, we develop ChipSong, a controllable lyric generation system, which can achieve fine-grained control over lyric generation by the proposed control methods for trigger words, format and rhyme. Especially, to the best of our knowledge, ChipSong is the first lyric generation system that can precisely control the word-level length format.

2 Related Work

Recent lyric generation works can be broadly categoried into three groups according to their cared artistic genres: 1) *hip-pop* generation, creating hip-pop lyrics with distinctive rhymes and rhythms constrains (Manjavacas et al., 2019; Nikolov et al., 2020; Xue et al., 2021); 2) *poetry* generation, creating some special text paradigms, such as Shakespeare's Sonnet (Oliveira et al., 2017; Li et al., 2020), Chinese Classical Poetry (Guo et al., 2019; Hu and Sun, 2020; Li et al., 2020), and Chinese Couplet (Yan et al., 2016), etc; 3) *popular song* generation, creating full-text lyrics (Watanabe et al., 2018; Zhu et al., 2018; Lee et al., 2019; Fan et al., 2019; Zhang et al., 2020a; Sheng et al., 2021) or polishing draft lyrics (Zhang et al., 2020a) for popular songs. Our ChipSong is actually a lyric generation system within the third group, and especially for Chinese popular songs. Moreover, different from previous lyric generation works, which were mostly *model*-oriented for natural paragraphs generation and excluded explicit user profiles from practical application scenarios, ChipSong customizes functions to generate lyrics for users from practical short-video scenario with re-

[1]About Chinese 14-rhyme

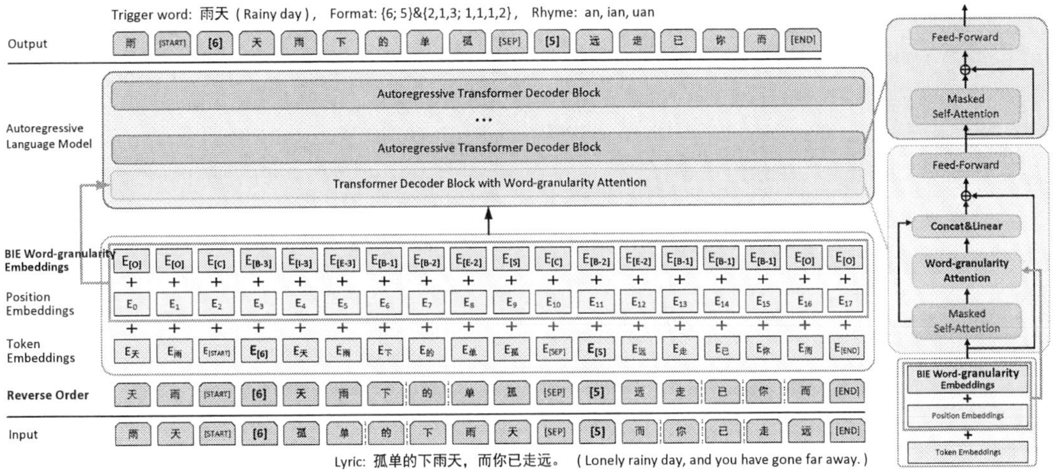

Figure 2: The left figure shows the overall architecture of ChipSong. The right figure shows the internal structure of layers; for simplicity, we've omitted the drawing of residual connection and layer normalization.

alistic demands regarding length format, trigger word, and rhyme, simultaneously.

Furthormore, detailed comparison between previous lyric generation works and ChipSong are conducted as follows, from implementation view. First, when it comes to length format control of lyrics, we only notice works (Shen et al., 2019; Li et al., 2020) with sentence-level length control, and no work currently with word-level length control. Second, most of previous works lacked sufficient abilities to deal with open-ended inputs to guide lyric content (Potash et al., 2015, 2018), as a result of the shortage of annotated training data. Fan et al. (2019) and Lu et al. (2019) regarded the user input as the first sentence and generate a continuation of lyric, but it tends to deviate from the initial input as the continuation progresses. Although, Zhang et al. (2020a) designed an interactive lyric creation system to handle the open-ended inputs, as a demo description work, it did not release sufficient implementation details and experimental evaluations. Third, in consideration of the creator's demand for rhyme control, previous works employed various rhyme modeling methods: Nikolov et al. (2020) selected output words from the a list of candidate rhyming words at the rhyming position, while forcibly adding a rhyming word could result in incoherent text in the rhyming position; SongNet (Li et al., 2020) proposed a rigid format control method to realize the rhyme modeling for Chinese lyrics; The recent DeepRapper (Xue et al., 2021) focused on continuous N-gram rhyme and rhythm modeling for rap generation, while we work on unigram rhyme control for popular songs.

3 Method

3.1 Overview

As shown in Figure 2, a Transformer-based autoregressive language model architecture is adopted as the backbone of ChipSong for lyric generation. And by modifying the internal model structure and utilizing processed external feature inputs, we apply the modeling of control conditions for length format, trigger word, and rhyme. In the subsequent section arrangement, we first describe the control condition inputs for ChipSong, and then describe the proposed condition control methods in detail.

3.2 User Inputs

As shown in Figure 1, the user specifies the conditional templates to formulate the lyric generation, and ChipSong generates the lyrics that meet the corresponding control conditions.

Trigger word: enter a few words that are separated by ";" to render the lyric content.

Format: enter each line length and each word (i.e., a combination of Chinese characters) length of each line in the lyric, where sentences' lengths are separated by ";", and words' lengths are separated by ",". For example, enter "7; 7; 9; 2, 2, 3, 1, 1" means to generate four lines of the lyric with lengths of 7, 7, 9, and 9, respectively, and in the last sentence, the word length arrangement is specified as 2,2,3,1,1. Users can also not specify the full template, and the system retrieves similar templates to complement the length format; or directly input a lyric, and the system extracts the length format for imitative writing.

Rhyme: enter the rhyme of the last word in each sentence. Rhymes are separated by ";". For example, input "ui;ui;ui;ui", the generated lyrics keep the rhyme of the last word of each sentence match with "ui". Users can also not specify rhymes, and the system freely generates sentences.

3.3 Sentence-level Format Control

An explicit character set C_S is designed to control the length of each line of the lyrics, just like "$[CLS]$" and "$[SEP]$" in BERT (Devlin et al., 2018), which is constructed as follows:

$$\ldots, [START], [4], a_1, a_2, a_3, a_4, [SEP], [5], a_1, a_2, a_3, a_4, a_5, [END]$$

where $[SEP]$ is the interline delimiter, a_i is the i-th character of a sentence, $[START]$ and $[END]$ are the beginning and end of a lyric, $[4]$ and $[5]$ represent that the next sentence length is 4 and 5, respectively. We assign 50 learnable character embeddings $\{[1], [2], [3], \ldots, [50]\}$ to C_S to represent the line length from 1 to 50, which are embedded in the lyric sequence as explicit supervisory information for training. The control character is placed after the sentence separator $[SEP]$ and before the beginning of the sentence to learn the correspondence between the control symbol and the sentence length. During prediction, the format control character entered by the user is inserted after the initial $[START]$ token and the generated $[SEP]$ token to achieve the length control of lines.

3.4 Word-level Format Control

Beyond the sentence-level format control, word-level format control arranges lyrics in a more refined way, benefiting fine-grained lyrics' adjustment or imitative writing lyrics. Unlike sentence-granularity format control, the explicit character control strategy makes input too verbose, and the unidirectional masked self-attention of autoregressive language model cannot model the uninput control symbols, which is difficult to reconcile and arrange the fixed-length words in fixed-length sentences. Therefore, we propose an implicit control method, *Begin-Internal-End* (BIE) word-granularity embedding with its guided attention mechanism to adjust the word-level length format.

3.4.1 BIE Word-granularity Embedding

As shown in Figure 2 (left), each lyric token is added with a learnable embedding to record word length information[2], just like position embeddings, that is "Begin-Internal-End (BIE) word-granularity embedding". The design of BIE embedding symbols is inspired by the sequence tagging task (Huang et al., 2015). We use $[B - \{length\}]$, $[I - \{length\}]$, $[E - \{length\}]$ to indicate the beginning, inside, and end of a word or term (i.e., a combination of Chinese characters), and specifically splice the "BIE" mark with a number to record word length. For example, "$[B - 1]$" indicates the word length is 1, and "$[B-4], [I-4], [I-4], [E-4]$" indicates the word length is 4. This labeling strategy can avoid word boundary confusion during training. We set additional embedding symbols $[S]$ (i.e., separator) and $[C]$ (i.e., count) to respectively correspond to the separator $[SEP]$ and sentence-level control characters, and $[O]$ (i.e., outside) to correspond to trigger words and the ending character $[END]$ in the lyric sequence.

Note that the lyric embedding sequence is not aligned with the BIE embedding sequence; it corresponds to the BIE embedding sequence shifted to the left. This setting aims to help the model learn to predict the word length of the next token for lyric sequence, and to learn when to stop sentence generation and feed new control characters.

3.4.2 Word-granularity Attention

The BIE word-granularity embeddings can only perceive the word length of the next lyric token in advance, but cannot predict the farther distance due to the unidirectional masked attention in autoregressive language model. When sentence length is fixed, BIE embeddings are difficult to reconcile and arrange the length of each word reasonably. Therefore, we design a word-granularity attention mechanism, which is guided by BIE embeddings, to perceive the word length information of all positions for the current token.

Concretely, the special decoder block with the word-granularity attention is placed at the bottom of the ChipSong model, on top of which the standard Transformer decoder block is stacked. The detailed structure is shown on the right of Figure 2 (right). The calculation process is as follows:

[2]Words length is obtained by the Chinese text segmentation tool, Jieba.

$$\hat{E}^{F_w} = E^{F_w} + E^P \quad (1)$$

$$C_w = Softmax(X'W_1\hat{E}^{F_w})\hat{E}^{F_w} \quad (2)$$

$$X_{out} = [X'; C_w]W_2 + X \quad (3)$$

First, the BIE embedding E^{F_w} and position embedding E^P are added to obtain $\hat{E}^{F_w}$, so that the BIE embedding sequence carries global position information. Then, after passing through the masked self-attention layer, a word-granularity attention layer is designed to compute the attention weights of the contextual lyric embeddings X' to the BIE embeddings $\hat{E}^{F_w}$, where a bilinear attention is applied, so as to obtain the contextual embedding C_w recording global words length for each lyric token. Finally, the contextual lyric embedding X' and global word-length embedding C_w are concatenated and pass through a linear layer to obtain fusion representation X_{out}, and a residual connection (He et al., 2016) is added to enhance the memory of the original input lyric embedding features X in decoder block. X_{out} is further modeled in subsequent Transformer decoder blocks.

3.5 Trigger Word Control

To produce enough trigger words during training to cover creators' input needs as much as possible, we adopt a two-stage strategy, establishing a candidate word list for each lyric in the first stage, and resampling the candidate list as trigger words during each training epoch in the second stage. Concretely, considering that general keyword extraction methods could result in a low coverage range of trigger words, all nouns, adjectives, and verbs[3] of the lyrics are reserved as the candidate word list after removing the stop words, and the candidate word list also preserves word frequency so that frequent words have a higher probability of being sampled. The number of trigger words sampled is determined according to the number of lyric sentences, and the rules are designed as follows:

$$\begin{cases} k = N_{sent}/2 - 1, & N_{sent} <= 12 \\ k = 5, & else \end{cases} \quad (4)$$

where k is the number of trigger words and N_{sent} is the number of sentences.

As shown in Figure 2, after building trigger words-lyric pair data, the trigger words sequence and lyric sequence are simply spliced and fed into the language model for training, guiding model self-supervisedly complements the lyric sequence according to partially-observed trigger word sequence, where trigger words are also separated by token "$[SEP]$". When prediction, feed trigger words, and the model complements the subsequent lyric part.

3.6 Rhyme Control

A paradigm of *reverse order training and shielding decoding* is designed to control rhymes. During training, we process the training data as inter-sentence normal order and intra-sentence reverse order, as shown in Figure 2. For example, when the original lyric sequence is "..., $[3], x_1, x_2, x_3, [SEP], [4], x_4, x_5, x_6, x_7, [SEP]$, ...", it is transformed into "..., $[3], x_3, x_2, x_1, [SEP], [4], x_7, x_6, x_5, x_4, [SEP]$, ...". In the same way, the BIE word-granularity embedding sequence is accordingly processed to keep consistency. The reverse order sentences input enables to learn a reverse language model, so that rhyming position is predicted first in a sentence, and the subsequent predictions coordinate the rhyming word for protecting the text fluency from being affected.

During prediction, the input pattern of "inter-sentence normal order, intra-sentence reverse order" is maintained; that is, the last word to rhyme in each sentence is predicted first, and then the rest of the sentence is predicted in reverse order. Then, a decoding shielding strategy is adopted to control the prediction of rhyming words. According to the Chinese 14-rhyme scheme, we build a rhyme dictionary whose key is the rhyme and value is the words that the rhyme matches. At the position of the last word in the sentence, the rhyme dictionary is queried according to the input rhyme, and the softmax output values corresponding to all non-rhymed words are reduced, so that the model selects outputs from rhyming words based on predicted probability distributions.

4 Experimental Setup

4.1 Data Preparation and Processing

We prepare a large lyric corpus to train the Chip-Song model. The lyric data is constructed with reference to ChineseLyrics[4], and we gather 848K Chinese popular lyrics, where the number of lyrics sentences is 27,181K, the average lyric length is

[3]POS-tagging information is obtained by the Jieba tool.

[4]https://github.com/dengxiuqi/ChineseLyrics

253 (excluding punctuation), the average number of sentences is 32, and the average length of each sentence is 8. To fit short-video durations, we tailor the lyrics into small segments of 8, 10, 12, 14, or 16 sentences in length, which considers that 8 to 12 lines of lyrics are generally required for a 60 sec. short-video song. Lyric tailoring also increases first line diversity. In addition, unsegmented lyrics are also incorporated as training data to preserve semantic integrity and learn long-range dependencies.

4.2 Evaluation Templates

To comprehensively evaluate the proposed system, we formulate multiple conditional templates for generation, which are provided in https://github.com/korokes/chipsong. Concretely, we build 15 groups of trigger words from users and construct 500 format templates from the format library, where the formats are extracted based on actual lyrics. Each format template is randomly assigned a rhyme pattern and a group of trigger words as a complete evaluation template for lyric generation. In addition, we sample the original lyrics corresponding to the format template to generate another group of trigger words as described in Section 3.5, which are only used to evaluate the effect of trigger words guiding content. The lyrics corresponding to these evaluation templates are eliminated from the training data.

For automatic evaluations, each template generates 20 samples, and a total of $500\times20=10{,}000$ samples are finally generated for evaluation. For human evaluations, 200 samples of 10 conditional templates are randomly reserved for evaluation.

4.3 Training settings

We use a 8-head, 8-layer, 512-dimensional Transformer to build the ChipSong model (39.5M). Actually, larger hidden layer dimensions can make the model perform better. For training, the Adam optimizer (Kingma and Ba, 2014) is used with an initial learning rate of 1.5e-4. The model is trained for about 3.5 days on two GTX 2080ti GPUs with a batch size of 8. The training data combines the segmented lyrics data and the raw lyrics data, eliminating lyrics corresponding to evaluation templates. Due to the large corpus and the duplication of segmented lyrics and original lyrics, we do not set too many training epochs, and set the training epochs to 3. Owing to sufficient lyrics gathering, we do not use the pretraining strategy. For prediction, we use Top$K$ decoding with a sampling value of 8.

4.4 Evaluation Metrics

Automatic Evaluation We use the trained lyric generation models on our corpus to evaluate the perplexity (PPL) and use the Distinct (MA-D1,D2, MI-D1,D2) metrics (Li et al., 2016) to evaluate the diversity of generated lyric texts. Moreover, we design the following metrics to evaluate the proposed conditional control ability: 1) sentence-level format accuracy (SA), the percentage of generated sentences with correct length. 2) word-level format accuracy (WA), the percentage of generated sentences whose words length arrangement is exactly the same as the label. 3) rhyme accuracy (RA), the percentage of generated sentences with correct rhymes. 4) word length accuracy (WA-N), the percentage of generated words containing N Chinese characters that are correct in position and length; as the Chinese word lengths are basically within 4, we evaluate the control accuracy of 1 to 5 word length. 5) trigger word effect, we first use trigger words extracted from the original lyrics to generate samples, and then use BLEU (Papineni et al., 2002) to compare content similarity between the original lyric and the generated lyric to evaluate the relevance of trigger words and contents indirectly.

Human Evaluation We recruit three postgraduates engaged in audio and music fields to score the generated lyrics on fluency, relevance, and listenability: (1) fluency (F), the quality of the generated lyrics, whether they are smooth, grammatical, and whether there are ill-formed sentences; (1=Bad to 3=Good). (2) relevance (R), the degree of relevance of the trigger words and the lyric content; (1=Bad to 3=Good). (3) listenability (L) (Watanabe et al., 2018), as lyrics, are the positions of words, lines, and segments natural? (1=Bad to 3=Good).

4.5 Baselines

For reference, a standard Transformer-based autoregressive language model (ALM) is trained as a baseline, with the same configuration as ChipSong. We also respectively train ALM-F, ALM-T, and ALM-R for observing a single conditional control effect, where the proposed control strategies of format (F), trigger word (T), and rhyme (R) are individually modeled into ALM for training (modeling all the three conditions into ALM is equal to ChipSong), with the same configuration

No.	Model	PPL (↓)	MA-D1	MI-D1	MA-D2	MI-D2	SA	WA	RA	WA-1	WA-2	WA-3	WA-4	WA-5
1	ALM	15.77	83.40	5.01	97.33	15.76	9.96	0.67	15.43	0.58	0.94	0.09	0.05	-
2	SongNet	12.33	88.05	4.77	98.05	18.92	97.80	5.89	13.82	3.67	6.82	0.75	0.59	-
3	ALM-F	8.49	89.24	4.47	**98.48**	17.39	98.38	**92.72**	16.44	**92.68**	**94.22**	**88.35**	**89.54**	**31.58**
4	ALM-T	14.78	86.27	3.49	97.20	14.84	10.68	0.51	12.01	0.45	0.59	0.07	-	-
5	ALM-R	15.55	**89.49**	4.76	98.28	19.63	9.57	0.36	98.38	0.35	0.46	0.08	-	-
6	ChipSong	**7.69**	89.20	**5.22**	98.04	**21.69**	**98.54**	86.64	**98.56**	86.04	89.03	78.74	76.11	18.42

Table 1: Automatic evaluation results of different models. SA: sentence-level format accuracy, WA: word-level format accuracy, RA: rhyme , WA-N: N-length word accuracy. Overall, ChipSong shows better control ability in all conditions. Note that single conditional control models perform better on corresponding conditions than ChipSong with full-conditional control applied, such as ALM-F on WA and WA-N metrics, because there are no constraints of other conditional controls, which is explained in result analysis.

No.	Model	BLEU-1	BLEU-2	BLEU-3	BLEU-4
1	ALM	23.50	7.63	2.61	0.90
2	SongNet	25.41	6.25	1.88	0.61
3	ALM-F	26.29	7.88	2.69	1.03
4	ALM-T	**29.84**	**11.33**	**4.53**	**1.83**
5	ALM-R	23.83	6.11	1.75	0.54
6	ChipSong	28.55	9.56	3.38	1.35

Table 2: Effects of trigger words controlling contents.

as ChipSong. In addition, we compare ChipSong with SongNet (Li et al., 2020) that proposes a rigid format and rhyme control method. Due to differences in model settings and usage data, we use our data to retrain the SongNet model. For the models that lack the trigger word mechanism, the input is used as the first sentence and let the model continue to write like previous methods.

5 Experimental Results

5.1 Results

Table 1 and Table 2 show the experimental results of different models under each evaluation metrics. As can be seen from Table 1, ChipSong demonstrates good conditional control ability on format and rhyme, where the sentence-granularity format accuracy (SA) is 98.54%, the word-level format accuracy (WA) is 86.64%, and the rhyme accuracy (RA) is 98.56%. Since SongNet's rhyming modeling method cannot actively select rhymes and requires specific rhyming corpus for training, it isn't easy to exert its role in rhyming modeling to achieve good rhyming accuracy. ChipSong also demonstrates better PPL and generative diversity. Interestingly, the reverse order training of rhyme control (No.5) has little impact on the model PPL, indicating that the reverse language model still learns language rules. As shown in Table 2, ChipSong embodies better content control capabilities via the trigger word mechanism.

It can also be observed that a single conditional control model (No.3,4,5) generally performs better on its corresponding control condition because there are no constraints of the other two conditional controls. For example, in Table 1, without the constraints of trigger words and rhyme decoding shielding, ALM-F can focus more on controlling length format and obtain higher WA and WA-N scores, even achieving 92.72 on WA; in Table 2, without format and rhyme constraints, ALM-T has more opportunities to generate content related to trigger words for better BLEU scores.

5.2 Ablation

To further analyze the effect of each proposed conditional control, we respectively remove the conditional control of 1) word-level format control (WC); 2) sentence-level format control (SC); 3) trigger word control (TC); 4) rhyme control (RC) to train the ablation models. Two internal structures of WC, 6) BIE embedding in WC (WC-Emb) and 7) word-granularity attention in WC (WC-Att), are also ablated for evaluation.

The experimental results are shown in Table 3 and Table 4. As can be observed from the tables, format (No.2,3,4,5) and rhyme control (No.7) increase the diversity of generation while trigger word control (No.6) decreases the diversity. The modeling of word-level format control, WC, WC-Att, and WC-Emb, plays an important role in reducing the PPL. When the modeling of WC, SC, RC, or TC is removed separately, the accuracy of the corresponding evaluations, SA, WA, RA, or BLEU, is obviously reduced, indicating the effectiveness of the proposed control methods. Although WC-Att and WC-Emb both play a positive role in word-level format control, trigger word control (TC) and rhyme control (RC) have a negative effect on word-

No.	Ablation Model	PPL (↓)	MA-D1	MI-D1	MA-D2	MI-D2	SA	WA	RA	WA-1	WA-2	WA-3	WA-4	WA-5
1	ChipSong	7.69	89.20	5.22	98.04	21.69	98.45	86.64	98.56	86.04	89.03	78.74	76.11	18.42
2	w/o WC-Emb	8.00	88.40	5.18	97.21	22.62	98.04	79.48	98.54	79.67	83.43	62.38	56.22	7.89
3	w/o WC-Att	9.75	88.89	4.94	97.90	21.53	97.98	78.95	98.53	77.94	82.75	66.88	58.01	15.79
4	w/o WC	12.55	85.51	4.11	96.65	15.99	98.36	5.39	98.22	3.79	6.55	0.78	0.36	-
5	w/o WC, SC	14.50	87.00	4.69	98.05	14.84	9.40	0.53	97.68	0.72	1.05	0.13	0.07	-
6	w/o TC	8.37	91.16	5.73	98.95	23.07	98.31	89.86	98.87	90.09	91.94	83.07	84.68	21.05
7	w/o RC	7.84	87.68	4.85	97.34	18.30	98.75	89.37	15.19	88.36	91.10	83.48	79.86	28.95

Table 3: Ablation results. WC: word-level format control, SC: sentence-level format control, TC: trigger word control, RC: rhyme control. Ablating one control of ChipSong causes the corresponding evaluation score to decrease, while evaluation scores of other controls increase due to the reduction of constraints for generation.

No.	Model	BLEU-1	BLEU-2	BLEU-3	BLEU-4
1	ChipSong	28.55	9.56	3.38	1.35
2	w/o WC-Emb	27.97	8.98	3.10	1.18
3	w/o WC-Att	26.93	8.01	2.67	1.02
4	w/o WC	27.49	8.39	2.81	1.00
5	w/o WC, SC	25.38	10.28	4.57	2.02
6	w/o TC	24.85	6.26	1.83	0.63
7	w/o RC	31.23	12.69	5.58	2.49

Table 4: Ablation results of trigger words controlling contents.

No.	Model	F	R	L	Avg
1	ALM	2.51	2.07	2.61	2.40
2	SongNet	2.53	1.82	2.96	2.44
3	ChipSong	2.56	2.44	2.96	2.65
4	ChipSong w/o WC	2.48	2.47	2.95	2.63
5	ChipSong w/o WC, SC	2.46	2.67	2.75	2.63
6	ChipSong w/o TC	2.51	1.75	2.97	2.41
7	ChipSong w/o RC	2.54	2.60	2.95	2.70

Table 5: Results of human evaluations. F: Fluency; R: Relevance; L: Listenability. Avg is the average score of F, R and L.

level format control, where the scores of WA and WA-N rise when TC or RC is ablated.

5.3 Human Evaluation

Table 5 shows the experimental results of human evaluation in fluency (F), relevance (R), and Listenability (L). On the whole, the fluency scores of the models are not much different (2.46-2.56 points), which is attributed to sufficient corpus for training. ChipSong scores far higher than baselines (No.1,2) in relevance evaluation due to the modeling of trigger word mechanism. It can also be seen that when the control of rhyme or format (No.4,5,7) is lifted, the relevance is improved; we conjecture that the model has more opportunities to generate related content when the format or rhyme is not restricted. ChipSong w/o RC (No.7) gain the best average score; this is because our human evaluation does not consider the evaluation of lyric rhymes. The listenability scores of the models without format control (No.1,5) drop from nearly full marks, because the free generation is prone to generate too short or too long sentences, or two consecutive sentences with large length differences, which is not conducive to fit songs.

5.4 Trigger word coverage

We count the sampled trigger words and the sampled trigger words without repetition in training, which aims to observe the trigger word coverage. The results are shown in Figure 3. Due to the two-stage strategies, a large number of trigger words are produced for training. The number of sampling words is 3.98e7, and is only 3.16e5 after deduplication. As shown in Figure 3, as the extracted trigger words increase, new trigger words increase very little, which shows that our method covers a relatively comprehensive range of trigger words to handle out-of-distribution and cover the general input needs for users.

5.5 Case Analysis

As shown in Figure 4, we enumerate some generated lyrics of the ChipSong system in several scenarios: 1) a Chinese Hanmai song with a specific format; 2) customizing format according to a song; 3) imitative writing a lyric for a cover song version, where the sentence- and word-level format are extracted from the original lyric, Han Hong's "Qingchun". For the first case in each template in the figure, we also provide the English translation for understanding the generated lyrics. For the first template in a given word-granularity length format, we provide a human-annotated word segmentation boundary with the green vertical line |. As can be seen from the generated results, ChipSong can fine-grainly adjust the generated lyrics' format to adapt to any song, render the content guided

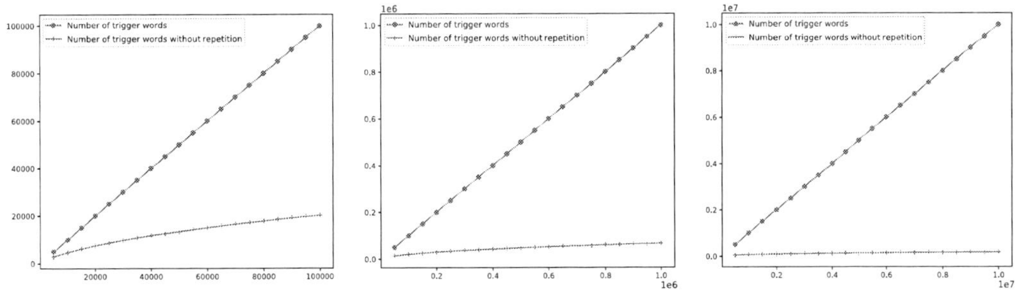

Figure 3: The count of sampled trigger words. Three figures use different scales. The total sampling number is 3.98e7, and is only 3.16e5 after deduplication. New trigger words increase very little as the increase of sampling trigger words, indicating that sampled trigger words cover a relatively comprehensive range to handle input needs.

<table>
<tr><th>Format</th><th colspan="3">Trigger word (T) & Rhyme (R) & Generated lyric</th><th>English Translation of the first case</th></tr>
<tr><td>Sentence granularity:
7;7;7;7;7;7;7;7
Word granularity:
2,2,1,2;
2,1,1,1,2;
2,2,1,2;
1,1,2,1,2;
2,1,1,1,2;
1,1,1,2,1,1;
2,2,2,1;
1,1,1,1,1,2</td><td>T: 今朝有酒今朝醉
R: ui, ei
良宵|不醉|亦|不归 (ui)
往日|与|你|共|举杯 (ei)
未知|哪日|再|相会 (ui)
只|为|来生|永|跟随 (ui)
再多|苦|我|也|无悔 (ui)
哥|只|想|努力|去|追 (ui)
人生|难得|几回|醉 (ui)
要|喝|倒|咱|再|举杯 (ei)</td><td>T: 今朝有酒今朝醉
R: ui, ei
不管|荣华|与|富贵 (ui)
只想|与|你|干|一杯 (ei)
走遍|千山|和|万水 (ui)
让|我|品尝|这|滋味 (ei)
女孩|你|让|我|心醉 (ui)
且|看|那|远方|多|美 (ei)
波涛|万里|长江|水 (ui)
风|又|吹|走|了|疲惫 (ei)</td><td>T: 今朝有酒今朝醉
R: ui, ei
痴心|爱过|这|一回 (ui)
如果|爱|你|学|不会 (ui)
当情|已经|被|摧毁 (ui)
还|能|怎么|去|挽回 (ui)
梦里|是|你|的|余味 (ei)
望|着|那|身影|才|美 (ei)
长夜|不知|何时|归 (ui)
我|又|为|谁|在|沉醉 (ui)</td><td>T: If there is liquor now, then drink now
R: ui, ei
Drink until thoroughly drunk in a good night
I raised the glass with you in bygone days
Do not know when will see you again
Hope is always with you in future life
No matter how difficult it is, no regrets
Try to pursue is the only thing I want
Life is rarely a few times drunk
Drink a toast again, just to get drunk</td></tr>
<tr><td>Sentence granularity:
10;8;10;8;10;8;10;8
Word granularity:
User-defined or complementing from the library</td><td>T: 玫瑰
R: ui, ei
那天你轻轻的拿着玫瑰(ui)
破碎的心日渐枯萎(ei)
告诉我温柔到底给了谁(ui)
最冷时有谁来安慰(ei)
不愿为我最后流一滴泪(ei)
有多少人今生无悔(ui)
就要说爱情能够再轮回(ui)
都说痴情叫人憔悴(ui)</td><td>T: 夏天
R: an, uan, ian
当樱花雨落在我的夏天(ian)
说好一起直到永远(uan)
夏日微风轻吻你们的脸(ian)
你总是笑得那么甜(ian)
绚烂白玫瑰开在心里边(ian)
让誓言永远不改变(ian)
爱像阵阵风吹过我胸前(ian)
飘进了片片彩云间(ian)</td><td>T: 红尘,流水,人世
R: ang, iang, uang
笑看落花流水一如往常(ang)
道不尽我此生轻狂(uang)
只身凡间游荡江湖渺茫(ang)
风花雪月你在何方(ang)
是谁倩影拂过一夜微凉(iang)
是否能将红尘遗忘(ang)
经年里看遍这人世匆忙(ang)
任谁淡墨染了云裳(ang)</td><td>T: Rose
R: ui, ei
You gently held the rose that day
The wounded heart slowly withers
Tell me who you gave your tenderness to
When it's cold, who is there to comfort me
Do not want to shed a single tear for me
How many people have no regrets in this life
Love can make life reincarnate
They say infatuation makes people gaunt</td></tr>
<tr><td>(Extracting format from original lyric)
也许不会再看见
离别时微黄色的天
有些人注定不会再见
那些曾青涩的脸
我拿起棕榈树的叶子
放在青涩的石板前
祭奠那些流逝的青春
和曾懵懂的誓言</td><td>T: 恋爱
R: an, uan, ian
星河日月共缠绵(ian)
清风拂去多少流年(ian)
不必问世间情缘深浅(ian)
江湖路尽头又见(ian)
你看那山高水也长远(uan)
时光穿行在云水间(ian)
刻下一张不老的容颜(an)
随你海角到天边(ian)</td><td>T: 酒
R: ui, ei
今朝拂尘再一醉(ui)
从此天涯远去不归(ui)
相爱过只求一生无悔(ui)
身旁的恋人是谁(ui)
让我在除夕夜又梦回(ui)
些许诗意比落花美(ei)
悠悠流水情匆似流水(ui)
等你滴入我心扉(ei)</td><td>T: 醉红颜, 酒
R: an, uan, ian
彼时把酒忆当年(ian)
记得那年桃花初见(ian)
或许你再续前生情缘(uan)
如今我轻语谁言(an)
人却在转瞬间霜满天(ian)
听到耳边箫声渐远(uan)
独饮一杯浊酒醉红颜(an)
都说往事化青烟(an)</td><td>T: In love
R: an, uan, ian
Stars, river, sun, and moon lingering together
The breeze blows, took away the years
Do not need to ask depth of love in the world
At the end of the road, we will meet
Look at the high mountains and far water
Time travels between clouds and water
Carve an ageless appearance of beauty
To the ends of the earth with you</td></tr>
</table>

Figure 4: Cases of lyrics generated by ChipSong. The generated results are marked in blue font. The rhymes are marked in grey font. T: Trigger words; R: Rhyme. For the fist template, the green vertical line | is used to manually annotate word segmentation boundaries. For the first case in each template, the English translation is given.

by open-ended trigger words, and maintain the rhyme. More generated cases are provided in https://github.com/korokes/chipsong.

6 Conclusion

In this work, we develop *ChipSong*, a lyric generation system, to assist musical short-video creators for **Chi**nese **p**opular **song** creation. ChipSong fine-grainly adjusts lyric generation to meet the creator's needs in various scenarios via the proposed strategies of sentence- and word-level format control, trigger word control, and rhyme control. In the future, we would like to consider melody generation and other attributions control of lyrics.

References

Jacob Devlin, Ming-Wei Chang, Kenton Lee, and Kristina Toutanova. 2018. Bert: Pre-training of deep bidirectional transformers for language understanding. *arXiv preprint arXiv:1810.04805*.

Haoshen Fan, Jie Wang, Bojin Zhuang, Shaojun Wang, and Jing Xiao. 2019. A hierarchical attention based seq2seq model for Chinese lyrics generation. In *Proceedings of the Pacific Rim International Conference on Artificial Intelligence*, pages 279–288.

Zhipeng Guo, Xiaoyuan Yi, Maosong Sun, Wenhao Li, Cheng Yang, Jiannan Liang, Huimin Chen, Yuhui Zhang, and Ruoyu Li. 2019. Jiuge: A human-machine collaborative Chinese classical poetry generation system. In *Proceedings of the 57th Annual Meeting of the Association for Computational*

Linguistics: System Demonstrations, pages 25–30, Florence, Italy. Association for Computational Linguistics.

Kaiming He, Xiangyu Zhang, Shaoqing Ren, and Jian Sun. 2016. Deep residual learning for image recognition. In *Proceedings of the IEEE conference on computer vision and pattern recognition*, pages 770–778.

Jinyi Hu and Maosong Sun. 2020. Generating major types of Chinese classical poetry in a uniformed framework. *CoRR*, abs/2003.11528.

Zhiheng Huang, Wei Xu, and Kai Yu. 2015. Bidirectional LSTM-CRF models for sequence tagging. *arXiv preprint arXiv:1508.01991*.

Diederik P Kingma and Jimmy Ba. 2014. Adam: A method for stochastic optimization. *arXiv preprint arXiv:1412.6980*.

Hsin-Pei Lee, Jhih-Sheng Fang, and Wei-Yun Ma. 2019. iComposer: An automatic songwriting system for Chinese popular music. In *Proceedings of the Conference of the North American Chapter of the Association for Computational Linguistics (Demonstrations)*, pages 84–88.

Jiwei Li, Michel Galley, Chris Brockett, Jianfeng Gao, and Bill Dolan. 2016. A diversity-promoting objective function for neural conversation models. In *Proceedings of the Conference of the North American Chapter of the Association for Computational Linguistics: Human Language Technologies*.

Piji Li, Haisong Zhang, Xiaojiang Liu, and Shuming Shi. 2020. Rigid formats controlled text generation. In *Proceedings of the Annual Meeting of the Association for Computational Linguistics*, pages 742–751.

Xu Lu, Jie Wang, Bojin Zhuang, Shaojun Wang, and Jing Xiao. 2019. A syllable-structured, contextually-based conditionally generation of Chinese lyrics. In *Proceedings of the Pacific Rim International Conference on Artificial Intelligence*, pages 257–265.

Enrique Manjavacas, Mike Kestemont, and Folgert Karsdorp. 2019. Generation of hip-hop lyrics with hierarchical modeling and conditional templates. In *Proceedings of the International Conference on Natural Language Generation*, pages 301–310.

Nikola I Nikolov, Eric Malmi, Curtis Northcutt, and Loreto Parisi. 2020. Rapformer: Conditional rap lyrics generation with denoising autoencoders. In *Proceedings of the International Conference on Natural Language Generation*, pages 360–373.

Hugo Gonçalo Oliveira, Raquel Hervás, Alberto Díaz, and Pablo Gervás. 2017. Multilingual extension and evaluation of a poetry generator. *Natural Language Engineering*, 23(6):929–967.

Kishore Papineni, Salim Roukos, Todd Ward, and Wei-Jing Zhu. 2002. Bleu: A method for automatic evaluation of machine translation. In *Proceedings of the annual meeting on association for computational linguistics (ACL)*, pages 311–318. Association for Computational Linguistics.

Peter Potash, Alexey Romanov, and Anna Rumshisky. 2015. Ghostwriter: Using an LSTM for automatic rap lyric generation. In *Proceedings of the Conference on Empirical Methods in Natural Language Processing*, pages 1919–1924.

Peter Potash, Alexey Romanov, and Anna Rumshisky. 2018. Evaluating creative language generation: The case of rap lyric ghostwriting. In *Proceedings of the Second Workshop on Stylistic Variation*, pages 29–38.

Liang-Hsin Shen, Pei-Lun Tai, Chao-Chung Wu, and Shou-De Lin. 2019. Controlling sequence-to-sequence models-a demonstration on neural-based acrostic generator. In *Proceedings of the Conference on Empirical Methods in Natural Language Processing and the International Joint Conference on Natural Language Processing*, pages 43–48.

Zhonghao Sheng, Kaitao Song, Xu Tan, Yi Ren, Wei Ye, Shikun Zhang, and Tao Qin. 2021. SongMASS: Automatic song writing with pre-training and alignment constraint. In *Proceedings of the AAAI Conference on Artificial Intelligence*, volume 35, pages 13798–13805.

Kento Watanabe, Yuichiroh Matsubayashi, Satoru Fukayama, Masataka Goto, Kentaro Inui, and Tomoyasu Nakano. 2018. A melody-conditioned lyrics language model. In *Proceedings of the Conference of the North American Chapter of the Association for Computational Linguistics: Human Language Technologies, Volume 1 (Long Papers)*, pages 163–172.

Lanqing Xue, Kaitao Song, Duocai Wu, Xu Tan, Nevin L Zhang, Tao Qin, Wei-Qiang Zhang, and Tie-Yan Liu. 2021. DeepRapper: Neural rap generation with rhyme and rhythm modeling. *arXiv preprint arXiv:2107.01875*.

Rui Yan, Cheng-Te Li, Xiaohua Hu, and Ming Zhang. 2016. Chinese couplet generation with neural network structures. In *Proceedings of the 54th Annual Meeting of the Association for Computational Linguistics (Volume 1: Long Papers)*, pages 2347–2357, Berlin, Germany. Association for Computational Linguistics.

Rongsheng Zhang, Xiaoxi Mao, Le Li, Lin Jiang, Lin Chen, Zhiwei Hu, Yadong Xi, Changjie Fan, and Minlie Huang. 2020a. Youling: An ai-assisted lyrics creation system. In *Proceedings of the Conference on Empirical Methods in Natural Language Processing*, pages 85–91.

Yuchao Zhang, Pengmiao Li, Zhili Zhang, Bo Bai, Gong Zhang, Wendong Wang, Bo Lian, and Ke Xu. 2020b. Autosight: Distributed edge caching in short video network. *IEEE Network*, 34(3):194–199.

Hongyuan Zhu, Qi Liu, Nicholas Jing Yuan, Chuan Qin, Jiawei Li, Kun Zhang, Guang Zhou, Furu Wei, Yuanchun Xu, and Enhong Chen. 2018. Xiaoice band: A melody and arrangement generation framework for pop music. In *Proceedings of the ACM SIGKDD International Conference on Knowledge Discovery & Data Mining*, pages 2837–2846.

Read, Revise, Repeat: A System Demonstration for Human-in-the-loop Iterative Text Revision

Wanyu Du[1]*, Zae Myung Kim[2]* , Vipul Raheja[3] , Dhruv Kumar[3] , Dongyeop Kang[2]
[1]University of Virginia, [2]University of Minnesota, [3]Grammarly
`wd5jq@virginia.edu`, `{kim01756,dongyeop}@umn.edu`
`{vipul.raheja,dhruv.kumar}@grammarly.com`

Abstract

Revision is an essential part of the human writing process. It tends to be strategic, adaptive, and, more importantly, *iterative* in nature. Despite the success of large language models on text revision tasks, they are limited to non-iterative, one-shot revisions. Examining and evaluating the capability of large language models for making continuous revisions and collaborating with human writers is a critical step towards building effective writing assistants. In this work, we present a human-in-the-loop iterative text revision system, $\mathcal{R}$ead, $\mathcal{R}$evise, $\mathcal{R}$epeat ($\mathcal{R}$3), which aims at achieving high quality text revisions with minimal human efforts by reading model-generated revisions and user feedbacks, revising documents, and repeating human-machine interactions. In $\mathcal{R}$3, a text revision model provides text editing suggestions for human writers, who can accept or reject the suggested edits. The accepted edits are then incorporated into the model for the next iteration of document revision. Writers can therefore revise documents iteratively by interacting with the system and simply accepting/rejecting its suggested edits until the text revision model stops making further revisions or reaches a predefined maximum number of revisions. Empirical experiments show that $\mathcal{R}$3 can generate revisions with comparable acceptance rate to human writers at early revision depths, and the human-machine interaction can get higher quality revisions with fewer iterations and edits. The collected human-model interaction dataset and system code are available at `https://github.com/vipulraheja/IteraTeR`. Our system demonstration is available at `https://youtu.be/lK08tIpEoaE`.

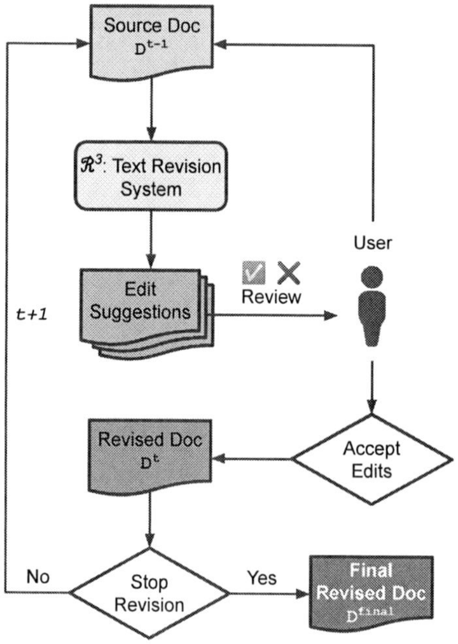

Figure 1: System overview for $\mathcal{R}$3 human-in-the-loop iterative text revision.

1 Introduction

Text revision is a crucial part of writing. Specifically, text revision involves identifying discrepancies between intended and instantiated text, deciding what edits to make, and how to make those desired edits (Flower and Hayes, 1981; Faigley and Witte, 1981; Fitzgerald, 1987). It enables writers to deliberate over and organize their thoughts, find a better line of argument, learn afresh, and discover what was not known before (Sommers, 1980; Scardamalia, 1986). Previous studies (Flower, 1980; Collins and Gentner, 1980; Vaughan and McDonald, 1986) have shown that text revision is an *iterative* process since human writers are unable to simultaneously comprehend multiple demands and constraints of the task when producing well-written texts – for instance, covering the content, following linguistic norms and discourse conventions of written prose, etc. Therefore, writers resort to performing text revisions on their drafts iteratively to

*Equal contributions.

Proceedings of the First Workshop on Intelligent and Interactive Writing Assistants (In2Writing 2022), pages 96 - 108

reduce the number of considerations at each time.

Computational modeling of the iterative text revision process is essential for building intelligent and interactive writing assistants. Most prior works on the development of neural text revision systems (Faruqui et al., 2018; Botha et al., 2018; Ito et al., 2019; Faltings et al., 2021) do not take the iterative nature of text revision and human feedback on suggested revisions into consideration. The direct application of such revision systems in an iterative way, however, could generate some "noisy" edits and require much burden on human writers to fix the noise. Therefore, we propose to collect human feedback at each iteration of revision to filter out those harmful noisy edits and produce revised documents of higher quality.

In this work, we present a novel human-in-the-loop iterative text revision system, $\mathcal{R}$ead, $\mathcal{R}$evise, $\mathcal{R}$epeat ($\mathcal{R}3$), which reads model-generated revisions and user feedbacks, revises documents, and repeats human-machine interactions in an iterative way, as depicted in Figure 1. First, users write a document as input to the system or choose one from a candidate document set to edit. Then, the text revision system provides multiple editing suggestions with their edits and intents. Users can accept or reject the editing suggestions in an iterative way and stop revision when no editing suggestions are provided or the model reaches the maximum revision limit. The overall model performance can be estimated by calculating the acceptance rate throughout all editing suggestions.

$\mathcal{R}3$ provides numerous benefits over existing writing assistants for text revision. First, $\mathcal{R}3$ improves the overall writing experience for writers by making it more interpretable, controllable, and productive: on the one hand, writers don't have to (re-)read the parts of the text that are already high quality, and this, in turn, helps them focus on larger writing goals (§4.2); on the other hand, by showing edit intentions for every suggested edit, which users can further decide to accept or reject, $\mathcal{R}3$ provides them with more fine-grained control over the text revision process compared to other one-shot based text revision systems (Lee et al., 2022), and are limited in both interpretability and controllability. Second, $\mathcal{R}3$ improves the revision efficiency. The human-machine interaction can help the system produce higher quality revisions with fewer iterations and edits, and the empirical experiments in §4.2 validate this claim. To the best of our knowledge, $\mathcal{R}3$ is the first text revision system in literature that can perform *iterative* text revision in collaboration by human writers and revision models.

In this paper, we make three major contributions:

- We present a novel human-in-the-loop text revision system $\mathcal{R}3$ to make text revision models more accessible; and to make the process of iterative text revision efficient, productive, and cognitively less challenging.
- From an HCI perspective, we conduct experiments to measure the effectiveness of the proposed system for the iterative text revision task. Empirical experiments show that $\mathcal{R}3$ can generate edits with comparable acceptance rate to human writers at early revision depths.
- We analyze the data collected from human-model interactions for text revision and provide insights and future directions for building high-quality and efficient human-in-the-loop text revision systems. We release our code, revision interface, and collected human-model interaction dataset to promote future research on collaborative text revision.

2 Related Work

Previous works on modeling text revision (Faruqui et al., 2018; Botha et al., 2018; Ito et al., 2019; Faltings et al., 2021) have ignored the iterative nature of the task, and simplified it into a one-shot "original-to-final" sentence-to-sentence generation task. However, in practice, at every revision step, multiple edits happen at the document-level which also play an important role in text revision. For instance, reordering and deleting sentences to improve the coherence.

More importantly, performing multiple high-quality edits at once is very challenging. Continuing the previous example, document readability can degrade after reordering sentences, and further adding transitional phrases is often required to make the document more coherent and readable. Therefore, one-shot sentence-to-sentence text revision formulation is not sufficient to deal with real-world challenges in text revision tasks.

While some prior works on text revision (Coenen et al., 2021; Padmakumar and He, 2021; Gero et al., 2021; Lee et al., 2022) have proposed human-machine collaborative writing interfaces, they are mostly focused on collecting human-machine interaction data for training better neural models, rather than understanding the iterative nature of the text revision process, or the model's ability to adjust editing suggestions according to human feedback.

Another line of work by Sun et al. (2021); Singh et al. (2022) on creative writing designed human-machine interaction interfaces to encourage new content generation. However, text revision focuses on improving the quality of existing writing and keeping the original content as much as possible. In this work, we provide a human-in-the-loop text revision system to make helpful editing suggestions by interacting with users in an iterative way.

3 System Overview

Figure 1 shows the general pipeline of $\mathcal{R}3$ human-in-the-loop iterative text revision system. In this section, we will describe the development details of the text revision models and demonstrate our user interfaces.

We first formulate an iterative text revision process: given a source document[1] $\mathcal{D}^{t-1}$, at each revision depth t, a text revision system will apply a set of edits to get the revised document $\mathcal{D}^t$. The system will continue iterating revision until the revised document $\mathcal{D}^t$ satisfies a set of predefined stopping criteria, such as reaching a predefined maximum revision depth t_{max}, or making no edits between $\mathcal{D}^{t-1}$ and $\mathcal{D}^t$.

3.1 Text Revision System

We follow the prior work of Du et al. (2022) to build our text revision system. The system is composed of edit intention identification models and a text revision generation model. We follow the same data collection procedure in Du et al. (2022) to collect the iterative revision data.[2] Then, we train the three models on the collected revision dataset.

Edit Intention Identification Models. Following Du et al. (2022), our edit intentions have four categories: FLUENCY, COHERENCE, CLARITY, and STYLE. We build our edit intention identification models at each sentence of the source document $\mathcal{D}^{t-1}$ to capture the more fine-grained edits. Specifically, given a source sentence, the system will make two-step predictions: (1) whether or not to edit, and (2) which edit intention to apply. The decision whether or not to edit is taken by an edit-prediction classifier that predicts a binary label of whether to edit a sentence or not. The second model, called the edit-intention classifier, predicts which edit intention to apply to the sentence. If the edit-prediction model predicts "not to edit" in the first step, the source sentence will be kept unchanged at the current revision depth.

Text Revision Generation Model. We fine-tune a large pre-trained language model like PEGASUS (Zhang et al., 2020) on our collected revision dataset to build the text revision generation model. Given a source sentence and its predicted edit intention, the model will generate a revised sentence, conditioned on the predicted edit intention. Then, we concatenate all un-revised and revised sentences to get the model-revised document $\mathcal{D}^t$, and extract all its edits using *latexdiff*[3] and *difflib*.[4]

In summary, at each revision depth t, given a source document $\mathcal{D}^{t-1}$, the text revision system first predicts the need for revising a sentence, and for the ones that need revision, it predicts the corresponding fine-grained edit intentions – thus, generating the revised document $\mathcal{D}^t$ based on the source document and the predicted edit decisions and intentions.

3.2 Human-in-the-loop Revision

In practice, not all model-generated edits are equally impactful towards improving the document quality (Du et al., 2022). Therefore, we enable user interaction in the iterative text revision process to achieve high quality of text revisions along with a productive writing experience. At each revision depth t, our system provides the user with suggested edits, and their corresponding edit intentions. The user can interact with the system by choosing to accept or reject the suggested edits.

Figure 2 illustrates the details of $\mathcal{R}3$'s user interface. First, a user enters their id to login to the web interface as shown in Figure 2a. Then, the user is instructed with a few guidelines on how to operate the revision as demonstrated in Figure 2b. After getting familiar with the interface, the user can select a source document from the left drop-down menu in Figure 2c. By clicking the source document, all the edits predicted by the text re-

[1] The source document can be chosen by a user in the candidate set of documents or written from scratch by a user.

[2] See §4.1 for the detailed data collection.

[3] https://ctan.org/pkg/latexdiff

[4] https://docs.python.org/3/library/difflib.html

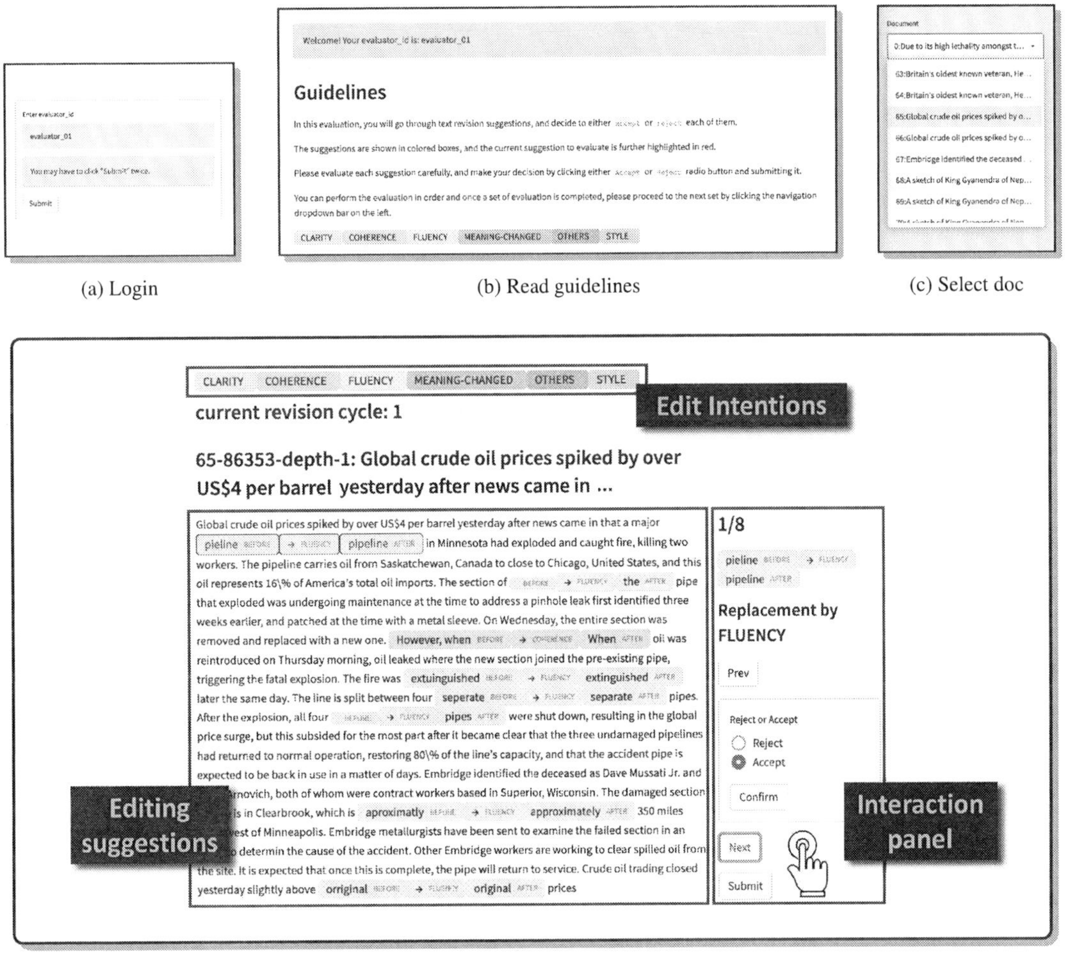

(a) Login (b) Read guidelines (c) Select doc

(d) Editing suggestions and interaction panel

Figure 2: User interface demonstration for $\mathcal{R}3$. Anonymized version available at `https://youtu.be/1K08tIpEoaE`.

vision model, as well as their corresponding edit intentions will show up in the main page as illustrated in Figure 2d (left panel). The user is guided to go through each suggested edits, and choose to accept or reject the current edit by clicking the *Confirm* button in Figure 2d (right panel). After going through all the suggested edits, the user is guided to click the *Submit* button to save their decisions on the edits. Then, the user is guided to click the *Next Iteration!* button to proceed to the next revision depth and check the next round of edits suggested by the system. This interactive process continues until the system does not generate further edits or reaches the maximum revision depth t_{max}.

4 Experiments

We conduct experiments to answer the following research questions:

- RQ1 How likely are users to accept the editing suggestions predicted by our text revision system? This question is designed to evaluate whether our text revision system can generate high quality edits.
- RQ2 Which types of edit intentions are more likely to be accepted by users? This question is aimed to identify which types of edits are more favored by users.
- RQ3 Does user feedback in $\mathcal{R}3$ help produce higher quality of revised documents? This question is proposed to validate the effectiveness of human-in-the-loop component in $\mathcal{R}3$.

4.1 Experimental Setups

Iterative Revision Systems. We prepare three types of iterative revision systems to answer the above questions:

1. HUMAN-HUMAN: We ask users to accept or reject text revisions made by human writers, which are directly sampled from our collected iterative revision dataset. This serves as the baseline to measure the gap between our text revision system and human writers.
2. SYSTEM-HUMAN: We ask users to accept or reject text revisions made by our system. Then, we incorporate user accepted edits to the system to generate the next iteration of revision. This is the standard human-in-the-loop process of $\mathcal{R}3$.
3. SYSTEM-ONLY: We conduct an ablation study by removing user interaction in reviewing the model-generated edits. Then, we compare the overall quality of final revised documents with and without the human-in-the-loop component.

In both HUMAN-HUMAN and SYSTEM-HUMAN setups where users interacted with the system, they were not informed whether the revisions were sampled from our collected iterative revision dataset, or generated by the underlying text revision models.

User Study Design. We hired three linguistic experts (English L1, bachelor's or higher degree in Linguistics) to interact with our text revision system. Each user was presented with a text revision (as shown in Figure 2d) and asked to accept or reject each edit in the current revision (users were informed which revision depth they were looking at). For a fair comparison, users were not informed about the source of the edits (human-written vs. model-generated), and the experiments were conducted separately one after the other. Note that the users were only asked to accept or reject edits, and they had control neither over the number of iterations, nor over the stopping criteria. The stopping criteria for the experiment were set by us and designed as: (1) no new edits were made at the following revision depth, or (2) the maximum revision depth $t_{max} = 3$ was reached.

Data Details. We followed the prior work (Du et al., 2022) to collect the text revision data across three domains: ArXiv, Wikipedia and Wikinews. This data was then used to train both the edit intention identification models and the text revision generation model. We split the data into training, validation and test set according to their document ids with a ratio of 8:1:1. The detailed data statistics are included in Table 1. Note that our newly collected revision dataset is larger than the previously proposed dataset in Du et al. (2022) with around 24K more unique documents and 170K more edits (sentence pairs).

	# Docs	Avg. Depths	# Edits
Training	44,270	6.63	292,929
Validation	5,152	6.60	34,026
Test	6,226	6.34	39,511

Table 1: Statistics for our collected revision data which has been used to train the edit intention identification model and the text revision generation model. **# Docs** means the total number of unique documents, **Avg. Depths** indicates the average revision depth per document (for the human-generated training data), and **# Edits** stands for the total number of edits (sentence pairs) across the corpus.

For the human evaluation data, we randomly sampled 10 documents with a maximum revision depth of 3 from each domain in the test set in Table 1. For the evaluation of text revisions made by human writers (HUMAN-HUMAN), we presented the existing ground-truth references from our collected dataset to users. Since we do not hire additional human writers to perform continuous revisions, we just presented the static human revisions from the original test set to users at each revision depth, and collected the user acceptance statistics as a baseline for our system.

For the evaluation of text revisions made by our system (SYSTEM-HUMAN), we only presented the original source document at the initial revision depth ($\mathcal{D}^0$) to our system, and let the system generate edits in the following revision depths, while incorporating the accept/reject decisions on model-generated edit suggestions by the users. Note that at each revision depth, the system will only incorporate the edits accepted by users and pass them to the next revision iteration.

For text revisions made by our system without human-in-the-loop (SYSTEM-ONLY), we let the system generate edits in an iterative way and accepted all model-generated edits at each revision depth.

Model Details. For both edit intention identification models, we fine-tuned the RoBERTa-large (Liu et al., 2020) pre-trained checkpoint from HuggingFace (Wolf et al., 2020) for 2 epochs with a learning rate of 1×10^{-5} and batch size of 16. The edit-

	Human-Human				System-Human (ours)			
t	# Docs	Avg. Edits	Avg. Accepts	% Accepts	# Docs	Avg. Edits	Avg. Accepts	% Accepts
1	30	5.37	2.77	51.66	30	**5.90**	**2.90**	49.15
2	30	4.83	3.00	62.06	24	3.83	2.57	**67.02**
3	20	3.80	2.67	70.39	20	3.43	1.94	56.71

Table 2: Human-in-the-loop iterative text revision evaluation results. t stands for the revision depth, **# Docs** shows the total number of revised documents at the current revision depth, **Avg. Edits** indicates the average number of applied edits per document, **Avg. Accepts** means the average number of edits accepted by users per document, and **% Accepts** is calculated by dividing the total accepted edits with the total applied edits.

prediction classifier is binary classification model that predicts whether to edit a given sentence or not. It achieves an F1 score of 67.33 for the edit label and 79.67 for the not-edit label. The edit-intention classifier predicts the specific intent for a sentence that requires editing. It achieves F1 scores of 67.14, 70.27, 57.0, and 3.21[5] for CLARITY, FLUENCY, COHERENCE and STYLE intent labels respectively.

For the text revision generation model, we fine-tuned the PEGASUS-LARGE (Zhang et al., 2020) pre-trained checkpoint from HuggingFace. We set the edit intentions as new special tokens (e.g., <STYLE>, <FLUENCY>), and concatenated the edit intention and source sentence together as the input to the model. The output of the model is the revised sentence, and we trained the model with cross-entropy loss. We fine-tuned the model for 5 epochs with a learning rate of 3×10^{-5} and batch size of 4. Finally, our text revision generation model achieves 41.78 SARI score (Xu et al., 2016), 81.11 BLEU score (Papineni et al., 2002) and 89.08 ROUGE-L score (Lin, 2004) on the test set.

4.2 Result Analysis

Iterativeness. The human-in-the-loop iterative text revision evaluation results are reported in Table 2. Each document is evaluated by at least 2 users. **We find that $\mathcal{R}3$ achieves comparable performances with ground-truth human revisions at revision depth 1 and 2, and tends to generate less favorable edits at revision depth 3.** At revision depth 1, $\mathcal{R}3$ is able to generate more edits than ground-truth human edits for each document, and gets more edits accepted by users on average. This shows the potential of $\mathcal{R}3$ in generating appropriate text revisions that are more favorable to users.

At revision depth 2, while $\mathcal{R}3$ generates less edits than human writers on average, it gets a higher acceptance rate than human writers. This result suggests that for the end users, more edits may not necessarily lead to a higher acceptance ratio, and shows that $\mathcal{R}3$ is able to make high-quality edits for effective iterative text revisions. At revision depth 3, $\mathcal{R}3$ generates even less edits compared both to human writers and its previous revision depths. This result can be attributed to the fact that our models are only trained on static human revision data, while at testing time they have to make predictions conditioned on their revisions generated at the previous depth, which may have a very different distribution of edits than the training data. Table 7 shows an example of iterative text revision in ArXiv domain generated by $\mathcal{R}3$. We also provide some other iterative revision examples generated by $\mathcal{R}3$ in Appendix A.

Edit Intentions. Table 3 demonstrates the distribution of different edit intentions, which can help us further analyze the which type of edits are more likely to be accepted by end users. For human-generated revisions, we find that FLUENCY edits are most likely to be accepted since they are mainly fixing grammatical errors.

For system-generated revisions, we observe that CLARITY edits are the most frequent edits but end users only accept 58.73% of them, which suggests that our system needs further improvements in learning CLARITY edits. Another interesting observation is that STYLE edits are rarely generated by human writers (1.2%) and also gets the lowest acceptance rate (33.33%) than other intentions, while they are frequently generated by our system (16.7%) and surprisingly gets the highest acceptance rate (64.6%) than other intentions. This observation indicates that $\mathcal{R}3$ is capable for generating favorable stylistic edits. Table 4 shows some examples of edit suggestions generated by $\mathcal{R}3$.

Role of Human Feedback in Revision Quality. Table 5 illustrates the quality comparison results of

[5] We note that the F1 score for STYLE is low as the number of training samples for that intent is particularly small.

	HUMAN-HUMAN			SYSTEM-HUMAN (ours)		
	# Edits	**# Accepts**	**% Accepts**	**# Edits**	**# Accepts**	**% Accepts**
CLARITY	197	119	60.40	**332**	195	58.73
FLUENCY	178	146	**82.02**	91	41	45.05
COHERENCE	103	41	39.80	141	68	48.22
STYLE	6	2	33.33	113	73	**64.60**

Table 3: The distribution of different edit intentions. **# Edits** indicates the total number of applied edits under the current edit intention, **# Accepts** means the total number of edits accepted by users under the current edit intention, and **% Accepts** is calculated by dividing the total accepted edits with the total applied edits.

Edit Intention	**Edit Suggestion**
CLARITY	Emerging new test procedures ~~, such as antigen or RT-LAMP tests,~~ might enable us to protect nursing home residents.
FLUENCY	For Radar tracking, we show how a model can reduce the tracking errors.
COHERENCE	However, ~~we show that~~ even a small violation can significantly modify the effective noise.
STYLE	There has been ~~numerous~~extensive research focusing on neural coding.

Table 4: Edit suggestion examples generated by $\mathcal{R}3$.

	Avg. Depths	**# Edits**	**Quality**
SYSTEM-HUMAN (ours)	2.5	148	**0.68**
SYSTEM-ONLY	2.8	175	0.28

Table 5: Quality comparison results of final revised documents with and without human-in-the-loop. **Avg. Depths** indicates the average number of iterations conducted by the system, **# Edits** means the total number of accepted edits by the system, and **Quality** represents the human judgements of the overall quality of system-revised final documents.

final revised documents with and without human-in-the-loop for $\mathcal{R}3$. We asked another group of three annotators (English L2, bachelor's or higher degree in Computer Science) to judge whether the overall quality of system-generated final document is better than the ground-truth reference final document. The quality score ranges between 0 and 1. We evaluated 10 unique documents in ArXiv domain, and took the average score from all 3 annotators. As shown in Table 5, **SYSTEM-HUMAN produces better overall quality score for the final system-generated documents with fewer iterations of revision and fewer edits**, which validates the effectiveness of the human-machine interaction proposed in $\mathcal{R}3$.

User Feedback. We also collected qualitative feedback about $\mathcal{R}3$ from the linguistic experts through a questionnaire. The first part of our questionnaire asks participants to recall their experience with the system, and evaluate various aspects of the system (in Table 6). They were asked to rate how easy it was to get onboarded and use the system (*convenience*), whether they were satisfied with the system (revision quality and usage experience) (*satisfaction*), whether they felt it improved their productivity for text revision (*productivity*), and whether they would like to use the system again (*retention*) for performing revisions on their documents.

In general, the users gave positive feedback towards the ease of use of the system. However, they were neutral on the potential productivity impact, owing to the lack of domain knowledge of the documents they were evaluating. This issue could be mitigated by asking users to revise their own documents of interest. The retention and satisfaction scores were leaning slightly negative, which was explained as primarily attributed to gaps in the user interface design (eg. improperly aligned diffs, sub-optimal presentation of word-level edits, etc.).

We also asked them to provide detailed comments on their experience, and the potential impact of the system on their text revision experience. Specifically, upon asking the users whether using the system to evaluate the model-suggested edits would be more time-efficient compared to actually revising the document themselves, we received many useful insights that help better design better interfaces and features of our system in future work, as some users noted:

> *I think it would be faster using the system, but I would still be checking the text myself in case edits were missed. The system made some edits where there were letters and parts of words being added/re-*

Criterion	Avg. Score	Std. Deviation
Convenience	3.66	0.58
Satisfaction	2.33	0.58
Productivity	3.00	1.00
Retention	2.66	0.58

Table 6: User feedback survey ratings. Ratings are on 5-point Likert scale with 5 being strongly positive experience, 3 being neutral, and 1 being strongly negative. However, we'd like to point out that as the number of users (linguists) who participated in the study is small, the statistical significance of the results should be taken lightly.

> *moved/replaced, which sometimes took some time to figure out. That wouldn't be the case if I were editing a document.*
>
> *Ultimately, I would use the system for grammar/coherence/clarity edits, and then still research (a lot) to ensure that meaning was preserved throughout the document. For topics that I was more familiar with/more general topics, using the system would probably reduce my time by a third or so. For topics that required more in-depth research for me, the time saved by using the system might be minimal.*

5 Discussion and Future Directions

When $\mathcal{R}3$ generates revisions at deeper depths, we observe a decrease in the acceptance ratio by human users. It is crucial to create a text revision system that can learn different revision strategies at each iteration and generate high quality edits at deeper revision levels.

Editing suggestions provided by our text revision generation models could be improved. Particularly, FLUENCY edits show a huge gap between human and system revisions (45.05% and 82.02%). Future work could focus on developing more powerful text revision generation models.

In our human-machine interaction, we restrict the users' role to accept or reject the model's predictions. Even with minimal human interaction, our experiment shows comparable or even better revision quality as compared to human writers at early revision depths. A potential future direction for human-machine collaborative text revision would be to develop advanced human-machine interaction interfaces, such as asking users to re-write the machine-revised text.

Also, a larger-scale user study could be carried out to derive more meaningful statistics (e.g. optimal number of revision depths and edit suggestions) and investigate if there is any intriguing user behavior in the iterative revision process. For example, as mentioned in the users' feedback, it would be interesting to check if users behave differently when they are asked to accept/reject edit suggestions provided for their own texts as opposed to the texts written by a third party.

6 Conclusion

In this work, we develop an interactive iterative text revision system $\mathcal{R}3$ that is able to effectively assist users to make revisions and improve the quality of existing documents. $\mathcal{R}3$ can generate higher quality revisions while minimizing the human efforts. Users are provided with a reviewing interface to accept or reject system suggesting edits. The user-validated edits are then propagated to the next revision depth to get further improved revisions. Empirical results show that $\mathcal{R}3$ can generate iterative text revisions with acceptance rates comparable or even better than human writers at early revision depths.

Acknowledgments

We thank all linguistic expert annotators at Grammarly for participating in the user study and providing us with valuable feedback during the process. We also thank Karin de Langis at University of Minnesota for narrating the video of our system demonstration. We would like to extend our gratitude to the anonymous reviewers for their helpful comments.

References

Jan A. Botha, Manaal Faruqui, John Alex, Jason Baldridge, and Dipanjan Das. 2018. Learning to split and rephrase from Wikipedia edit history. In *Proceedings of the 2018 Conference on Empirical Methods in Natural Language Processing*, pages 732–737, Brussels, Belgium. Association for Computational Linguistics.

Andy Coenen, Luke Davis, Daphne Ippolito, Emily Reif, and Ann Yuan. 2021. Wordcraft: a human-ai collaborative editor for story writing. *arXiv preprint arXiv:2107.07430*.

Allan Collins and Dedre Gentner. 1980. A framework for a cognitive theory of writing. In *Cognitive processes in writing*, pages 51–72. Erlbaum.

t	Human-Human	System-Human (ours)
0	Due to its high lethality amongst the elderly, nursing homes are in the eye of the COVID-19 storm. Emerging new test procedures , such as antigen or RT-LAMP tests, might enable us to protect nursing home residents by means of preventive screening strategies. Here, we develop a novel agent-based epidemiological model for the spread of SARS-CoV-2 in nursing homes to identify optimal preventive testing strategiesto curb this spread . The model is microscopically calibrated to high-resolution data from actual nursing homes in Austria, including the detailed networks of social contacts of their residents and information on past outbreaks.	Due to its high lethality amongst the elderly, nursing homes are in the eye of the COVID-19 storm. Emerging new test procedures , such as antigen or RT-LAMP tests, might enable us to protect nursing home residents by means of preventive screening strategies. Here, we develop a novel agent-based epidemiological model for the spread of SARS-CoV-2 in nursing homes to identify optimal preventive testing strategiesto curb this spread . The model is microscopically calibrated to high-resolution data from actual nursing homes in Austria, including the detailed networks of social contacts of their residents and information on past outbreaks.
1	Due to its high lethality amongst the elderly, nursing homes are in the eye of the COVID-19 storm. ~~Emerging new~~ With test procedures becoming available at scale , such as antigen or RT-LAMP tests, might enable us to protect nursing home residents by means of preventive screening strategies. Here, we develop a novel agent-based epidemiological model for the spread of SARS-CoV-2 in nursing homes to identify optimal ~~preventive testing strategiesto curb this spread~~ prevention strategies . The model is microscopically calibrated to high-resolution data from actual nursing homes in Austria, including the detailed networks of social contacts of their residents and information on past outbreaks.	Due to its high lethality amongst the elderly, nursing homes are in the eye of the COVID-19 storm. Emerging new test procedures ~~, such as antigen or RT-LAMP tests,~~ might enable us to protect nursing home residents by means of preventive screening strategies. Here, we develop a novel agent-based epidemiological model for the spread of SARS-CoV-2 in nursing homes to identify optimal preventive testing strategies ~~to curb this spread . The model is microscopically.~~ The model is calibrated to high-resolution data from actual nursing homes in Austria, including the detailed networks of social contacts of their residents and information on past outbreaks.
2	Due to its high lethality amongst the elderly, nursing homes are in the eye of the COVID-19 ~~storm~~ pandemic . Emerging new test procedures , such as antigen or RT-LAMP tests, might enable us to protect nursing home residents by means of preventive screening strategies. Here, we develop a ~~novel~~ detailed agent-based epidemiological model for the spread of SARS-CoV-2 in nursing homes to identify optimal preventive testing strategiesto curb this spread . The model is microscopically calibrated to high-resolution data from actual nursing homes in Austria, including ~~the detailed networks of social contacts of their resident~~ detailed social contact networks and information on past outbreaks.	~~Due to its high lethality amongst the elderly, n~~ N ursing homes are in the eye of the COVID-19 storm. Emerging new test procedures might enable us to protect nursing home residents by means of preventive screening ~~strategies~~ . Here, we develop a novel agent-based epidemiological model for the spread of SARS-CoV-2 in nursing homes to identify optimal preventive testing strategies. The model is calibrated to high-resolution data from actual nursing homes in Austria, including ~~the~~ detailed networks of social contacts of their residents and information on past outbreaks.
3	-	Due to its high lethality amongst the elderly, nursing homes are in the eye of the COVID-19 storm. Emerging new test procedures might enable us to protect nursing home residents by means of preventive screening. Here, we develop a ~~novel~~ n agent-based epidemiological model for the spread of SARS-CoV-2 in nursing homes to identify optimal preventive testing strategies. The model is calibrated to high-resolution data from actual nursing homes in Austria, including detailed networks of social contacts of ~~their~~ residents and information on past outbreaks.

Table 7: A sample snippet of iterative text revisions in ArXiv domain generated by $\mathcal{R}3$, where t is the revision depth and $t = 0$ indicates the original input text. Note that ~~text~~ represents user accepted deletions, text represents user accepted insertions, and text represents user rejected edits.

Wanyu Du, Vipul Raheja, Dhruv Kumar, Zae Myung Kim, Melissa Lopez, and Dongyeop Kang. 2022. Understanding Iterative Revision from Human-Written Text. In *Proceedings of the 60th Annual*

Meeting of the Association for Computational Linguistics. Association for Computational Linguistics.

Lester Faigley and Stephen Witte. 1981. Analyzing revision. *College composition and communication*, 32(4):400–414.

Felix Faltings, Michel Galley, Gerold Hintz, Chris Brockett, Chris Quirk, Jianfeng Gao, and Bill Dolan. 2021. Text editing by command. In *Proceedings of the 2021 Conference of the North American Chapter of the Association for Computational Linguistics: Human Language Technologies*, pages 5259–5274, Online. Association for Computational Linguistics.

Manaal Faruqui, Ellie Pavlick, Ian Tenney, and Dipanjan Das. 2018. WikiAtomicEdits: A multilingual corpus of Wikipedia edits for modeling language and discourse. In *Proceedings of the 2018 Conference on Empirical Methods in Natural Language Processing*, pages 305–315, Brussels, Belgium. Association for Computational Linguistics.

Jill Fitzgerald. 1987. Research on revision in writing. *Review of Educational Research*, 57(4):481–506.

Linda Flower. 1980. The dynamics of composing: Making plans and juggling constraints. *Cognitive processes in writing*, pages 31–50.

Linda Flower and John R. Hayes. 1981. A cognitive process theory of writing. *College Composition and Communication*, 32(4):365–387.

Katy Ilonka Gero, Vivian Liu, and Lydia B Chilton. 2021. Sparks: Inspiration for science writing using language models. *arXiv preprint arXiv:2110.07640*.

Takumi Ito, Tatsuki Kuribayashi, Hayato Kobayashi, Ana Brassard, Masato Hagiwara, Jun Suzuki, and Kentaro Inui. 2019. Diamonds in the rough: Generating fluent sentences from early-stage drafts for academic writing assistance. In *Proceedings of the 12th International Conference on Natural Language Generation*, pages 40–53, Tokyo, Japan. Association for Computational Linguistics.

Mina Lee, Percy Liang, and Qian Yang. 2022. Coauthor: Designing a human-ai collaborative writing dataset for exploring language model capabilities. *arXiv preprint arXiv:2201.06796*.

Chin-Yew Lin. 2004. ROUGE: A package for automatic evaluation of summaries. In *Text Summarization Branches Out*, pages 74–81, Barcelona, Spain. Association for Computational Linguistics.

Yinhan Liu, Myle Ott, Naman Goyal, Jingfei Du, Mandar Joshi, Danqi Chen, Omer Levy, Mike Lewis, Luke Zettlemoyer, and Veselin Stoyanov. 2020. RoBERTa: A robustly optimized BERT pretraining approach. In *International Conference on Learning Representations*.

Vishakh Padmakumar and He He. 2021. Machine-in-the-loop rewriting for creative image captioning. *arXiv preprint arXiv:2111.04193*.

Kishore Papineni, Salim Roukos, Todd Ward, and Wei-Jing Zhu. 2002. Bleu: a method for automatic evaluation of machine translation. In *Proceedings of the 40th Annual Meeting of the Association for Computational Linguistics*, pages 311–318, Philadelphia, Pennsylvania, USA. Association for Computational Linguistics.

M. Scardamalia. 1986. Research on written composition. *Handbook of reserch on teaching*.

Nikhil Singh, Guillermo Bernal, Daria Savchenko, and Elena L. Glassman. 2022. Where to hide a stolen elephant: Leaps in creative writing with multimodal machine intelligence. *ACM Trans. Comput.-Hum. Interact.*

Nancy Sommers. 1980. Revision strategies of student writers and experienced adult writers. *College composition and communication*, 31(4):378–388.

Simeng Sun, Wenlong Zhao, Varun Manjunatha, Rajiv Jain, Vlad Morariu, Franck Dernoncourt, Balaji Vasan Srinivasan, and Mohit Iyyer. 2021. IGA: An intent-guided authoring assistant. In *Proceedings of the 2021 Conference on Empirical Methods in Natural Language Processing*, pages 5972–5985, Online and Punta Cana, Dominican Republic. Association for Computational Linguistics.

Marie M. Vaughan and David D. McDonald. 1986. A model of revision in natural language generation. In *24th Annual Meeting of the Association for Computational Linguistics*, pages 90–96, New York, New York, USA. Association for Computational Linguistics.

Thomas Wolf, Lysandre Debut, Victor Sanh, Julien Chaumond, Clement Delangue, Anthony Moi, Pierric Cistac, Tim Rault, Remi Louf, Morgan Funtowicz, Joe Davison, Sam Shleifer, Patrick von Platen, Clara Ma, Yacine Jernite, Julien Plu, Canwen Xu, Teven Le Scao, Sylvain Gugger, Mariama Drame, Quentin Lhoest, and Alexander Rush. 2020. Transformers: State-of-the-art natural language processing. In *Proceedings of the 2020 Conference on Empirical Methods in Natural Language Processing: System Demonstrations*, pages 38–45, Online. Association for Computational Linguistics.

Wei Xu, Courtney Napoles, Ellie Pavlick, Quanze Chen, and Chris Callison-Burch. 2016. Optimizing statistical machine translation for text simplification. *Transactions of the Association for Computational Linguistics*, 4:401–415.

Jingqing Zhang, Yao Zhao, Mohammad Saleh, and Peter Liu. 2020. PEGASUS: Pre-training with extracted gap-sentences for abstractive summarization. In *Proceedings of the 37th International Conference on Machine Learning*, volume 119 of *Proceedings of Machine Learning Research*, pages 11328–11339. PMLR.

A $\mathcal{R}3$ Iterative Revision Samples

We present more iterative revision examples generated by $\mathcal{R}3$ in Table 8 and Table 9.

t	HUMAN-HUMAN	SYSTEM-HUMAN(ours)
0	Corporal Nathan Hornburg. A Reserve soldier serving with Canadian Forces in Afghanistanwas killed on September 24, 2007. Four others were injured in the incident which killed 24-year-old Corporal Nathan Hornburg of Calgary, Alberta. A Canadian Forces statement said Cpl. Hornburg was killed during Operation Sadiq Sarbaaz (Honest Soldier) approximately 47 kilometres west of Kandahar City in Panjwaii District. Media reports indicated he died from mortar fire at around 4 :30 p.m. local time (12:00 UTC) while he was repairing the track on a Canadian Leopard tank near a cluster of villages known as Zangabad.	Corporal Nathan Hornburg. A Reserve soldier serving with Canadian Forces in Afghanistanwas killed on September 24, 2007. Four others were injured in the incident which killed 24-year-old Corporal Nathan Hornburg of Calgary, Alberta. A Canadian Forces statement said Cpl. Hornburg was killed during Operation Sadiq Sarbaaz (Honest Soldier) approximately 47 kilometres west of Kandahar City in Panjwaii District. Media reports indicated he died from mortar fire at around 4 :30 p.m. local time (12:00 UTC) while he was repairing the track on a Canadian Leopard tank near a cluster of villages known as Zangabad.
1	~~Corporal Nathan Hornburg. A Reserve soldier serving with Canadian Forces in Afghanistanwas killed on September 24, 2007~~ On MOnday, a 24-year old Calgary Reservist became the 71st Canadian soldier killed in Afghanistan . Four others were injured in the incident which killed ~~24-year-old~~ Corporal Nathan Hornburg ~~of Calgary, Alberta. A Canadian Forces statement said Cpl. Hornbur was killed during~~ , who was operating as part of Operation Sadiq Sarbaaz (Honest Soldier) approximately 47 kilometres west of Kandahar City in Panjwaii District. Media reports indicated he died from mortar fire at around 4 :30 p.m. local time ~~(12:00 UTC)~~ while he was repairing the track on a Canadian Leopard tank near a cluster of villages known as Zangabad.	~~Corporal Nathan Hornburg. A Reserve~~ A Canadian soldier serving with Canadian Forces in Afghanistanwas killed on September 24, 2007. Four others were injured in the incident which killed 24-year-old Corporal Nathan Hornburg of Calgary, Alberta. ~~A Canadian Forces statement said Cpl.~~ Nathan Hornburg was killed during Operation Sadiq Sarbaaz (Honest Soldier) approximately 47 kilometres west of Kandahar City in Panjwaii District. Media reports indicated he died from mortar fire at around 4 :30 p.m. local time (12:00 UTC) while he was repairing the track on a Canadian Leopard tank near a cluster of villages known as Zangabad.
2	Corporal Nathan Hornburg. A Reserve soldier serving with Canadian Forces in Afghanistanwas killed on September 24, 2007. Four others were injured in the incident which killed 24-year-old Corporal Nathan Hornburg of Calgary, Alberta. A Canadian Forces statement said Cpl. Hornburg was killed during Operation Sadiq Sarbaaz ~~(Honest Soldier) approximately 47 kilometres west of Kandahar City in Panjwaii District~~ , a joint Afghan-NATO mission designed to "set the conditions for a continuous security presence and the establishment of a new police sub-station in the northern part of (Panjwaii)." . Media reports indicated he died from mortar fire at around 4 :30 p.m. local time (12:00 UTC) while he was repairing the track on a Canadian Leopard tank near a cluster of villages known as Zangabad.	A Canadian soldier serving with the Canadian Forces in Afghanistanwas killed on September 24, 2007. Four others were injured in the incident which killed 24-year-old Corporal Nathan Hornburg of Calgary, Alberta. Nathan Hornburg was killed during Operation Sadiq Sarbaaz (Honest Soldier) , approximately 47 kilometres west of Kandahar City in Panjwaii District. Media reports indicated he died from mortar fire at around 4 :30 p.m. local time (12:00 UTC) while he was repairing the track on a Canadian Leopard tank near a cluster of villages known as Zangabad.
3	-	A Canadian soldier serving with the Canadian Forces in Afghanistan was killed on September 24, 2007. Four others were injured in the incident which killed 24-year-old ~~Corporal~~ Cpl. Nathan Hornburg of Calgary, Alberta. Nathan Hornburg was killed during Operation Sadiq Sarbaaz (Honest Soldier), approximately 47 kilometres west of Kandahar City in the Panjwaii District. Media reports indicated he died from mortar fire at around 4 :30 p.m. local time (12:00 UTC) while he was repairing the track on a Canadian Leopard tank near a cluster of villages known as Zangabad.

Table 8: A sample snippet of iterative text revisions in Wikinews domain generated by $\mathcal{R}3$, where t is the revision depth and $t = 0$ indicates the original input text. Note that ~~text~~ represents user accepted deletions, text represents user accepted insertions, and text represents user rejected edits.

t	HUMAN-HUMAN	SYSTEM-HUMAN(ours)
0	Jecon Gregory is or was a nomadic artist, whose autobiographical fragments and poems, dictated to an acquaintance, were published as the book "History of a Nation of One" (Harcourt Brace, New York, 1969, and Michael Joseph, London, 1971). Jecon apparently did not know his place, date, language or even name of birth, began his wanderings as a child in Malta; walked through many lands, barefoot, tall and thin, pulling all his possessions in a basket on wheels, sleeping on the ground, and making a living by drawing portraits.	Jecon Gregory is or was a nomadic artist, whose autobiographical fragments and poems, dictated to an acquaintance, were published as the book "History of a Nation of One" (Harcourt Brace, New York, 1969, and Michael Joseph, London, 1971). Jecon apparently did not know his place, date, language or even name of birth, began his wanderings as a child in Malta; walked through many lands, barefoot, tall and thin, pulling all his possessions in a basket on wheels, sleeping on the ground, and making a living by drawing portraits.
1	Jecon Gregory is or was a nomadic artist, whose autobiographical fragments and poems, dictated to an acquaintance, were published as the book "History of a Nation of One : An Unlikely Memoir " (Harcourt Brace, New York, 1969, and Michael Joseph, London, 1971). .. Jecon apparently did not know his place, date, language or even name of birth, began his wanderings as a child in Malta; walked through many lands, barefoot, tall and thin, pulling all his possessions in a basket on wheels, sleeping on the ground, and making a living by drawing portraits.	Jecon Gregory is or was a nomadic artist, whose autobiographical fragments and poems, dictated to an acquaintance, were published as the book ~~"~~ History of a Nation of One" (Harcourt Brace, New York, 1969, and Michael Joseph, London, 1971). Jecon apparently did not know his place, date, language or even name of birth, began his wanderings as a child in Malta; walked through many lands, barefoot, tall and thin, pulling all his possessions in a basket on wheels, sleeping on the ground, and ~~making a living by~~ drawing portraits.
2	-	Jecon Gregory is or was a nomadic artist, whose autobiographical fragments and poems, dictated to an acquaintance, were published as the book "History of a Nation of One" (Harcourt Brace, New York, 1969, and Michael Joseph, London, 1971). Jecon apparently did not know his place, date, language or even name of birth, began his wanderings as a child in Malta; walked through many lands, barefoot, tall and thin, pulling all his possessions in a basket on wheels, sleeping on the ground, and ~~making a living by~~ drawing portraits.
3	-	-

Table 9: A sample snippet of iterative text revisions in Wikipedia domain generated by $\mathcal{R}3$, where t is the revision depth and $t = 0$ indicates the original input text. Note that ~~text~~ represents user accepted deletions, text represents user accepted insertions, and text represents user rejected edits.

Author Index

Association for Computational Linguistics
209 N. Eighth Street
Stroudsburg, Pennsylvania 18360

ISBN 978-1-7138-6740-1

CURRAN ASSOCIATES INC.
proceedings.com